Affirming Black Students' Lives and Literacies

Bearing Witness

Arlette Ingram Willis

Gwendolyn Thompson McMillon

Patriann Smith

Foreword by Theresa Perry

TEACHERS COLLEGE PRESS

TEACHERS COLLEGE | COLUMBIA UNIVERSITY
NEW YORK AND LONDON

Published by Teachers College Press,® 1234 Amsterdam Avenue, New York, NY 10027

Library of Congress Cataloging-in-Publication Data

Names: Willis, Arlette Ingram, author. | McMillon, Gwendolyn Thompson, author. | Smith, Patriann, 1982– author.
Title: Affirming Black students' lives and literacies : bearing witness / Arlette Ingram Willis, Gwendolyn Thompson McMillon, Patriann Smith.
Description: New York : Teachers College Press, 2022. | Includes bibliographical references and index. | Summary: "Drawing on the authors' experiences as Black parents, researchers, teachers, and teacher educators, this timely book presents a multi-pronged approach to affirming Black lives and literacies. The authors believe change is needed-not within Black children-but in the way they are perceived and educated, particularly in reading, writing, and critical thinking across grade levels. To inform literacy teachers and school leaders, they the authors provide a conceptual framework for reimagining literacy instruction based on Black philosophical and theoretical foundations, historical background, literacy research, and authentic experiences of Black students. This important book includes counter-narratives about the lives of Black learners; research conducted by Black scholars among Black students, examples of approaches to literacy with Black children that are making a difference; conversations among literacy researchers that move beyond academia; and a model for engaging all students in literacy. Affirming Black Students' Lives and Literacies advocates for adopting a standard of care that will improve and support literacy achievement among today's Black students by rejecting deficit presumptions and embracing the fullness of these students' strengths. Book Features: A critique addressing the miseducation of Black children that points to the array of available scholarship that should inform reading praxis and research. An anti-deficit framework to help teachers and school leaders provide cultural support for literacy achievement among Black students. Narrative examples of current Black literacy scholarship by Black scholars who embrace their faith-walk as an integral part of their holistic approach. Discussion questions to spur conversations among school administrators, parents/caregivers, politicians, reading researchers, teacher educators, and classroom teachers"—Provided by publisher.
Identifiers: LCCN 2021048643 (print) | LCCN 2021048644 (ebook) | ISBN 9780807766989 (paperback) | ISBN 9780807766996 (hardcover) | ISBN 9780807781043 (ebook)
Subjects: LCSH: African American children—Education—Language arts. | Language arts—United States. | Culturally relevant pedagogy—United States.
Classification: LCC LC2778.L34 W55 2022 (print) | LCC LC2778.L34 (ebook) | DDC 371.829/96073—dc23/eng/20211109
LC record available at https://lccn.loc.gov/2021048643
LC ebook record available at https://lccn.loc.gov/2021048644

ISBN 978-0-8077-6698-9 (paper)
ISBN 978-0-8077-6699-6 (hardcover)
ISBN 978-0-8077-8104-3 (ebook)

Printed on acid-free paper
Manufactured in the United States of America

We purposefully begin our dedication page giving all the glory, honor, and praise to our Lord and Savior, Jesus Christ, from whom all blessings flow. We thank You, Lord, for putting Your love in our hearts to share with others. We are grateful that You have chosen us for such a time as this, to bless Your children, their parents and families, and the teachers who are privileged to teach them.

Arlette Ingram Willis dedicates this book to her parents, Adell and Angie Ingram; brothers; husband, Leonard; sons, Lenny, Justin, and Jacob; daughters-in-laws; grandchildren; and to Black student readers I have been honored to learn from and with.

Gwendolyn Thompson McMillon dedicates this book to her parents and siblings:

Rev. Dr. M. T. & Mother Pecola Thompson, Randy, Myron, Billy, M.T. Jr., Phyllis, Bessie, and Leon, her first teachers and literacy role models.

She also dedicates this book to her loving husband of 35 years—Rev. Dr. Vincent McMillon, her sounding board and confidante—and to her sons, Joshua, David, Morgan, Brian, and Vincent II, who continue the Legacy of Literacy.

Patriann Smith dedicates this book to our Black ancestors who came before and fought for freedom through literacy. She also dedicates this book to her father—Patrick Smith, former preacher and school principal who invested in literate children; mother—Maryanna Smith, who taught her how to read; daughter—Karice Smith, who pursues a literate future through screenwriting; nieces—Jaeda, Gheryl, Jainy, Ella, and Bella, and nephews—Jayden, Zain, and Nathaniel—who redefine literacy daily.

Contents

Foreword   *Theresa Perry*   ix

Preface   xi

Acknowledgments   xxi

1. Introduction: Theoretical Perspectives   1

Black Epistemology, Ideology, and Theory   2

Conceptual and Theoretical Foundations   2

Conceptual Foundations: Moral Courage and Moral Licensing   4

Theoretical Foundations: Black Liberation Theology, Black Radical
Tradition, Critical Race Theory, and Decolonization   7

Black Liberation Theology   8

Black Feminism   10

The Black Radical Tradition   12

Critical Race Theory   13

Decolonial Theories   15

Reading Research and Black Students   16

2. Black Women Activist Teachers   19

Literacy and Freedom   21

Literacy and Civil Rights   35

Literacy and Liberation   40

Literacy and Justice: Black Independent Schools   45

9-11/15

9/18-22

| | Our Teachers | 50 |
| | Conclusion | 50 |

3. The Mis-Education of a High-Performing Black Girl — **53**

Shawyn's Narrative: A Summary	53
The Study	55
Aesha	56
Discussion	64
Conclusion	67
In Conversation	68
Critical Discussion Questions	72
Suggested Readings	73

4. Cultural Dissonance in a First-Grade Classroom — **75**

Gwen's Narrative: A Summary	75
Setting	76
Tony	77
Travis	80
A Closer Look Inside Ms. Rudolph's First-Grade Classroom	83
Conclusion	92
In Conversation	93
Critical Discussion Questions	99
Suggested Readings	100

5. Transcending (Dis)Belief: Black (Immigrant) Youth Literacies — **101**

Patriann's Narrative: A Summary	101
An Invitation From a Black Immigrant Educator	102
Black Immigrant Educator Literacies	105
Jorge: A Black Immigrant Latinx Youth	107

S 10/16
10/16-20

S 10/16
10/16-20

S 10/23
10/16-20

Contents

Black American Youth Literacies 110

Excerpts From Black American Youth 112

Conclusion 118

In Conversation 119

Critical Discussion Questions 122

Suggested Readings 123

6. **It's Never Too Late** **125**

Arlette's Narrative: A Summary 126

It Is Never Too Late . . . 126

A Brief Backstory 127

Meeting Clemente 129

Twenty Years Later 132

Perspective 134

Conclusion 135

In Conversation 136

Critical Discussion Questions 139

Suggested Readings 140

7. **Conceptual Framework: Toward a Standard of CARE** **141**

Foundations 141

Race and Culture 143

Equity Pedagogies 146

CARE 148

References **159**

Index **175**

About the Authors **183**

S10/23
10/23-11/3

S10/30
10/23-11/3

Foreword

This is an outstanding, compelling, and complicated book. It challenges us to deal squarely with the political nature of literacy and education in the United States, historically and contemporarily. It provides a road map for how we can center the lives of Black women educators, who have made enormous contributions to the field of education.

Early in the book, the authors, Black women scholars, use the historical narratives of Black women educators to effectively illustrate and contend that for these women education was inextricably linked to freedom.

This is a critical and important gendered movement in the text. All too often, and understandably, Frederick Douglass is seen as the most powerful voice linking education to freedom. By now, we all know the story. His enslaver saw him reading, snatched the book from his hand, articulating that reading would make him unfit to be a slave. We all know the rest of the story. This increased his desire to become literate. He started schools for other enslaved individuals. And indeed, literacy did make him even more motivated to see his freedom.

On another note, our students should know and pass on the stories of the Black women chronicled in this book. To be more specific, our students should read the narrative of Harriet Jacobs' *Incidents in the Life of a Slave Girl* and the narrative of Septima Clark's *Ready From Within*.

From among the women that Willis and her colleagues include in the texts, the question for us as educators is: How, and in what ways can we tell the stories of these Black women, these historical legends, who saw education as inextricably linked to freedom? Are they best told in chapter books? Will we eventually have illustrated classroom materials that capture their lives and work? Do we need to create a study group in which interested teachers can work with scholars to research and examine what more is knowable about these women? Can some of these stories be told in picture books that are as compelling as the books written and illustrated by Derrick Barnes and Gordon C James, *Crown: An Ode to the Fresh Cut* and *I Am Every Good Thing?*

Willis and her coauthors are to be commended for laying out the multidisciplinary theoretical and ideological underpinnings of their intellectual work and research: Black Liberation Theology, Black Feminism, and the Black Radical Tradition. It is important here to note that in articulating the theoretical underpinnings, they have courageously and in an intellectually rigorous way chosen, not only not to ignore, but more importantly, to foreground how anti-Blackness affects the education of Black children. At the same time, they acknowledge that a singular theoretical framework is not likely to be powerful enough to sufficiently capture the multiplicity of forces affecting the lives of Black people and by extension Black children.

As in perhaps no other research I have read, in Chapter 3, "The Mis-Education of a High-Performing Black Girl," and Chapter 4, "Cultural Dissonance in a First-Grade Classroom," the authors lay out and graphically capture how schools affect Black children. The chapters are compelling, heartbreaking, and instructive. We get a window of how a smart, extremely literate Black girl is treated when she goes to school. In Chapter 4, we are offered an equally compelling and illuminating portrait of cultural conflict when smart, engaging Black boys enter a classroom.

I want to compliment the researchers. They have allowed us to see up-close what happened to smart, prepared, engaged, young Black children when they entered classrooms in America. I know of no other context where this has been accomplished as effectively as it has in this book.

In closing, this book should be mandatory reading for all teachers, teacher educators, and pre-service students. It is a theoretically and historically grounded book. It provides a powerful, heartbreaking, and textured window into what happens to Black children who go to school more than prepared to learn. It indicates how we, as a society, can develop an ethic of care for Black children and youth.

—Theresa Perry

Preface

The inception of this book has been years in the making, although it is being published at a time of disunity and a time of racial awakening in our nation. As Black women educators, we have had numerous conversations among ourselves, and with family and friends, about why there is a clear disconnect between the creative, humorous, intelligent, loving, and thoughtful Black children in our lives and the depiction of Black students as readers and learners. We are aghast at the inhumane legislation aimed at forestalling Black students' reading performance, while little is being done to disrupt notions about who Black children are and the assets they bring to learning. For answers, we have therefore turned to our own experiences as Black parents, researchers, teachers, and teacher educators. Our individual and collective experiences reveal that often discussions about our children's learning, and especially their progress as readers, are conducted in isolation, at parent-teacher conferences where we are informed about reading development, levels, progress, and test scores, with little insight about our children as real human beings.

In conversations among like-minded folks, we do not need to convince them, nor do we try to convince them, that Black students are as smart as other students, and are not in need of fixing or change. We love Black students for who they are and all they can become. We believe change is needed—not within Black children, but in the way they are educated in general and taught to read specifically. We ask: If not now, when? As the Honorable U.S. Representative Ayanna Pressley (2020) reminds us, our truths are worth sharing: "We belong at every table where decisions are made about our lives, our livelihood, and our justice. Our lives, our stories, and our struggles matter" (n.p.). Black student readers are the focus of this book. We envisage Black students as complete and whole humans who are loved and deserving of appropriate and high-quality literacy instruction that is authentic and informed (culturally, linguistically, and racially). We

see Black students as learners who come to school ready to read. We
much prefer to prevent Black students from becoming victims of literacy policies at federal, state, and local levels—*not* based on research
about Black literacy learners.

We approached this book as a way to provide information about
Black epistemology, history, and lives as a prelude to explanations of
why it is important that everyone learns about Black literate lives. We
provide a conceptual framework to reimagine literacy instruction for
Black students, based on Black philosophical and theoretical foundations, historical background, literacy research, and authentic conversations about literacy experiences of Black children in schools to
inform educators as well as reading researchers. For students who are
currently experiencing reading difficulties in schools, it is our hope
that this text will address cultural, knowledge, and racial misunder-
standings about the brilliance of Black students as literacy learners.

We provide an alternative perspective about Black literacy
achievement by detailing historic and contemporary struggles for
equal and quality literacy (assessments, funding, praxis, and research)
in the United States. More subtly, we also address the current political struggle to gain access to quality literacy instruction promulgated
within the literacy research community at large (which ignores the
positive research on literacy among Black children) and promoted by
the politically powerful in and beyond the U.S. (negative views of
Black children as literacy learners). The text provides (a) counternarratives about the lives of literacy learners through narratives, (b) literacy research conducted by Black scholars among Black students as
an alternative knowledge base, and (c) examples of researchers and
teachers whose approach to literacy with Black children is making a
difference.

The text is a critique addressing the miseducation of Black children
by pointing to the array of available scholarship that is ignored but
should inform reading praxis and research. Although it is tempting to
separately address the "irresponsible whitesplaining and blacksplain-
ing" and its negative impact on the lives of Black children, we believe
that a more productive approach, which is likely to spur change, can
occur using authentic counternarratives. We believe our approach an-
ticipates and refutes arguments for maintaining the status quo. More
importantly, it provides Black philosophical and theoretical foundations needed to inform change, and is informed and anchored within
a Black cultural experience. The text includes research that should be
a part of the current discussion of reading praxis as well.

The book presents a multipronged approach to Black literacy by acknowledging that we are Black women, mothers, teachers, and researchers. We value Black life and the lives of Black children. We understand what school life is like for Black children and value who they are and what they bring to literacy learning. We document a history of contributions made by Black women who were activists and teachers in the pursuit of equity and access to literacy. We also include literacy research among Black students today. We argue that research is available to inform literacy research, policies, and praxis but that this research is unacknowledged and unused in the struggle for literacy equity. Moreover, the book provides conversations influenced by experience and research to inform educators and teachers about how to care for Black students and provide cultural support for literacy achievement among Black students. We understand that every student and every classroom and school context is different and will need specific solutions. We provide some guidelines for parents and caregivers, as we also seek sustainable solutions to the miseducation of Black students. We are aware of current solutions and some proposed solutions that are based more on logic, theories, and randomized experiments than on the care and education of Black students. We seek to provide all readers who "walk the talk" with information that will be useful.

As we know, there is a limited number of literacy researchers who have lived experiences as Black, Indigenous, and People of Color (BIPOC), and academics. We also know that to be taken seriously in academia it is necessary to articulate the epistemological, ideological, and theoretical scholarship that informs your thinking. Thus, we begin this book with a theoretical chapter to clarify our positioning and explicate how foundational Black scholarship is to our work. Next, we include a chapter focused on the history of Black women activist teachers and reading access. As Black women we know how often our work and scholarship are overlooked and undervalued, so we provide a genealogical perspective as we honor the lives and sacrifices of our foremothers. From their teaching and writings, we appreciate their contributions to Black literacy: love and care for Black students, belief in the intellect of Black readers, and investment and philosophies about teaching. These ideas help us to craft our conceptual framework.

All readers bring their complex lives to the task, as Morrison (2019) observes: "the way that a reader participates in a text—not how she interprets it, but how she helps write it" (p. 347). This idea reimagines Black students' engagement in reading, especially but not solely with regard to "required to read" texts in which Black people are either invisible or marginal. At some level, each reader decides to accommodate the text, as they disregard, distance, ignore, or surrender to life and literacy in a racialized society. The process is reminiscent of Hall's (1980) articulation of how readers respond to text: (a) agreement, (b) negotiation, or (c) opposition. Over the last 3 decades, reading research and accompanying instruction have not informed or improved the reading performance of Black readers. The present-day political and legal maneuvering alleging support of Black students' reading improvement is misguided, rhetorical, and unethical. This book is guided by the following questions:

- What can our narratives tell us about Black students' reading experiences and instruction in schools?
- How can Black students' experiences, interests, languages, and preferences inform reading instruction?
- What can we learn from the affordances within Black communities, families, and languages that support reading instruction and research?

In chapters 3 through 6, we present research narratives as a way to bridge the town-and-gown divide and to inform all readers—particularly Black caregivers/parents. We are acutely aware of the day-to-day struggles of parenting Black children who attend schools in White public spaces because we have been/are in the same space. We present literacy research conducted among Black students by Black researchers that parents/caregivers as well as administrators and teachers may be unaware exist. Chapters 3 through 6 ends with two subsections, "In Conversation" and "Critical Discussion Questions," to push readers to think beyond their own experiences and to make clear that many Black children in classrooms across the nation are having similar literacy experiences. As such, "In Conversation" is a space where we extend the research examined in a conversation among ourselves, and "Critical Discussion Questions" presents questions to be discussed among all stakeholders: Black parents and caregivers, teachers, educational administrators, policymakers, and reading researchers. These chapters conclude with short lists of additional available readings and resources published by numerous Black scholars.

We present the insights in this book as an extension of decades of conversation repeatedly put forward among Black and Brown scholars to address inequities in curriculum and in literacy practice. We

stand on the shoulders of giants whose efforts to advance multiculturalism, social justice, and cultural awareness in literacy research
and otherwise have paved the way for us to unequivocally name
race and explicitly focus on anti-Blackness as a basis for moving
toward racial justice in literacy research today. Our emphasis on centering Blackness in literacy research represents a multifaceted and
unique lens through which to dismantle and disrupt harm while
portraying the humanizing potential of literacy research and practice for Black students. It is possible only because of the ground-
work laid by cultural and educational activists. Because of our Black
forerunners, we can now call for an immediate transition beyond
decades of dehumanization of Black children through literacy research, practice, and assessment. Because of these giants who pre-
ceded us, we can now call for a reckoning of our nation and its
use of literacy as a vehicle for rehumanization and CARE for Black
children. Increasingly, other nations are openly confronting how
racism has functioned in their past through acknowledgment, cor-
recting racist wrongs in school curricula, and restoration. We remain hopeful, like our ancestors, that the same is possible in the
United States. In the absence of naming a wrong done for what it
was and continues to be, how can we possibly address it? Where
there is hope, there is possibility.

After reading this text, parents/caregivers will be able to confi-
dently reframe generic responses about their child's literacy development, directly engage in the literacy decision-making, and be prepared
to offer alternative suggestions. After reading this text, literacy and
reading researchers, politicians, and stakeholders will be able to more
accurately produce research studies framed by foundational Black
ideological and theoretical understandings as well as perspectives that
are historically, culturally, and linguistically accurate. After reading
this text, school administrators, school personnel, and teachers will be
able to respectfully engage with Black parents/caregivers and provide
responsible and practical suggestions to improve Black students' literacy development. After reading this text, classroom teachers, literacy
coaches, and school personnel will be able to care for Black children
and teach them as fellow humans who are complete and not in need
of "fixing."

Readers can read from beginning to end or begin and move to
where their particular interests and needs take them within the chapters to come, which offer the following:

CHAPTER 1: INTRODUCTION: THEORETICAL PERSPECTIVES

The book begins with an introduction that outlines our ideological and theoretical grounding that provides the foundation of our thinking. Our thinking is informed by Black Liberation Theology, Black Feminism, Black Radical Tradition, and Decolonial Theory. We acknowledge that there is no monolithic Black experience nor a definitive knowledge base: We present our interpretations and understandings herein.

CHAPTER 2: BLACK WOMEN ACTIVIST TEACHERS

This chapter provides a historical overview and description of select Black girls/women who sought to provide access to reading in the United States, 1700–2020. The chapter presents a seldom-acknowledged narrative history of literacy teaching undertaken by Black girls/women. Their narratives are contextualized to illustrate the goals and purposes for teaching literacy as expressed by Black girls/women and foreground concepts and themes that arise in subsequent chapters.

CHAPTERS 3–6:

Chapters 3 through 6 are research studies that are presented in narrative style to appeal to all readers, as well as to illustrate that Black researchers conduct research among Black students. Collectively, the research studies serve as counternarratives to the half-truths, myths, and negative stereotypes about Black students as learners, readers, and writers. The chapters consist of four distinct sections:

1. Each chapter begins with a research study (described below).
2. "In Conversation" is a follow-up to research studies. It is also where we share our thoughts about the lived experiences described in each study and explicate how each study is reflexive and reflective of the reality of many Black students' reading experiences. We do so in part to debunk myths about Black communities, families, readers, and students as we tell our truths, our way. The process of sharing the lived experiences of Black students' reading provides us with an opportunity to "speak the truth to the people," as

Evans (1994) encourages, and we work toward collective knowledge. Moreover, this section provides alternative and rich descriptions of Black readers and allows us to reimagine in a way that respects Black students as human, valuable, and worthy.

3. Critical discussion questions are posed for stakeholders: Black parents and caregivers, as well as teachers, educational administrators, policymakers, and reading researchers. The queries are crafted to challenge readers to re-envisage Black readers and writers. Readers should read the chapter and our conversation and then discuss the questions so that the book becomes a teaching tool as opposed to a set of instructions.

4. A selective list of additional readings concludes each chapter, as readers are encouraged to read more about research conducted by Black scholars about Black literacy in schools. We have selected literature that supports Black literacy learners.

CHAPTER 3: THE MIS-EDUCATION OF A HIGH-PERFORMING BLACK GIRL

This narrative centers on a Black girl, Aesha, whose early schooling (preschool, kindergarten, and 1st grade) reveals that she is intelligent and a strong early reader. Over this 3-year period, observations of Aesha's home life describe a loving home life that undergoes changes as well as a consistent commitment to education, and observations of her school life document a shift in Aesha's level of engagement and responsiveness as a learner and a reader. Interviews with her mother describe an awareness of Aesha as a growing Black girl who is embarking on an education in a racialized society, and interviews at school with classroom teachers reveal varying perceptions of Aesha as a person, learner, and reader. Interviews were conducted at her home and in the schools she attended. Among the findings that emerge are (1) Aesha's teachers' dismissal of her intellectual acuity and high reading performance and (2) an array of interlocking institutional structures that prohibit Aesha's continual growth as a high-performing Black reader. Using both critical race and colonial theory, this study documents how "(a) restrictive organizational and structural conditions present within schools serving Black students; (b) disconnection between Black parents and teachers; and (c) narrow, low-level reading instruction, collectively work to create an oppressive infrastructure within schools that contributes to the educational neglect of high performing students" (Williams, 2007, p. iv).

CHAPTER 4: CULTURAL DISSONANCE IN A
FIRST-GRADE CLASSROOM

This chapter's narrative invites the audience into the lives of two brilliant 1st-grade African American boys, Tony and Travis, who were assessed by the literacy coach at a 5th-grade reading level. Despite their reading ability, Tony and Travis were suspended multiple times during their 1st-grade year. Their teacher believed that Tony and Travis were academically smart, but their behavior prevented her from being able to teach them. They spent most of their classroom experience in time-out. The boys' parents eventually became ambivalent toward the teacher and the school when they were unable to effectively teach their smart 1st-grade sons. This narrative illuminates the tragic undereducation of Black boys in classrooms with teachers who are unable to build effective relationships with them and their parents. Disciplinary actions such as time-out prevented Tony and Travis from receiving important instructional time; and denied privileges such as recess and field trips eventually became learning denied to Tony and Travis.

CHAPTER 5: TRANSCENDING (DIS)BELIEF:
BLACK (IMMIGRANT) YOUTH LITERACIES

This chapter's narrative is designed to engage the audience with the literacies of a Black/Latinx immigrant youth, Jorge, and with the literacies of Black American youth. First, the chapter describes the journey of a Black immigrant woman writer of color, Patriann, coming into the role of supporting Black (immigrant) children's writing in school. Second, the chapter presents insights into the literate activities of and conversations with Black children who became dear to her heart as she worked with them to develop their literacies. The chapter ends with understandings about race, language, literacies, and learning, which are necessary to believe that all Black children can read and write.

CHAPTER 6: IT'S NEVER TOO LATE

Arlette's narrative rests at the intersection of theory and praxis. She shares the story of a young Black male who was a focal student in a research project that she conducted. The student was charming and engaging, whose postsecondary plans were uncertain when she met him during the last semester of his senior year in high school. In the study, she enacted culturally responsive teaching and used Black literature. Two decades later, she received an email from him that detailed his life since the research project and how he believed his participation changed his life.

CHAPTER 7: CONCEPTUAL FRAMEWORK: TOWARD A STANDARD OF CARE

Chapter 7 is the appropriate place to share a conceptual framework that flows from the preceding chapters on Blackness, the abbreviated history of Black literacy, and Black literacy research. We understand that change, substantive, radical change, must begin long before student/teacher interactions. It begins when teachers and other stakeholders understand the history of racism that is embedded within the history of literacy in the United States and how structural racism has thwarted literacy access and achievement for Black people. In so doing, we hope to normalize perceptions of Black students as readers and literacy learners.

We summarize key concepts, ideas, and themes about literacy among Black learners as described in the research conducted among Black learners (chapters 3 through 6). Next, we use the research as part of an alternative knowledge base to describe a conceptual framework for teachers and stakeholders moving forward.

We believe that Black students, both in the United States and beyond, are worthy of high-quality literacy instruction. Our approach is one among many ways to reconceptualize the lives of Black children and to reframe literacy approaches to teaching Black students. In Chapter 7, we unpack our philosophical framework informed by each proceeding chapter and our conceptual framework of CARE. We also explicate CARE as a pedagogical concept. Moreover, we provide an example of how to implement CARE and improve the educational experiences of Black students and readers.

Acknowledgments

Arlette Ingram Willis acknowledges that research support for this project was made possible through funding provided by the Spencer Foundation Small Grants Program, the National Council of Teachers of English, and the University of Illinois College of Education's Bureau of Educational Research. She acknowledges two former doctoral students, the late Dr. Shawyn O. (Williams) Jenkins (1978–2018), whose dissertation focused on the literacy of three Black girls in and out of school, and Dr. Julia Burke, whose support as graduate research assistant was invaluable during our research project, along with an anonymous classroom teacher who graciously permitted us time with her students.

Gwendolyn Thompson McMillon acknowledges the Spencer Dissertation Fellowship for Research Related to Education program and the Spencer Research Training Grant Fellowship program sponsored by Michigan State University. She also acknowledges the students and parents who willingly shared their stories, as well as the principal, teachers, and staff who opened the doors of the school and allowed her to have total daily access to conduct research.

Patriann Smith acknowledges the United States Department of Education Promise Neighborhood Grants program and Dr. Tala Karkar Esperat, whose commitment to excellence as a research assistant made it possible to participate as a research partner with the beautiful Black youth referenced in this book. She acknowledges the stories and voices of the Black youth with whom she engaged in this book, and whose brilliance shone brightly as a basis for the insights presented.

CHAPTER 1

Introduction:
Theoretical Perspectives

The true evil of American slavery was the narrative we created to justify it. They made up this ideology of white supremacy that cannot be reconciled with our Constitution, that cannot be reconciled with a commitment to fair and just treatment of all peoples. They made it up so they could feel comfortable while enslaving other people . . . [S]lavery didn't end in 1865, it just evolved. (Stevenson, 2017, n. p.)

We enter this project as three Black women scholars who also are daughters, mothers, teachers, and researchers. We unapologetically bring all of whom we are to this process, including our spiritual selves, our understanding of God and His view of humanity, and our collective understandings that influence this scholarship. Our thinking also is grounded in our life experiences as three Black women who have strong roots in the Black Church as well as in our lives as academic researchers and members of Black communities. We are women with Black families who have been Black teachers (preschool–graduate school) and have taught Black children here in and beyond the United States. We have varied yet common experiences as Black women in the academy and community; "ours is an amazing, spectacular, journey in the Americas. It is so remarkable one can only be thankful for it, as bizarre as that may sound" (Walker, 2018, p. ii). Collectively, our life experiences, intellectual insights, academic training, and founts of cultural knowledge help guide our thinking as we look at the history of Black folk in the Americas to find patterns of attitudes, behaviors, customs, languages, knowledge, and wisdom. We understand that this history is tainted by racism and White supremacy; thus, we provide a counternarrative exposing injustices and pain, as well as highlighting joy and strengths. We applaud creative minds of Black people who for centuries have struggled to simply learn to read.

BLACK EPISTEMOLOGY, IDEOLOGY, AND THEORY

All research is grounded in someone's conceptual, ideological, philosophical, or theoretical thinking. Teasing these out is a process, and we invite you to wander with us through the scholarship that informs our project of understanding literacy (communicating, reading, and writing) among Black people and ways to improve reading instruction for Black readers. We draw on research narratives and counternarratives of Black lived experiences to describe our humanity and the right to be understood as fellow humans. We talk about Blackness and what that means for Black students who are learning to read and write, for students who know how to read and write, and for people who seriously accept the responsibility for teaching Black students to read and write. We acknowledge Blackness is a concept, and a lived reality that is historically, geographically, politically, and socially constructed. We embrace all that Blackness brings and means as a cultural and racial phenomenon and as a means of survival. Herein, Blackness centers on authenticity, behaviors, being, emotions, languages, literacies, and life. Barajas (2019) notes that in a Charlie Rose documentary, Toni Morrison declares "we don't want to speak for black people. We want to speak to and be among. It's us" (n.p.). To be clear, the lens through which we view reading is rooted within Blackness, while acknowledging that what it means to be Black carries with it a heterogeneity we cannot claim to fully capture in this book.

CONCEPTUAL AND THEORETICAL FOUNDATIONS

We briefly examine theories that ground and inspire our work. We are not philosophers; however, as like-minded social scientists, we are in one accord regarding select concepts and theories to communicate, frame, and inform. We identify ideas foundational to our thinking, drawing from multiple and intersecting concepts, philosophies, and theories. To identify one or two concepts or theories would be to shortchange what we believe, how we think, and how we conduct and interpret research. We reject Western linear formats, preferring more robust and multiperspective, prismatic, and transformable approaches. We engage Blackness—as a heuristic—to capture the foundational concepts and theories we draw upon to describe our experiences, lives, and scholarship as well as to acknowledge historical and contemporary renderings of Blackness. We add our voices to claim, embrace, and dignify

Blackness in all of its "perfect imperfections." We lean into Blackness as we embrace Black feminism, liberation theology, the radical tradition, and decolonial theories. We draw from Black love and care, from Mother Wit and Othermothering, from moral courage and responsibility—from deep within and from ever-changing.

No single concept, ideology, philosophy, or theory adequately captures our approach to thinking about Blackness, nor is it our intent to present exhaustive summaries of any concept or theory. We offer brief descriptions of concepts and theories that inform our understandings of being and being Black, because of and despite our geographies, as these are our roots. We maintain that these collective ideas work in concert and help us to articulate and frame our thinking, as three Black female literacy scholars, about what literacy means, who has access to literacy, and what literacy research and practice should be. We take seriously the moral imperative to bringing an end to the inadequate and unproductive educational experiences and discourses surrounding millions of Black readers, as well as the abuse and trauma they have endured in the name of reading: reading assessment, reading instruction, and reading research.

We envisage our stance as a *moral imperative*, which the *Macmillan Dictionary* (2009–2020) defines as "something that must happen because it is the right thing" (n. p.). As Black literacy researchers, we must speak out and not wait until the inevitable happens. Thousands of Black children are languishing in classrooms with "universal" curricula and weathering trauma—at a tender age—when faced with current reading assessments. Students should not be held accountable for failing to learn; the system should be held accountable for failing to adequately teach and assess student learning. This text is written to save the lives of Black students/readers.

We write also to save ourselves—our humanity and the values we espouse—and to provide authentic, culturally and linguistically rich descriptions and interpretations of Black culture, language, literacies, lives, and values to inform reading assessment, instruction, praxis, and research. We refuse, as Morrison (2019) advises, "to continue to produce generation after generation of people trained to make expedient decisions rather than humane ones" (p. 72). We write from where Black cultures, languages, literacies, knowledges, and voices create, grow, live, and produce. As fellow humans occupying the world and as all Black women of African descent, we "dream the world as it ought to be, imagine what it would be like" (Morrison, 2019, p. 70). We write to right wrongs where Blackness is peripheral in reading research. In our lives and scholarship, Blackness is centralized, and we argue that where Black readers are concerned, Blackness must be central. Our collective wisdom acknowledges that humans need one another to move forward.

CONCEPTUAL FOUNDATIONS: MORAL COURAGE AND MORAL LICENSING

What moral foundation is needed in reading research to inform assessment and instruction: agency, articulation, choice, commitment, compass, courage, imagination, impetus, imperative, judgments, responsibility, sense, support, truth, or understanding? According to Miller (2000), moral courage represents one's willingness to defend a conviction regardless of how others respond. Individuals who show moral courage may be aware of the risks, hazards, and obstacles associated with their actions such as disapproval, derision, or harm to self and family, but they are nonetheless compelled to act because of their insistence on virtue, value, and a sense of what is right (Kidder, 2005; Miller, 2000). Among the key factors that affect moral courage is the power of the situations one faces (Zimbardo, 2005). For instance, powerful situations may lead individuals who otherwise tend to operate from a moral compass to overlook and reject their convictions in favor of group or authority norms. This tendency, referred to as the inoculation hypothesis (Cialdini & Trost, 1998), leads many individuals to choose these norms so that they can avoid fear and ridicule or because they lack confidence about how to behave in given situations.

We are witnesses to the moral courage of our forebears of African descent who endured unknown anti-Black racism, hardships, and indignities as they sought a better life for their progeny. Glaude (2016) notes that "we learn race in the places we live not as rules, but as habits—as a kind of general know-how that enables us to get about" (p. 57). Conversely, powerful situations also create an environment where individuals defy group norms and privilege their convictions because they believe in what is right (Zimbardo, 2005). Individuals who are capable of following their convictions and moral compasses regardless of authority or group norms tend to be driven by the notion of duty to uphold standards of rightness that transcend the societal obligations and guidelines on which these standards are based. They choose to follow their moral convictions, often do not keep company with those who do not also hold these convictions, and tend to be less reliant on the group norms or what others think to determine how they will behave in a given situation (Skitka, 2012). This notion has been referred to as the *authority independence hypothesis* (Milgram, 1974). Such individuals might view the need to advocate for the rights of a Black child to use their literacies as more important than legislation dictating that no Black person should be allowed to — *history* read and write. In this sense, the individual is more concerned with the right to literacy being allowed to every human and thus a Black child, and therefore chooses to overlook or resist the law of the land legislating against this right. Moreover, the individual's convictions involve a belief that authority's rules and laws on the issue should allow for the right of the Black child to literacy.

Overall, individuals who have stronger moral convictions have less desire to conform to group or authority norms and are not likely to be influenced by the majority but rather will choose these moral convictions above all. Such individuals, like Rosa Parks back then on the bus, are therefore more likely to reflect moral courage (Skitka, Bauman, & Lytle, 2009). In thinking about moral courage, it is important to consider what happens when individuals, as a society, take a certain moral stance as opposed to others regarding disenfranchised groups. What is the consequence, for instance, when inoculation supersedes authority independence in the approaches to Black readers in schools? And what happens when, in the mind of groups, the moral duties that are taken up are justified as good when they are evil? Warrican (2020) presents the notion of moral licensing (Khan & Dhar, 2006) as one where "in the minds of people, the good that they do for others far outweighs any negative effects that may be incurred" (p. 1). Such a situation is visible in many former British colonies where granting independence (i.e., the good act) was seen to have somehow been a recompense for the evils of slavery (i.e., the negative effects). With such a perspective, "dominant groups feel that doing an act of good counterbalances an unfavorable act" (Warrican, 2020, p. 15), and individuals point to an act they consider to be good as a means of excusing behavior that they know is bad or immoral. Warrican observes:

> . . . moral licensing is a psychological phenomenon that allowed, for example, slave owners to feel virtuous when they claimed that they treated their slaves well, feeding, clothing and sheltering them in ways that others did not, while overlooking the fact that they were depriving these kept individuals of their freedom . . . The application of moral licensing

to excuse certain behaviors may be a deliberate and public act, but some-times it is subconscious. There is no doubt that there are those who are aware of how doing a moral act can allow them to get away with future immoral actions, and they may use this awareness to their advantage. Others may stumble into this advantage, recognize its benefits and decide to utilize it while disregarding the fact that they are performing immoral actions. (p. 17)

Applying the perspective of moral licensing to how Black readers are treated in schools, it is easy to question "whether moral licensing provides people with a way of reassuring themselves that they are moral people" (Warrican, 2020, p. 8).

Think of an educational system with schools and policymakers who present an appearance of virtue by providing educational op-portunities to Black students while at the same time insisting on disregarding, and sometimes instituting legislation, such as the "3rd-grade reading" laws that detrimentally affect Black youth. Or think of an educational system where the languages and literacies of Black youth are said to be valued but at the same time, legislation about the instruction provided on a daily basis is not modified to ensure that teachers have provisions to advocate for the translanguaging of Black students in classrooms. Glaude (2016) articulates that such po-sitions represent moral failure. He argues that a "value gap (the be-lief that White people are valued more than others) and racial habits (the things we do, without thinking, that sustain the value gap) un-dergird racial inequality, and how White and Black fears block the way to racial justice in this country" (p. 6). This value gap is daily visible in the ways that the languages of Black students are racial-ized, and they are repeatedly rejected despite being expected to ap-proximate Eurocentric literacy norms (Rosa & Flores, 2017). Glaude proffers that "the value gap has both moral and political significance. We have to be better people by fundamentally transforming the con-ditions of our living together" (p. 46). For a society bent on inocula-tion that disregards moral conviction regarding Black readers, moral licensing appears to play a legitimate role. As observed by Warrican (2020):

Those who engage in moral licensing seem to think that they accumulate moral credits from past good deeds which they can then draw down on as license to do bad or immoral acts. It may be the thought of such moral credits that drives many to dehumanize Black [youth]. (p. 17)

Such accumulated moral credits may also be related to continuous attempts to silence and ignore Black researchers' voices in conversations about best practices in the teaching of Black students (Delpit, 1988; Willis, Smith, Kim, & Hsieh, 2021). Attempts to silence and ignore Black researchers who challenge privileged perspectives are made by gatekeepers who exert power to retain the status quo. From the perspective of moral licensing, the very notion that Black students and researchers do receive instruction in classrooms, workplaces, communities, and universities allows such gatekeepers to feel justified in determining if and how Black folks contribute to given conversations. One might argue that such reasoning, based on moral licensing, helps explain the persistent and unjust treatment of Black readers and the continued disregard for their plight that has persisted for decades, despite the abolition of slavery.

THEORETICAL FOUNDATIONS: BLACK LIBERATION THEOLOGY, BLACK RADICAL TRADITION, CRITICAL RACE THEORY, AND DECOLONIZATION

There are complex, multiple, and overlapping philosophical, ideological, and theoretical schools of thought that inform our thinking. We use the notion of parallax to help explain our stance. The *Oxford Dictionary* (Oxford University Press, 2020) defines *parallax* as "the effect whereby the position or direction of an object appears to differ when viewed from different positions" (n.p.). As Black women, we each possess different histories and from different places, offering varied lenses of the world. We draw from a deep well of schools of thought: Black Feminist Theory, Black Liberation Theology, Black Mother Wit, Black Radical Tradition (from David Walker's rebellion to the #BlackLivesMatter movement); Critical Race Theory (counternarratives, intersectionality, interest convergence), and Decolonial Theory, among others.

We draw upon myriad sources and resources, just as we do when we engage Black students as readers. No single source of knowledge is sufficient to meet all the needs of every student: we listen, probe, correct, and hear with our hearts and souls, along with our academic knowledge and expertise. What is important to take away from this text is that Black scholars framing reading research may draw from sources that are unknown (but not unknowable) to mainstream readers, because of their understanding of Blackness and to correct and reframe Black students as readers. We acknowledge that our stance is unconventional, as is our goal: to improve and accurately reflect the reading achievement of Black students. Next, we offer a brief overview of foundational theory, Black Liberation Theology, as well as insights drawn from the Black Radical Tradition, Critical Race Theory, and Decolonial Theory.

BLACK LIBERATION THEOLOGY

> No theology, Black or White, Protestant or Catholic can become Christian theology in North America or the world that does not engage White supremacy in society and the Church. To remain silent about the deadly consequences of White racism in the modern world automatically invalidates any theology's claim to Christian identity. (Cone, 2000, p. 731)

Although it is a common belief that Black Liberation Theology emerged out of the civil rights and Black Power movements as a way for Black Christians to reconcile their belief in the Holy Bible and their struggle with the connection of Christianity to whiteness and White supremacy, no one knows for certain the inception of Black Liberation Theology. We are aware that Black ministers and laity in Protestant and Catholic churches organized themselves inside and outside of predominantly White churches and organizations. They "identified and critiqued the structures and patterns of relationships that continued to marginalize, devalue, exploit, and otherwise perpetuate the oppression and dehumanization of Black people in the United States as antithetical to the gospel of Jesus Christ" (Phelps, 2000, p. 673). This theology focuses on racism and fights against oppressive forms of hypocrisy displayed by White Christians who have historically misused biblical texts to justify their inhumane acts. It demands action on the part of the oppressed and oppressor. The oppressed must rise up and fight against the injustices they experience at all costs, and the oppressor must confess their wrongs and turn from their wicked ways. Black Liberation Theology is built on the understanding that there is no separation between the Black Church and the Black Community (Lincoln & Mamiya, 1990). Instead, the Black Church is a safe space where Black people can find solace, support, and affirmation (Calhoun-Brown, 1999). We approach our research from a Black Liberation Theological perspective because we have been raised in Black churches that teach the importance of participating in social justice movements.

The Black Church is the "Mother Womb" of the Black Community, the institution from which many other institutions have grown, such as banks, colleges, nonprofit organizations, schools, and social justice movements (Frazier, 1963; McMillon, 2001). Before 1794 and Richard Allen's (1760–1831) founding of Bethel African Methodist Episcopal Church (AME) in Philadelphia, Pennsylvania, and beyond the 2015 murder of nine Black parishioners at Emanuel AME in Charleston, South Carolina, the Black Church has nurtured and supported Black families throughout their struggles against the many facets of institutionalized racism, reminding them of their strength and their duty to resist. We were taught from an early age that it is our responsibility to become educated but not allow our education to taint our beliefs and understandings about who we are as Black women of God and our responsibility to our Black community. We were taught to aim high, accomplish our goals, and reach back to help others. We were taught that we must stand up and fight the injustices that we see wherever we find ourselves. We were taught that silence is consent and that we cannot be complicit in the immoral, degrading injustices that we see in the teaching of reading for Black students.

We choose to speak out to honor our ancestors on whose shoulders we stand. We stand on the shoulders of many giants who share(d) our Black Liberation Theological perspective, including Reverend Nat Turner; Reverend George Liele; Reverend Richard Allen; Alberta Williams King; Rt. Excellent Samuel Sharpe; Dr. Martin Luther King Jr.; Dr. Marian Wright Edelman; Dr. Samuel DeWitt Proctor; Dr. Otis Moss Jr.; Reverend C. T. Vivian; Reverend Jeremiah Wright; Bishop Vashti McKenzie; Dr. Renita Weems; Reverend Dr. M. T. and Pecola Thompson; Adell and Angie Ingram; and Patrick and Maryanna Smith; along with many others, too numerous to name. They went before us, paving the way, tearing down strongholds, building bridges, and challenging White supremacist mindsets of people who tried to keep Black folks in their "place." They incited revolts; founded Black churches, schools, organizations, and movements; demanded seats at decision-making tables; and challenged racist mindsets by becoming "firsts" and mentoring others to follow in their footsteps. They taught us to rise up and respond to our "calling" from God to faithfully and fearlessly fight for equity and justice for our people. Anything less would be sinful. Our list includes Black heroes whose work precedes the civil rights and Black Power movements. Their "acts of resistance" provided the foundation for the continued resistance that occurred during that time, and the organized acts of resistance during the civil rights and Black Power movements sparked a fire in us to continue their work.

For our current work, understand that "resistance" is not unfamiliar to us or the Black students whom we love so dearly. In fact, bell hooks (1994) defines Black students' unwillingness to complete assignments as "resistance" to the oppressive actions that they experience in America's schools. She asserts that we should not confuse their resistance as an inability to do the work but understand it as their way of articulating their refusal to submit to oppressive actions and mindsets that they encounter daily. We have seen these actions in our own children while trying to negotiate their educational experiences. We join Black children in their resistant outcry to stop treating them like dispensable guinea pigs and laboratory rats. They are neither. It is not acceptable to use them to test the latest reading program developed by literacy researchers seeking fame and fortune from the perpetuation of institutionalized racism. We stand on our Black Liberation Theological beliefs, surrounded by a great cloud of witnesses—past and present—and demand that these acts of racism, intentional or unintentional, cease!

BLACK FEMINISM

I am my Sister's keeper. (Anna Julia [Haywood] Cooper, 1886)

Black feminist ideology was first introduced by Anna Julia (Haywood) Cooper, the Mother of Black Feminism, in the late 19th century. Her work, which was greatly influenced by her enslaved mother, emphasized (a) commitment to family and to others in the community; (b) strategies to assist race, class, and gender oppression; and (c) a strong religious belief in God's benevolence. Cooper was a teacher who believed that higher education could help to uplift the race, and she believed that Black women were uniquely qualified to deliver such an education to Black youth. As an activist, Cooper defied ideological and cultural hegemony and challenged the use of science as proof of racial intellectual and moral inferiority. Her unvarnished writings acknowledge Black women's intellect and role in society. Bonnick (2007) notes that "historically the field of education is intimately connected to black people's struggles to improvise agency out of conditions they were not expected to survive" (pp. 179–180) and believes the position exemplifies Cooper's stance.

Collins (1990, 1998a, 1998b, 2000) further clarifies Black Feminism in her writings, outlining four tenets: (a) specialized epistemology, (b) dialogue to assess knowledge claims, (c) an ethic of caring, and (d) an ethic of personal responsibility. Collins observes that Black women have shared their knowledge and evolving critical consciousness in what she identifies as "safe spaces" (p. 100), where subjugated and oppositional knowledges are welcomed and affirmed. She proffers that subjugated knowledge is "secret knowledges generated by oppressed groups . . . hidden because revealing it weakens its purpose of assisting them in dealing with oppression" (p. 301) and that oppositional knowledge is "a type of knowledge developed by, for, and/or in defense of an oppressed group's interests. . . .[It] fosters the group's self-definition and self-determination" (p. 299). Our text is informed by the four tenets of Black Feminism, as well as Collins's notion of a matrix of domination, which serves as a lens to understand how power operates in society. She also identifies four domains of power: (a) structural (an organization's laws, policies, and practices), (b) disciplinary (rules/bureaucracies), (c) hegemonic (ideas and ideologies), and (d) interpersonal (lived experiences of discrimination). Collins explains that within the matrix of domination, there is: "(1) a particular arrangement of intersecting systems of oppression, e.g., race, social class, gender, sexuality, citizenship, status, ethnicity, and age; and (2) a particular organization of its demands of power; e.g., structural, disciplinary, hegemonic, and interpersonal" (pp. 299–300).

Crenshaw's body of scholarship extends our thinking about Black Feminism and establishes connections with Critical Race Theory. She was among the organizers of the Critical Race Theory workshop during the 1987 critical legal studies (CLS) conference. She sought to encourage legal scholars to "reexamine the terms by which race and racism have been negotiated in the American consciousness, and to recover and revitalize the radical tradition of race-consciousness among African-Americans and other peoples of color" (Crenshaw, Gotanda, Peller, & Thomas, 1995, p. xiv). Crenshaw is best known for exposing the intersections of oppression that occur in the lives of Black women, "where systems of race, gender, and class domination converge" (Crenshaw, 1991, p. 1241). As she articulates: "Black feminism emphasized the role of structures in constituting the conditions of life in which racially and economically marginalized women were situated" (Cho, Crenshaw, & McCall, 2013, p. 797). For example, she publicly acknowledges the names of Black women and girls who have been killed by police officers. Moreover, she challenges the mischaracterization of Black women into single categories and insists on understanding their lives as existing at points of intersection. To be clear, though Crenshaw's focus has been on the lives of Black women, she is not immune to the lives of all Black suffering. She writes that "we must also absorb the bone-chilling truth . . . of the everyday disregard for our lives. . . . It has to be squarely confronted for what it is: One more chapter in the annals of American racial power, in which the bodies of some are sacrificed en masse for the privilege and convenience of others" (Crenshaw, 2020, n.p). Crenshaw carefully details how interlocking political systems work to obfuscate as well as privilege dominant groups, groups who dismiss, ignore, and minimalize anti-Black racism—whether intentional and overt discrimination or underprosecuted and unpunished murder. Crenshaw recognizes that Black lives are not valued and that the lack of concern for Black life concretizes the contemporary Jim Crow miscarriage of justice. She reflects this idea in the midst of a racial reckoning in the United States and her understanding of the impact of the murder of Breonna Taylor: "If #Breonna Taylor's story serves as a cornerstone for a generation of activism, it will foreground something new in the freedom struggle: It will make Black women central to any analysis of and challenge to anti-Blackness" (Crenshaw, 2021c).

THE BLACK RADICAL TRADITION

We were never meant to survive. (Audre Lorde, 1978)

A complete list of the Black scholarship that informs our writing is beyond the scope of this introduction. Our work is inspired by Michelle Alexander; Maya Angelou; James Baldwin; Gloria Ladson-Billings; Eduardo Bonilla-Silva; Tehama Lopez Bunyasi; Septima Clark; Patricia Hill Collins; James Cone; Anna Julia (Haywood) Cooper; Kimberlé Crenshaw; Fredrick Douglass, W. E. B. Du Bois: Frantz Fanon; Henry Louis Gates Jr.; Eddie Glaude; Stuart Hall; Fannie Lou Hamer; Cheryl Harris; bell hooks; C. L. James, Robin D. G. Kelly; Ibram X. Kendi; Martin Luther King Jr.; Alaine Locke; Manning Marable; Toni Morrison; Fred Moten; Nell Painter; Rosa Parks: Cedric Robinson; Candis Watts Smith; Geneva Smitherman; Claude Steele; Alice Walker; Cornel West; Carter G. Woodson; and Richard Wright, among others. These scholars exemplify the Black radical intelligentsia who reveal how political structural racism reproduces itself and alerts us to the pervasiveness of anti-Black racism. Robinson (2000), for example, examines resistance by Africans in Africa, European genocide, imperialism, and racism in the United States:

> The Black Radical Tradition was an accretion, over generations, of collective intelligence gathered from struggle. In daily encounters and petty resistances to domination, slaves had acquired a sense of the calculus of oppression as well as its organization and instrumentation. These experiences lent themselves to a means of preparation for more epic resistance movements. (p. xxx)

Marable (2011) also traces the evolution of the Black Radical Tradition and summarizes: "Its essential characteristics were strong opposition to structural racism; and its political economy, and the advocacy of robust state interventions to protect blacks' lives and improve their material and social conditions" (p. 2). We are cognizant that each generation builds upon the former—for example, Black resistance bears witness to the civil rights movement as well as the #BlackLivesMatter movement. Bunyasi and Smith (2019) argue that the Black Lives Matter movement is "an effort to bring attention to the precarious nature of Black lives in the United States" (p. 1). For centuries, the Black Radical Tradition has sought to improve the plight of people of African descent. This collective body of scholarship informs our thinking and significantly differs from the scholarship typically used to inform reading.

CRITICAL RACE THEORY

We engage Critical Race Theory (CRT) as espoused by Bell (1980, 1995), Crenshaw et al. (1995), and Delgado and Stefancic (2001). Crenshaw et al. (1995) argue that race is 'real' in the sense that there is material dimension and weight to the experience of being 'raced' in American society (p. xxvi). CRT centers on race and acknowledges that intersectionality or multiple forms of oppression—class, ethnicity, gender, immigration rights, language, nationality, sexual orientation, and sovereignty—exist and are experienced among People of Color. CRT scholarship is premised on two foundational ideas: to understand how a regime of White supremacy and its subordination of People of Color have been created and maintained in the United States and, in particular, to examine the relationship between social structures and professed ideals such as the "rule of law" and "equal protection." The second is a desire not merely to understand the vexed bond between law and racial power but to change it (p. xiii). De La Garza and Ono (2016) also suggest that CRT "assumes that the production, dissemination, and evaluation of knowledge is fundamentally political and, as such, CRT researchers challenge objectivity, neutrality, and scholarly authority and the way these objectives may be used to distance and separate researchers from material life" (p. 2). To be clear, CRT centers on race, acknowledges that intersectionality exists, and focuses on race experienced among People of Color. Matsuda, Lawrence, Delgado, and Crenshaw (1993) identify six defining elements that capture basic themes in CRT legal scholarship: (a) recognizes that racism is endemic to American life; (b) expresses skepticism toward dominant legal claims of neutrality, objectivity, color blindness, and meritocracy; (c) challenges ahistoricism and insists on a contextual/historical analysis of the law; (d) insists on recognition of the experiential knowledge of People of Color and our communities of origin in analyzing law and society; (e) is interdisciplinary and eclectic; and (f) works toward the end of eliminating racial oppression as part of the broader goal of ending all forms of oppression (p. 6). CRT can be used in reading research to deconstruct context and text, to expose how, and how often, issues of race are linked to "claims of color blindness, neutrality, and meritocracy" (Love, 2004, p. 228). When used as a lens to examine reading research and Black readers, we find helpful Delgado's (1989) description of how master narratives represent "the bundle of presuppositions, received wisdoms, and shared understandings against a background of which legal and political discourse takes place. These matters are rarely focused on" (p. 2413). In addition, we draw on Crenshaw's (1991) theory of intersectionality, as well as extensions of the concept, to understand how institutional and structural political processes and procedures have helped to shape reading reforms and the veneer of equity that obscures the reality of the reform laws. We also consider discursive structures "where systems of race, gender, and class domination converge" (Crenshaw, 1991, p. 1241) to expose commonplace disparaging, inaccurate, and racially ignorant discourses used to describe Black readers as well as their communities, families, and languages.

DECOLONIAL THEORIES

> A basic task of decolonial thought has been to use the analysis of modernity/coloniality to identify the primary drivers of colonial relations of power, or the causes of modern/colonial forms of social classification, relations, and structures. (Drexler-Dreis, 2019, p. 2)

We draw on decolonial theories that function as a "deeply subaltern form of qualitative research practice; one which seeks to formidably challenge and disrupt the one-dimensional Eurocentric epistemicides prevalent in traditional theories of schooling and society" (Darder, 2015, p. 64; Paraskeva, 2011). Functioning as critical bicultural researchers, we

> . . . engage the dominant literature on pedagogy, curriculum, methodology, and schooling in ways that treat these writings as data to be systematically and qualitatively analyzed, based upon [our] own (autoethnographic) historical experiences of difference, as both historical subjects in their self-determination and bicultural critical educators in [our] field[s]. (Darder, 2015, p. 64)

Drawing from the philosophy of Ubuntu—"'I am we; I am because we are; we are because I am'" (Chilisa & Ntseane, 2010, p. 619), we adopt a humanist approach that reflects respect and compassion while emphasizing human dignity and support for the community (Lituchy & Michaud, 2017). We give precedence to the collective social (i.e., Indigenous) over the individual (i.e., Western-European), aware that knowledge from a decolonizing perspective is perceived as "eternal," retrieved based on "observation and interaction with the biological and social environments, as well as from visions, stories, and spiritual insights" and "receding from consciousness when not required" (Ibrahima & Mattaini, 2019, p. 9).

Acknowledging that most of our scholarship thus far and the scholarship on which our work is premised utilizes "Western" methodologies, where evidence of knowledge is gained from hearing, sight, smell, taste, and touch, we challenge the notion that non-Western ways of knowing rooted in aesthetics or in spirituality such as gods or spirits be disregarded in our legitimate understandings of how we, as Black sisters, come to know the world and how our Black children read it (Ibrahima & Mattaini, 2019; Matsinhe, 2007). In doing so, we come against notions that suggest relying solely on:

. . . conclusions that privilege reasoning shaped by an underlying belief in the superiority of an either/or, linear, reductionist, hierarchical, concrete, object/subject or nature/human separation, and neutral, decontextualized, ahistorical, and apolitical methodologies in the ways we construct knowledge about social phenomenon. (Darder, 2015, p. 66)

Our decolonizing approach has the potential to radically change the field of reading and the lives of millions of Black students. This framework emphasizes the dialectic critical to acknowledging the interplay between decolonizing methods that foreground non-Western Eurocentric epistemologies about Black youth and hegemonic Westernized perspectives that consistently redefine Black readers as ill-equipped, inadequate, incapable, and underperforming. We deconstruct Westernized ways of viewing Black readers while simultaneously interrogating these notions through contextual knowledge, historical values (i.e., past, present, future), and insider realities of non-Westernized thought. We stand in accord with Ella Baker (1964) as we end this section with a "call to remembrance" of those who proceeded us in this journey:

Until the education of a black mother's son becomes as important to the rest of the country as the education of a white mother's son, we who believe in freedom shall not rest. (Baker, quoted in Glaude, 2016, p. 235)

READING RESEARCH AND BLACK STUDENTS

We write this book at a unique time in our nation's history, a time in which the voices of Black women are being listened to, not just heard, as never before. The recent murders of unarmed Black American citizens Ahmaud Arbery, George Floyd, and Breonna Taylor have brought into sharp relief the importance and value of Black people's lives. What is being written, and what will be written about this time in U.S. history, depends in part on the perspective of the writer as well as the interpretation of the reader. We write not only amid political disunity, including the continuous public lynching of Black bodies by police, but also during a period when the COVID-19 pandemic has exposed economic and racial disparities in health care and education. As schools closed due to stay-at-home state mandates and were forced to turn to online instruction, the "digital divide" among communities became more apparent. Students without access to computers or

Internet service also lacked greater access to equitable educational opportunities. Media commentators have drawn reference to the nation's sin of racism as well as the legacy of slavery that has tarnished the democratic notions of fairness and equity. Attention also has been given to implicit and systemic racism that exists in institutions as well as in all fields of study, including reading, in the United States.

Why this book, and why now? We write to save Black readers from the current system and false promises of an equitable education that continually traumatize and deny Black students educational justice. We find it inconceivable that the plight of Black readers is flying under the radar of political candidates and pundits. Nationally, a shocking number of state laws and policies target "struggling" readers, most of whom are Black, to read on their grade level by the end of grade 3. If students fail to do so, they are retained in grade 3. How does a nation reconcile penalizing 9-year-old children, but not holding accountable administrators, teachers, and researchers for the processes and systems they create? What psychological trauma will these children endure from the outcomes of reading assessments on which such laws are premised? The assessments emerging from such processes and systems, underpinned by racist ideologies and methods (Willis, 2009, 2018), appear to reemerge cyclically with new rationalizations, or reinventions of past methods, and a renaming of the purpose. To date, there has been little change in the results and outcomes for many Black readers, both in and beyond the United States, on standardized reading assessments. It is important to ask: who benefits, and what institutions benefit, from the failure of Black students to learn to read and perform well on standardized tests? We acknowledge that although this book has been years in the making, it is being published at a time of disunity and within a horrific sociopolitical environment. We ask: If not now, when?

As literacy researchers, we too value the lives of Black people and seek to ensure that Black readers matter. Historically, literacy research has pathologized Blackness and continues to promote misinterpretations of Black readers and their life experiences that are accepted, promoted, repeated, and published. Given our conceptual and theoretical framing of Blackness, we write understanding how brinksmanship in academia works. We have also talked about how authentic interpretations of Black readers by Black researchers are disavowed, derided, and dismissed as "identity politics." In short, we realize that within the reading research community, our positionality may come at a cost; however, it is one that we are willing to pay. Drawing from

Tayari Jones's (2019) we do not need to "search for common ground; but to look for the true path forward" (n.p.). We believe the path forward begins with understanding that Black readers, like all readers, are human and should be valued. We affirm our Blackness framework as a starting point, not in comparison to, or in competition with, other racial groups, because Blackness is complete in and of itself.

We seek to redirect reading research away from sanctimonious "universal" notions of readers that infantilize students' cultures, languages, literacies, and knowledge systems. By way of contrast, there is a rich body of overlooked research on Black student reading conducted and interpreted by Black scholars since the late 1800s. The research, and the stories the research tells, differs markedly from the negative racialized depictions of Black readers, communities, and families, polluting reading research. This alternative body of research offers a culturally and linguistically attuned stance toward Black readers as we say, "They tell it right." We also offer a more authentic understanding of Black students' experiences as readers, along with descriptions of communities and families struggling against an oppressive system. This book offers support to parents/caregivers, politicians, teachers, and researchers seeking ways to help improve reading development and assessment for Black students.

In the next chapter, we center on Black women's lives, teaching, and depths of wisdom in its complexity as activists and teachers. We also celebrate and value the scholarship of Black scholars who have contributed to our understanding of Black excellence, worthy of unvarnished attention in its own right.

CHAPTER 2

Black Women Activist Teachers

> This traditional system—built on the logics of heteropatriarchal white supremacy—inherently erases the invisible labor of those who helped to build the genealogies of thought that contribute to all knowledge. Within this rubric, Black women have been systematically unnamed. Therefore, naming is an act of rebellion. (C. A. Smith et al., 2021, p. 1)

In this chapter, we provide an overview of the historic "roots and routes" (Hall, 1980) Black women have taken in support of educational justice, racial justice, and access to literacy for Black people. The roots of denying education and the access to literacy are entangled in the dominant ideas held by those in power before the founding of the nation as well as in contemporary times. Anderson (1988) observes that "Blacks emerged from slavery with a strong belief in the desirability of learning to read and write" (p. 5). He also notes that Black people held literacy in high regard; "historically African Americans have relied heavily on schooling to eliminate illiteracy . . . ," and consequently, "the denial of opportunities for schooling has translated into the denial of access to literacy" (pp. 35–36). Black people have:

> . . . demanded, created, funded, and maintained educational institutions that would (a) provide literacy for all; (b) apprise individuals of and prepare them for the dominating culture's institutions; (c) counteract their pernicious and venal images of African Americans prevalent in popular culture; and (d) engender group solidarity and commitment to uplift. (Harris, 1992, p. 276)

To be clear, decisions to deny enslaved Black people's literacy have always been calculated decisions that were politicized and legalized with incalculable human costs.

The routes to literacy are grounded in Black Liberation Theology, Black feminist theory, and the Black Radical Tradition. They include the intersection of cultural, historical, political, social, and racial routes navigated by Black women to gain access to literacy and to teach literacy. Black women teachers often expressed their epistemological understandings through acceptance, love, and respect for our humanity and the harrowing life experiences so many endured. Collectively, they advocated for freedom and leadership training, as well as racial justice and uplift. They sought to improve access, opportunity, and the quality of education for Black students through the concepts, ideas, and strategies they embraced, acknowledging and understanding cultural roots and the history of enslavement of Black people. We include them in this book, in part, because of their ordinariness—that is, they did not seek fame, they were not (at the onset) academics; they were Black women on a mission. And we include them because they provide insight into the long history of literacy in the United States and how Black women activist teachers approached literacy.

We examine intersecting contexts (cultural, political, social, racial, and religious) as Black women activist teachers navigated to gain access to literacy. The narrative is constructed to share autobiographical and biographical information about each woman's life and their contributions to provide and to extend literacy access to Black people in their geographical areas/spheres of influence. The efforts of these seemingly ordinary Black women activist teachers offer an often-overlooked historical perspective of literacy in the United States. Their lives and accomplishments, along with those of countless other unsung Black people, highlight how hard we have fought for literacy. The efforts of these seemingly ordinary Black women who became freedom fighters and extraordinary activists, community leaders, and teachers offer a unique historical perspective of reading and writing education in the United States. Their lives and accomplishments, along with those of countless other Black people, highlight how hard we have fought for education and for access to literacy.

Methodologically, historical research "attempts to systematically recapture the complex nuances, the people, meanings, events, and even ideas of the past that have influenced and shaped the present" (Berg & Lune, 2012, p. 305). Historical research consists of several well-defined steps: (1) reading secondary sources, (2) formulating a research question, (3) conducting background research, (4) refining the question, (5) using historical methods, (6) locating primary and secondary data, (7) evaluating the authenticity of the sources, (8) analyzing the data, and (9) crafting a narrative. We use autobiographical and biographical information about the experiences of Black women and girls who sought access and opportunity for education in general, and reading in particular. Primary data sources include diaries, journals, letters, newspaper articles, and various government documents. As such, these written documents and eyewitness accounts of Black women activist teachers have been evaluated for external criticism or authenticity (verifying the author's legitimacy and document) and internal criticism or accuracy (determining what the document means). Secondary sources (articles, biographies, books, newspaper articles, and periodicals) were evaluated similarly. Data analysis centers on content analysis and interpretation of the data (reviewing sources for patterns, establishing categories, and developing themes).

In the United States, fear of the liberatory power of literacy has fueled efforts historically, politically, socially, and racially to sanction who, and under what circumstances, Black people would be permitted to learn to read. In 2021, learning to read should be recognized as a civil right, influenced by the 14th Amendment's adherence to equal protection under the law, but is still debated in the court of public opinion and federal courts. Black women activist teachers were more than witnesses to change; they were change agents. They were hopeful— despite the historical moment and circumstances of their lives—that access to caring and compassionate education in general, and literacy in particular, would provide Black people with a path forward to freedom, civil rights, liberation, and justice.

LITERACY AND FREEDOM

Therefore if the Son makes you free, you shall be free indeed. (John 8:36)

Too often the history of slavery, "which continues to evolve" (Stevenson quoted in Chotiner, 2020, n. p.), is minimized to protect the oppressors. Enslaved Africans arrived from various African nations and did not have a shared culture, language, or religion. Once in the New World, they were expected to learn the language of their oppressors, but they were forbidden to learn to read and write in the oppressor's language. As early as 1664, colonies enacted a series of slave laws for people of African descent, legalizing slavery, determining a person's birthright, separating parents and children, outlawing miscegenation, ordering servitude for life, restricting enslaved people's behavior and movement, and forbidding meetings and the use of weapons. The Virginia Slave Law of 1667 also declared that enslaved Africans could be baptized, making them Christians, and their status as Christians was not in conflict with biblical scriptures that declare Christians should not enslave one another. The law was established to ease concerns of slaveholders and to permit them to legally, if not morally, continue chattel slavery unencumbered by religious beliefs. In 1740, in the landmass that is now known as South Carolina, legislation also passed outlawing teaching enslaved Africans to read and write:

> Whereas, the having slaves taught to write, or suffering them to be employed in writing, may be attended with great inconveniences; Be it enacted, that all and every person and persons whatsoever, who shall hereafter teach or cause any slave or slaves to be taught to write, or shall use or employ any slave as a scribe, in any manner of writing whatsoever, hereafter taught to write, every such person or persons shall, for every such offense, forfeit the sum of one hundred pounds, current money. (Simkin, 2020, n.p.)

There was a greater emphasis on teaching Black people to read and a reticence to teaching Black people to write (Bly, 2011; Monaghan, 2005), as literacy historians argue that White Christians believed that teaching Black people to write would stop rebellions. Others held that teaching Black people to write made them appear more human, with the ability to think, reason, and understand what was happening to them in ways that were not complimentary portrayals of the actions of White people.

Likewise, it was against the law for enslaved people to be taught and to teach other enslaved people to read and write in many Southern colonies. Browne-Marshall (2013) observes a twofold argument against the education of Black people: (a) Black people were characterized as "uneducable," and (b) "an educated person who learned to read and write would be rendered unfit for slave labor" (p. 19). The education of Black people was somewhat different in the North; in the state of New York, the African Free School was established in 1788. In addition, in Boston, there were segregated schools for Black students. White people, identified by their Christian beliefs, established schools for Black people in an effort to spread Christianity. Other parts of the country, including Williamsburg, Virginia, also took up the mantle of spreading Christianity to enslaved Black people. White Christians in Williamsburg established the Bray School for enslaved and formerly enslaved African children, and the school's mission extended beyond altruism, reading, and writing: "Christianizing people . . . as a way of controlling them to making sure that they understood their place in society" (Allen quoted in Heim [2021], para. 9).The version of the Bible being read by slaves, however, may be more akin to a version used in the British West Indies: *Select Parts of the Holy Bible, for the use of the Negro Slaves, in the British West-India Islands* (1807).This version included most of the Old Testament and nearly half of the New Testament, although throughout it was heavily redacted and used to persuade enslaved and formerly enslaved Black people of their racial hierarchical place. For example, missing in this version is "there is neither Jew nor Greek, there is neither bond nor free, there is neither male nor female: for ye are all one in Christ Jesus" (Galatians 3:28), to discourage Black people from seeing themselves as equal to Whites. By contrast, the verse "servants, be obedient to them that are your masters according to the flesh, with fear and trembling, in singleness of your heart, as unto Christ" (Ephesians 6:5) was used to forestall rebellion.

The goals of Black and White Christians to extend literacy to enslaved and formerly enslaved Black people were in opposition. Williams (2005) notes that "literacy constituted one of the terrains on which slaves and slave owners waged a perpetual struggle for control" (p. 13). In his 1854 autobiography, Frederick Douglass observed, "I would at times feel that learning to read had been a curse rather than a blessing. It had given me a view of my wretched condition, without the remedy. It opened my eyes to the horrible pit, but to no ladder upon which to get out" (p. 55). He also articulated the differences he understood between Christians' actions and love in the Bible, the misinterpretations offered to control enslaved Black people: "a justifier of the most appalling barbarity—a sanctifier of the most hateful frauds—and a dark shelter under, which the darkest, foulest, grossest, and most infernal deeds of slaveholders find the strongest protection" (p. 86). Baker (2020) insightfully observes that Douglass understood the psychological toll of Black freedom and the desire for integration.

Black women also were active in efforts by Black Christian church-affiliated groups, some identified by denominations and others more generic in nature, such as the American Missionary Association (AMA). Sarah "Sallie" Daffin, for instance, taught in schools, whereas Nannie Helen Burroughs opened a school for Black girls in Washington, D.C. with the support of the Baptist Church. In addition, the federal government, under the Bureau of Refugees, Freedmen, and Abandoned Lands (Freedmen's Bureau), and philanthropic agencies (Negro Rural School Fund/Jeanes Fund, Phelps-Stokes Fund, Rosenwald Fund) also established schools for Black people after the Civil War.

Black people, nonetheless, learned to read, through the benevolence of Whites or being taught by other Black people. Those who learned to read shared their new knowledge and skills with other enslaved Black people. Williams (2005), for instance, shares an interview with Mattie Jackson, a woman who was born enslaved, by noting Jackson's desire to learn, as it "illustrates the radical potential that enslaved African Americans perceived in literacy" (p. 8). Williams also articulates that Black teachers understood that literacy was accompanied by "other ways of knowing. They relied heavily on oral and aural systems of information" (p. 9). Jackson, for example, learned to read, used the knowledge she gained to resist her owners, and eventually "refused to acquiesce in her enslavement" (p. 10). Williams does not offer details of how Jackson learned to read.

Individual narratives of Black women activist teachers follow and consist of brief snippets of their lives, teaching, and thoughts, with a focus on literacy. Their discussions on literacy vary, and there are few clear descriptions of literacy instruction. What is shared in many autobiographical and primary sources are descriptions of their intent: why they taught Black people to read and how they describe Black people as learners. In general, but not exclusively, Black women activist teachers accepted Black people as fellow humans struggling under oppressive living conditions. They treated Black people with dignity and respect; they valued their experiences and what they brought to the reading process, without question, without challenge, and without demeaning negative characterizations. We realize that these brave Black women were not always free to say exactly what they wanted; as such, their narratives were often tempered so as not to offend White benefactors, editors, publishers, and readers. Each woman used her opportunity and voice to express her beliefs about Black people as caring, loving, thoughtful, and generous people who were interested in learning literacy. We are grateful for their sacrifices and the paths they have left us to follow, like rose petals leading our way to reclaim Black literacy.

Harriet Ann Jacobs (1813–1897)

Harriet Ann Jacobs, born in Edenton, North Carolina, captures the effect of slave laws on the lives of enslaved people. Because she was an enslaved person, it was illegal for her to be taught to read and write. However, she describes being taught to read and write by her first White mistress. In her narrative, *Incidents in the Life of a Slave Girl:*

Written by Herself (1861), Jacobs acknowledges that she also taught other enslaved Black people to read and write. She shared an experience with an elderly enslaved man, Uncle Fred:

> I asked him if he didn't know it was contrary to law; and that slaves were whipped and imprisoned for teaching each other to read. This brought the tears into his eyes. "Don't be troubled uncle Fred," said I. "I have no thoughts of refusing to teach you. I only told you of the law, that you might know the danger, and be on your guard." He thought he could plan to come three times a week without its being suspected. I selected a quiet nook, where no intruder was likely to penetrate, and there I taught him his A, B, and C. Considering his age, his progress was astonishing. As soon as he could spell in two syllables he wanted to spell out words in the Bible. The happy smile that illuminated his face put joy into my heart. After spelling out a few words, he paused, and said, "Honey, it 'pears when I can read dis good book I shall be nearer to God." (p. 112)

Jacobs lived 6 years in her grandmother's attic to evade sexual harassment from her owner, all the while watching her two children grow and flourish. She eventually fled to New York, where she taught enslaved people to read and write. With the support of Lydia Maria Child, a White abolitionist, Jacobs published her narrative. Jacobs wrote for a largely White audience, and her narrative replicates a pattern within slave narratives meant to endear the reader to (a) the plight of enslaved Black women, (b) a description of the horrors of slavery, (c) temperate descriptions of sexual abuse, (d) pacification of White guilt and sensibilities, (e) a strong pronouncement of Christian beliefs, and (f) the importance and value of literacy.

There is a rich body of research about Black women activist teachers (Jean Deveaux in South Carolina, Lucinda Jackson in Georgia, and Blanche Harris in Mississippi, among others) who provided literacy training to Black people in the 1800s. Next, we share a brief narrative about several other Black women activist teachers: Mary S. Peake, Charlotte Forten Grimké, Georgia Washington, Lucy Craft Laney, Ruby Middleton Forsythe, Katherine Crosby, and Bertha Maxwell-Roddey.

Mary Smith Kelsey Peake (1823–1862)

Mary Smith was born in Virginia to a free woman and an Englishman. She learned to read as a young child and attended a select school for

Black children taught by White teachers until it was closed by law (Lockwood, 1862). She was a member of the Black upper class in Hampton, Virginia, and married Thomas Peake, a formerly enslaved man. She secretly taught enslaved people to read and write in her home. She was hired by the AMA to teach at Fortress Monroe, under a tree, Emancipation Oak, in the summer of 1861, now Hampton University. As Lockwood (1862) recalled,

> I soon found from observation, as well as information, that we had in her a teacher of the choicest spirit, and of peculiar qualifications. She was happy in having pupils as ready to learn as to request instruction. Her school numbered at first only about half a dozen, but in a few days she had between fifty and sixty. These scholars were found to have generally very fair intellectual capabilities, and a few evinced quite rare talents. Among these was her own little daughter, . . . She learned to read simple lessons fluently in a very short time. Others also exhibited a precocity which from day to day rewarded and stimulated that ardor of this devoted teacher.
>
> Mrs. Peake was not satisfied with the ordinary routine of the week-day school room but felt that the teacher of a mission school should aim to educate the children for eternity as well as for time. She found great assistance in the primer, catechism, and other elementary religious books, with which she had been furnished. She felt that the teachings of the week-day school ought to be largely preparatory to the rehearsals of the Sabbath school . . .
>
> While Mrs. Peake attached prime importance to the training of the rising generation, she felt that great improvement might be made among the adults. . . .She was accordingly very ready to gratify the desire of a number of adults for an evening school, . . . The result is, that several, who scarcely knew the alphabet before, now begin to read with considerable readiness.
>
> Mrs. Peake deeply realized that every undertaking, and especially the training the young, should be begun and continued with prayer. She not only prayed with her pupils, but taught them to pray. (pp. 30–33)

Among the early Black female teachers was a free Black woman, Charlotte Forten, whose grandfather and father financed abolitionist efforts and fought for equal rights for Black people. The women in her family were involved members of literary societies, and Forten worked under the auspices of the Freedmen's Bureau.

Charlotte L. Bridges Forten Grimké (1837–1914)

Charlotte Lottie Bridges Forten, known as "Lottie," was born into a well-resourced and respected Black family in Philadelphia. She received her education from private tutors before attending Higginson Grammar School, and she endured racial harassment while the only Black student at Salem Normal School. Later, she returned to teach at Epes and Higginson grammar schools as the first Black teacher. She was very committed to racial uplift and advancing education for Black people. Forten was a poet and published author before she taught on St. Helena Island in 1861. While teaching there, she kept a journal and later published excerpts about her experiences in *The Atlantic Monthly* (1864):

> After the lessons, we used to talk freely to the children, often giving them slight sketches of some of the great and good men. Before teaching them the "John Brown" song, which they learned to sing with great spirit, Miss T. told them the story of the brave old man who had died for them. I told them about Toussaint, thinking it well they should know what one of their own color had done for his race. They listened attentively, and seemed to understand. (para 15)

Forten's characterization and descriptions of the Black people and students emphasized their intelligence, eagerness to learn, desire for access to education, and genuinely thoughtful deportment. Likewise, the Black community relished their time with Forten. The relationship between Black teachers, even those who were not local community members, led Alvord (1866), a Freedmen Bureau supervisor, to observe:

> Throughout the entire South an effort is being made by the colored people to educate themselves. In the absence of other teaching they are determined to be self-taught; and everywhere some elementary textbook, or fragment of it, may be seen in the hands of negroes. They quickly communicate to each other what they already know, so that with very little learning many take to teaching. (quoted in Brosnan, 2019, p. 235)

In general, the Black community's support for Black education was unwavering. Johnson (1991) reveals that during Reconstruction, Black people often preferred schools established by other Black people, as they were "distrustful of whites, while whites were disdainful of black teachers and dismayed at the popularity of black-controlled schools among black families who preferred them to the white-managed counterparts, even when the latter were free and the former charged tuition" (p. 90). The American Missionary Association reported in 1870 that "most effective teachers of freedmen came from among themselves. They have the readiest access to their own race, and can do a work for them no teachers sent from the North can accomplish" (quoted in Johnson [1991], p. 92).

After the Civil War, Black girls and women took on the monumental tasks of teaching literacy, for example at Calhoun Colored School (Willis, 2002). Calhoun Colored School (CCS) was established in conjunction with the 1865 Congressional mandate known as the Freedmen's Bureau. The mandate was issued to support education that included addressing illiteracy among formally freed enslaved Black people. CCS was one among thousands of racially segregated schools established after the Civil War to offer Black students an education.

The founders of Calhoun were not educated as teachers; thus, their efforts were largely experimental and characterized by infantilizing the students in unflattering ways. The education offered to Black students was based on the Hampton-Washington model, a model that offered a rudimentary education (Anderson, 1988) and nurtured a complacent attitude of continual subservient labor in the South. Although it was a vast improvement over the one-room, seasonal classes offered to Black students, it was woefully inadequate. A scene as described in the following was not uncommon:

> The teacher of the only (so called) school in the neighborhood, a young girl of 17 or 18, had gathered a number of children about her to share the benefits of six months of schooling in which she had obtained learning. (Alice Bacon, 1892, quoted in Willis, 2002, p. 36)

The students who received their instruction were in the day or boarding school and paid a modest tuition or worked at the school. The literacy programs at CCS emphasized "(a) oral reading; (b) elocution; (c) rote memory; (d) appreciation for literature; and (e) connecting home, school, and community life to schoolwork" (Willis, 2002, p. 21). To be clear, at Calhoun students did not read texts (books, broadsides, or newspapers) written by Black people, although such texts were available. In this school for Black children, education and literacy were being framed as non-Black.

The faculty, however, made special efforts to include "(a) outside materials to interest students, (b) extensive discussions of words and allusions, (c) memorization of poetry, (d) help with articulation and expression, and (e) practice of written work" (Willis, 2002, p. 21). These efforts were aimed at helping students to put their thoughts into words, to write, and to spell correctly. All of the texts the students read, however, were written by European/White American authors, e.g., *Freedmen's Speller* (American Tract Society, 1865). Calhoun's teaching staff consisted of Black and White females and males, a very uncommon occurrence in the South.

Strategically, the curriculum at Calhoun took students—most of whom were adults, not children—12 years to complete 8 years of education. The idea under the Hampton-Washington model was to ensure that Black students learned to be compliant, dependent residents of the South. According to Anderson (1988), the model held an "ideological force that would provide instruction suitable for adjusting blacks to a subordinate social role in the emergent New South" (p. 36). He also mentions that at Hampton it was "part and parcel of the plan to train a corps of teachers with a particular social philosophy relevant to the political and economic reconstruction of the South" (p. 77). Black teachers, men and women, envisaged a different, more independent life for Black students.

Georgia Washington (1851–1952)

Among the teachers brought to Calhoun was Georgia Washington, a graduate of the Hampton Institute. Her early life underscores the sacrifice and struggle endured by Black women during the late 1800s. Her autobiographical memories were published in *The Southern Workman*, as part of an article by Ludlow (1893), which shared Washington's 1878 letter to an unknown Hampton supporter from New England. Washington shared her harrowing journey as a Black child, especially a female, to obtain an education. Her remembrances illustrate the daily sacrifices (child labor, gender discrimination, hunger, and poverty) endured to obtain an education and to provide one to other Black people. Washington writes that "my chief desire is to get an education that I may be a help to my race" (Washington, quoted in Ludlow [1893], pp. 225–227). Despite her many hardships, Washington graduated from Hampton in 1882, and she was regarded as an exemplary teacher.

Ten years later, she traveled to Calhoun, Alabama, as a teacher, where she taught the free night school classes. These classes were established to offer the mothers and fathers of the day-school children a chance to learn to read, write, and do simple arithmetic. Mabel W. Dillingham (1893), one of CCS's founders, in an editorial for *The Southern Workman*, described the night-school attendees: "It took one back to 'contraband days,' to see the class of old folks, toiling with dim eyes and stiff fingers over primer and copy books after a day's work in the field" (p. 12). More elderly Black people in the community were taught to read and write in their homes. Washington (1893) also published a letter in the journal in which she described the Black people in rural Alabama as mothers, fathers, and children who were "like the colored people everywhere, are very religious; some, I believe, are real Christians; they verily believe the Lord sent us all here in direct answer to their prayers" (Willis, 2002, p. 11). That same year, Washington left Calhoun and moved to Mount Meigs, Alabama, where she started her own school, People's Village Public School. She writes:

> When I went there in October I found the people busy picking cotton, and not a house for a school or a place for the teacher to live had been provided or thought of. The school opened October 9, 1893. On Sundays I talk to the people, and I held mothers meetings to try to reach the woman through the children. I was busy all week. It was the hardest work I've ever undertaken but the most enjoyable. I was happier than ever before in my life. The Lord just walked before me and made the rough places smooth. I learn to have confidence in the seeming impossible. (Washington, quoted in Ludlow, 1893, p. 230)

The school began with four young boys and grew steadily over the next few years. The Black people in the town helped to purchase land and build a new schoolhouse. It is unclear from the available sources how the literacy program at the People's Village Public School was framed. The legacy of Georgia Washington, however, remains as generations attended the school under Washington, who retired in 1932. Former students hold biannual reunions where they reconnected and remember their years under her leadership (Klass, 2017).

According to Kendi (2016), early assimilationists supported the concept of "uplift suasion," or the idea that Black people's thoughts and actions should be displayed in such a way as to "prove all the stereotypes about them were wrong" (Reynolds & Kendi, 2020, p. 65). The concept appears foundational to the ethos at Calhoun. Teachers and students appear to support the assimilationist notion that if Black people wanted to be seen as human, they must "make yourself small, make yourself unthreatening, make yourself the same, make yourself safe, make yourself quiet, to make White people comfortable with your existence" (p. 66). The acquisition of literacy was understood as a way to uplift oneself and the race.

Nationally, there were many other Black women teachers who courageously and unapologetically embraced their religious beliefs as well as their belief in the intellectual capacity of Black people, and took up the mantle to improve literacy among Black people in the schools they established.

Lucy Craft Laney (1854–1933)

Lucy Craft Laney was born in Macon, Georgia, to free parents: a Presbyterian minister and a skilled carpenter, and a mother who was a domestic worker. It was her mother's employer, Miss Campbell, who taught Laney to read at the age of four. After graduating from Atlanta University's normal school program, Laney opened a school of her own in the basement of Christ Presbyterian Church in Augusta, Georgia. Her early Christian training was a hallmark of her moral sense of responsibility to improve the plight of Black education. Laney's desire was to establish a school for Black girls, and her first class began with six girls, but she eventually permitted boys to attend. The school quickly grew and was renamed the Haines Normal Institute and Industrial School, in honor of a wealthy benefactor, Mrs. F. E. H. Haines, then president of the Women's Department of the Presbyterian Church USA (Georgia Women of Achievement, 1992, n.p.). It is believed that "the keynote of her teaching seems to have been a boundless faith in children's ability to learn, combined with the highest expectations of what they should achieve" (n.p.). Laney also argued, ". . . the educated Negro woman must teach the Black Babies. . . .many modern pedagogues and school keepers fail to know their pupils to find out their real needs" (quoted in Foster, 1997, p. xliv). The self-sacrifice and hard work of Washington, Laney, and untold other Black women teachers was grounded in a shared Christian foundation and hope in the future of Black people. Throughout the nation, in Black rural communities and urban cities, Black women founded schools and courageously provided access to literacy. Many knew one another, as McCluskey (1997) documents through an examination of correspondence among Laney, Bethune, and Burroughs. As King (2017) expresses, their collective experiences reflect the "Black Radical Tradition of returning what we learn to the people" (p. 95). Black women teachers desired to share what they knew with other Black people, and their shared relationships demonstrate how "Black women have generated alternative practices and knowledges that have been designed to foster U.S. Black women's empowerment" (P. Collins, 2000, p. 30). Their correspondence about shared experiences also was an acknowledgment of how Black women consulted and encouraged one another as they fought to shape educational opportunities in Black communities across the nation. These battles finally resulted in a federal law to address educational justice.

In 1954, the U.S. Supreme Court handed down a unanimous decision in *Brown v Board of Education of Topeka,* in which the judges ruled that separate facilities were in violation of the 14th Amendment, specifically the Equal Protection Clause. *Brown*'s initial case was part of a larger class-action suit seeking equal educational rights for Black children. The judges wrote that "in the field of public education, the doctrine of 'separate but equal' has no place. Separate facilities are inherently unequal." In 1955, Justice Warren approved "admission to public schools on racially nondiscriminatory basis with all deliberate speed" (*Brown v Board of Education II,* 1955). The intent of the Court was to end state-sponsored and -supported racial discrimination in public education and to guide the process of racial desegregation of education. The effective implementation of *Brown,* however, hinged not only on federal law, but also on state and local willingness to comply with the law. Although the U.S. Supreme Court had favorably ruled in support of the plaintiffs in *Brown,* the integration of the nation's public schools was met with violent controversy. The experiences of teaching literacy to Black students during this period are captured in the lives of Ruby M. Forsythe, Katherine Crosby, and Bertha Maxwell-Roddey.

Ruby Middleton Forsythe (1905–1992)

Ruby Middleton Forsythe (interview with Foster [1997]) began after she had taught for 60 years, mostly at Pawleys Island's Holy Cross Faith Memorial School in South Carolina. She conveys her pedagogical stance:

> The first thing I try to do is to become a mother to all of them. I let them know I care about them. I tell them, "as long as you are here with me

I'm your mama until you go back home, and when you go back home, you go to your other mother." Once you get the affection of those little ones you won't want to teach any other group. You have to be tender but firm and positive. So you show them that motherly affection. (quoted in Foster, 1997, p. 31)

Of particular interest are Forsythe's thoughts on teaching reading to Black students and her unflinching belief in their intelligence:

My children start reading as soon as they learn their alphabet. You will hear a lot of experts say that you must not teach the alphabet as alphabets. I don't care what the experts say, each teacher has to find her own way to teach the children she has. Some of the methods that the experts tell you to use don't work with the group you have. So, I don't pay attention to what the experts have to say. I teach the children to recognize the letters as letters and in words. I don't care what you get in college. When you come out and get in the classroom, you have to find your own ways to make sure that you reach the children you have in your classroom. It's up to you to find methods that work. (quoted in Foster, 1997, p. 32)

Ruby Forsythe was among the Black female teachers who taught prior to and through the desegregation of public schools. Not all Black teachers were employed after public schools were integrated (Foster, 1997), but Katherine Crosby and Bertha Maxwell-Roddey were, and they are featured next.

Bertha Maxwell Roddey (1931–) and Katherine Crosby (1925–2012)

Atwater and Gyant (2004) chronicled the amazing life of Bertha Maxwell Roddey (1931–), outlining her multiple accomplishments, a Black woman who broke many barriers serving as mentor, principal, professor, and teacher. She also was founder of the National Council of Black Studies.

Ramsey (2012) constructed oral histories from her interviews with two Black women teachers, Katherine Crosby and Bertha Maxwell-Roddey, who taught during the transition from segregated to integrated schools in the South. These Black women teachers accepted and understood the humanity within each Black student and the language their Black students spoke and the cultural references they used, as well

as the pain and joy they shared. Ramsey notes that they "struggled against discriminatory forces to fight for educational equality in the public schools and in academia. In addition to battling against racism, they often had to combat gender discrimination" (p. 245). Browne-Marshall (2013) observes that "Black communities bore the brunt of bussing efforts" and "Black public schools built during segregation were demolished. Black students were then bused to the formerly all-White schools" (p. 36). Maxwell-Roddey, like many Black people before her, moved her family because of racial discrimination: "they wanted to bus my little girl 15 miles to a black school and then I was going to [have to] go 15 miles to the other side. So I quit . . ." (quoted in Atwater & Gyant, 2004, p. 119). Black teachers endured these conditions for years under the constant oversight and pressure of losing their teaching positions.

Ramsey (2012) captures their experiences: "[T]hese teachers practiced a form of caring activism that not only encouraged gender equality but also adopted concepts of cultural nationalism to help Black children develop a positive self-identity after desegregation" (p. 245). According to Ramsey, both women graduated from Johnson C. Smith University, a historically Black College, and continued their education with additional coursework. In 1966, Crosby received a master's degree in early childhood education. Maxwell-Roddey enrolled in corrective reading at Howard University. Their desire for racial uplift is perhaps best illustrated by Maxwell-Roddey's summer reading program aimed at Black children prior to attending 1st grade. She organized the Volunteer Teacher Corps, where "the instructors taught fundamental reading skills to 87 incoming first graders who could not afford the public preschool program's $30 fee" (Ramsey, 2012, p. 251). Her efforts were appreciated by the community, and later her tutoring program became a model for the local Head Start program, directed by Crosby. Access to reading and writing, limited for many decades before integration, appeared to be a way forward for Black education.

Black women teachers' love of Black people that compelled them to teach is captured by bell hooks (1994) in a personal memory:

> They were committed to nurturing intellect so that we could become scholars, thinkers, and cultural workers—Black folks who used our minds. We learned early that our devotion to learning, to a life of the mind, was a counter-hegemonic act, a fundamental way to resist every strategy of white racist colonization. Though they did not define or articulate these practices in theoretical terms, my teachers were enacting a

revolutionary pedagogy of resistance that was profoundly anti-colonial. Within these segregated schools, Black children who were deemed exceptional, gifted, were given special care. Teachers worked with and for us to ensure that we would fulfill our intellectual destiny and by so doing uplift the race. My teachers were on a mission. (p. 2)

Many Black adults had long been denied educational access and did not know how to read and write. During the early years of the civil rights movement, the lack of education in general, and literacy in particular, was used as a reason to disenfranchise Black citizens. Although the 15th Amendment granted Black men the right to vote, Jim Crow laws had denied their rights.

LITERACY AND CIVIL RIGHTS

The work of early civil rights activists included Black women who taught people literacy for human and civil rights and included the right to vote. Later, schools were established by Black empowerment organizations such as the Black Panther Party (BPP), the National Association for the Advancement of Colored People (NAACP), the Urban League, and the Student Nonviolent Coordinating Committee (SNCC), among others, to improve education for Black students. The efforts of these organizations, along with local support by Black families and community members, sought to improve access and opportunities for literacy attainment by Black people because literacy tests were often used to disenfranchise Black people from voting. Among the women fighting for the right to vote and to teach literacy skills were Septima P. Clark and Bernice Robinson.

Septima Poinsette Clark (1898–1987)

Septima Clark, born in Charleston, South Carolina, became a teacher and civil rights advocate. She recalls how in 1947, after teaching for years on St. John's Island, South Carolina, she was tasked with teaching remedial reading. However, she was dismissed from this position because of her involvement with the NAACP. Later, Clark joined the staff of Myles Horton's Highlander Folk School, where she met Rosa Parks and Dr. Martin Luther King Jr. As the director of the Leadership workshops at Highlander Folk School, Clark hired her cousin, Bernice Robinson, a beautician, to be a teacher. She recalls that she and Myles

Horton believed that Robinson was a "good listener" (Brown, 1991, p. 49) and would make a good teacher.

As Black women, Clark and Robinson understood the importance of acquiring and using the constitutional right to vote. Black men had won the right under the 15th Amendment, and White women under the 19th Amendment, but Black women had not received the right; thus, literacy, women's rights, and voting were intimately connected. Bernice Violanthe Robinson (1914–1994), as a noncertified teacher, was hired purposely to teach adults to read so that they could vote in South Carolina. She began teaching on St. John's Island, and since she did not have a teaching license, she could teach without fear of losing her job. The classes for adults were held in secret (two back rooms of a grocery store), for 2 months when people were not working in the fields.

To gain a sense of what students knew, Robinson asked her students to read a line of the voter registration form and to write their names in cursive. She quickly determined that most of the adults had very rudimentary literacy skills, and she learned how to work with the skills her students brought to class. Her approach to teaching reading focused on helping students understand the context of words as well as learning how to break words into syllables. In addition, she supported her students' desire to learn how to write in cursive—a skill helpful in daily life. One day, without conferring with Robinson, Clark was asked to teach a lesson, and surprisingly their reading instruction was identical.

Among the barriers to enfranchisement in the state of South Carolina was a "literacy test." A deputy registrar would require a person seeking to vote to explain a portion of the South Carolina state constitution. The literacy test essentially disenfranchised Black people who had not been taught to read or write. The veracity of responses on the literacy tests was decided at the discretion of the local registrar. Not surprisingly, responses by Black people were deemed unacceptable. Under Clark's leadership, Citizenship Schools taught "practical literacy along with political and economic literacy" (Charron, 2009, p. 5). The Citizenship Schools' literacy programs asserted literacy

> . . . should not isolate people's learning of reading, writing, and critical thinking from the community in which they reside; the historical roots from which they follow; the language they use in defining their existence; and the politics and economics that shape and reshape their critical thinking/reflections of themselves and others. (Peavy, 1993, p. 213)

The schools also provided Black people with information about federal, state, and local laws as well as their civil rights under the law. Although various reading approaches were attempted, instructors found that listening to Black people was a key to success. To gain the students' trust, teachers began by providing time and space for people to talk, share their stories, and express their ideas. Then, after teaching them to read and write and their rights under the law, Black people would be able to register to vote.

The right to vote hinged in part on the right to literacy, and denying literacy to children eventually resulted in the denial of voting rights to adults. Among the most oppressive educational opportunities for Black children were those in Mississippi. For example, Ida Mae Brandon Gladney's early school days in the early 1920s, as well as that of the other Black children, were scheduled around the production of cotton (Wilkerson, 2010). The school term lasted roughly 6 months a year, in a one-room school with grades 1–8 all taught by a single Black teacher (pp. 24–26), leaving Black students with a limited education.

During the summer of 1964, educational opportunities were extended through the Freedom Schools, organized by members of the Congress of Racial Equality (CORE), NAACP, SNCC, and the Southern Christian Leadership Conference (SCLC). The collective adopted the title Council of Federated Organizations (COFO). These schools were influenced by the work of the Highlander Folk School and Septima Clark's Citizenship Education School. The official Freedom School website provides a mimeographed copy of Charlie Cobb's (n.d.) writing, "Some Notes on Education." Cobb was a college student at Howard University and a member of SNCC (Jackson & Howard, 2014; Payne, 1997), who shared some of his fundamental beliefs:

> What we have discovered over the last few years of our activities in the South, is that oppression and restriction is not limited to the bullets of local racists shotgun blasts, or assaults at county courthouses, or the expulsion of sharecroppers from plantations, but that it (oppression and restriction) is embedded in a complex national structure, many of the specifics of which are oft times difficult to discern, but which govern every facet of our lives. What is relevant to our lives is constantly defined for us.

Cobb (n.d.) described the systematic use of race as a source of conflict in the political and social worlds in his thoughts on the importance of education and stated, "for education is not the development of intellectual skills, but a preparation for participation in living" (p. 3). To that end, in 1963 he articulated the purpose of the "Freedom Schools in A prospectus for a summer Freedom School program in Mississippi" to "fill an intellectual and creative vacuum in the lives of young Negro Mississippians, and to get them to articulate their own desires, demands and questions" (para 6).

The Freedom School program was a network of over 40 schools that served 2,000 Black students in Mississippi from July through August 1964. According to Hale (2011), the schools were focused on supporting educational change for elementary and secondary students. Cobb's 1963 proposal, intended for 10th and 11th graders, included "supplementary education, such as basic grammar, reading, math, typing, history, etc. Some of the already-developed programmed educational materials might be used experimentally" (n.p.). In addition, Cobb accounted for a remedial opportunity: "to improve comprehension in reading, fluency, and expressiveness in writing" (n. p.). Cobb (1963) articulated the joint effort in planning as follows:

> The aim of the Freedom School curriculum will be to challenge the student's curiosity about the world, introduce him to his particularly "Negro" cultural background, and teach him basic literacy skills in one integrated program. . . . By using the multi-dimensional, integrated program, the curriculum can be more easily absorbed into the direct experience of the student, and thus overcome some of the academic problems of concentration and retention. (para 20)

King (2017) emphasized that "both African and local histories were essential elements in the collectively constructed curriculum and pedagogy that was designed to raise the consciousness, political awareness, and civic engagement of Black youth" (p. 102). In this way, the development of students' literacy skills was foundational to the success of the Freedom School. In 1964, a Freedom School teacher orientation memo advised volunteer teachers as follows:

> The purpose of the Freedom schools is to provide an educational experience for students which will make it possible for them to challenge the myths of our society, to perceive more clearly its realities, and to find alternatives, and ultimately, new directions for action. (para 1)
>
> The kinds of activities you will be developing will fall into three general areas: 1) academic work, 2) recreation and cultural activities, 3)

leadership development. It is our hope that these three will be integrated into one learning experience, rather than being the kind of fragmented learning and living that characterizes much of contemporary education. (para 4)

In another section of the orientation materials, specific directions for teaching literacy included the following:

If you do not have reading material which matches your (each) student— and content is at least as important as reading level—I would suggest your having the students write their own material. Your labor is likely to bear more fruit if they, rather than you, do the writing. If you want to study a difficult novel, read it aloud to them, or have a student who enjoys read- ing aloud and does it well do part of the reading. As you read, encourage interruptions for questions and discussion. Then you can have some or all students write summaries or critiques or whatever you want. Read then aloud in class (each his own, perhaps) and discuss content. If it turns out to be something great, you can have the students edit the material and perhaps exchange a volume with another freedom school. (Freedom School Orientation Memo,1964)

Freedom School teachers consisted of classroom teachers, college students, and volunteers, both Black and White. The experiences of Black women who were college students and served as teachers in the Freedom Schools were captured by Kristal Moore Clemons (2014) through interviews with participants. Clemons used pseudonyms for her interviewees, Denise and Mildred. "Denise," for instance, offers insight into a teacher's pedagogical stance:

The children who came to the school felt special because there was a school made just for them . . . the Freedom Schools . . . were made, cre- ated, for those children and those children knew that. . . .And when you feel special, when you feel loved, you begin to see yourself in a way that you would not perhaps see yourself. And you begin to dream in a differ- ent way, you begin to believe in yourself. . . .
Our goal was to assist the students in giving voice to their feelings, giving voice to their goals, giving voice to an understanding of learning materials that were in our curriculum, but essentially it was just about them learning to love themselves. Also to believe that they had to know, not believe, that they had the right to the best education the best life

possible. Our goal was to make them understand that they were not to be denied anything—that there was nothing wrong with them. They were not inferior. (quoted in Clemons, 2014, p. 147)

Denise mentioned some of the instructional materials at the Freedom Schools that aligned with the broad curricular purposes outlined initially by Cobb and that were later refined:

[W]e worked with stories, fables and folktales and short stories, and all of which focus on achievement, dignity, character, and culture. We did a lot in the way of oral reading where they would read and interpret. We did journaling, they would write in the journal and they would write responses to some of the stories that we read with them . . . whatever the students want to bring to share became central to the learning process. (quoted in Clemons, 2014, p. 147)

The curricular materials for literacy activities included reading books by Black authors, Black history texts, case studies, newspaper articles, and political documents and writing articles for Freedom School newspapers, as well as producing books of poetry and short stories (Menkart and View (2021).

While many Black people sought integration of public schools, some leaders, like Dr. Martin Luther King Jr., held different views: "White people view black people as inferior . . . People with such a low view of the black race cannot be given free rein and put in charge of the intellectual care and development of our boys and girls" (quoted in Kendi, 2019, p. 173). The history of Black education records efforts to acquire a quality education also in Black Liberation schools.

LITERACY AND LIBERATION

Black liberation schools grew out of the efforts of the Citizenship Schools and the summer Freedom Schools in Alabama and Mississippi. They reimagined Black education as seen in efforts by the Black Panther Party (BPP). In 1966, BPP members Bobby Seale and Huey Newton articulated their *Ten-Point Program,* and among the first points were: "We want freedom. We want the power to determine the destiny of our Black and Oppressed Communities. We believe that Black people will not be free until we are able to determine our destiny" (p. 1). In terms of education, they stated, "We want decent education for our people that exposes the true nature of this decadent American society. We want education that teaches us our true history. And our role in the present-day society" (*Black Panther Party Ten Point Program*, 1966). They also mentioned the following:

> We believe in an educational system that will give to our people a knowledge of self. If a man does not have knowledge of himself and his position in society and the world, then he has little chance to relate to anything else. (*Black Panther Party Ten Point Program*, para, 10; Bloom & Martin, 2016, p. 72)

The efforts of the BPP to combat American imperialism and promote economic, educational, political, social, and racial justice were constantly under government surveillance. As quickly as the BPP rose, it declined as many founding members were arrested and jailed. The BPP created community-based schooling that focused on Black accomplishments; Black arts, culture, language, and literacy; the strengths and limitations of American democracy (anti-imperialism and oppression); and revolutionary Black consciousness (Lomotey, 2010, pp. 2–3). The first attempt to organize a BPP liberation school (in 1966) centered on the BPP's ideology; however, as the organization grew, the educational foci and pedagogical positioning shifted. The second attempt in educational programming (in 1971) had greater engagement in community organizing, grouping children by ability, and providing individual attention. The final phase (in 1973) appeared to be a mélange of BPP ideology and progressive education (Lomotey, 2010). Black children in the early programs had been removed from public schools by their parents as the schools sought to "prepare children and youth to join in the struggle to create a new society" (p. 2). One of the highlights of the BPP was the Oakland Community School, run mostly by Black women:

> They kept the community programs alive and did most of the painstaking day-to-day social labor necessary to sustain the chapters. Providing informal child-care networks and day-care centers, assisting elderly and infirm community members with their housing, food, medical, and even more personal concerns were generally the province of Panther women. (Bloom & Martin, 2016, p. 193)

Ericka Huggins and Angela D. LeBlanc-Ernest (2009) concur that the role of Black women within the movement, especially the education programs, was pivotal: Black women used "academic education and 'commonsense' experiences to combat social injustice" (p. 163). They also proffered:

> The activism of the BPP women who became the OCS (Oakland Community School) teaching staff and administrators during the 1970s and early 1980s was no less significant than that of women who organized and educated black and poor communities in the nineteenth and mid to early twentieth centuries. (p. 163)

The BPP offered practical aid to the needs of the Black community, such as clothing, food assistance, and medical screenings. Among their most important contributions was the education program, directed by Erica Huggins "with the help of Panther Regina Davis. Through their efforts, the school eventually offered top-notch education enrolling about 200 kids with twice as many on the waiting list" (p. 384). The education program evolved over time as described by one of its founders, who explains that the heart of the program was to honor and support the evolving sense of self among Black students, as completely whole and worthy.

Ericka Huggins (1948–)

Ericka Cozette Jenkins was born on January 5, 1948, in Washington, DC. She committed herself to the cause of Black Liberation after attending the March on Washington. As an undergraduate, she attended the historically Black institution Lincoln University, where she majored in education before moving to Los Angeles. After moving to Los Angeles, she joined the BPP and became aware that some members of the BPP could not read, so she taught them how (Rofel & Tai, 2016, p. 237). In 1967, she married John Huggins, the leader of the Los Angeles branch of the BPP, who was killed weeks after the birth of their daughter. Later, she and a fellow BP, Bobby Seale, were arrested and jailed on charges of conspiracy. After her release from jail with all charges dropped, she began life as a widow and single mother. Huggins recalled that:

> . . . from 1973–1981, I was the Director of the Oakland Community School, the groundbreaking community-run child development center

and elementary school founded by the Black Panther Party. Working with a team of incredibly talented party members and local educators a vision for the innovative curriculum for the school was written. This curriculum and the principles that inspired it became a model for and predecessor to the charter school movement. (Huggins, 2020, para 7)

Huggins became a central figure in the BPP. She revealed that Black women theorized "community and coalition-building through the lenses of gender, race, and class converged to create and sustain an alternative educational institution in the midst of the nationwide urban educational crisis" (Huggins & LeBlanc-Ernest, 2012, p. 166). Members of the BPP withdrew their children from public schools and established the Intercommunal Youth Institute. Gloria Smith crafted a curriculum, and Brenda Bay was appointed to lead the effort (1971–1973). The Institute was "designed to help our children think. All instruction is made relevant to the survival of Black and poor people. . . .Our objective is the development of the well-rounded human being" (*The Black Panther*, July 28, 1973, p. 14). Later, the Institute's name was changed to the Oakland Community School (OCS), and Ericka Huggins was appointed its director from 1973 to 1981. With a focus on the whole child, OCS students received breakfast, lunch, and dinner (Huggins, 2007). Also available were family counseling, health care screening, new clothes, and tutoring services. Huggins, in an interview with M. Phillips (2014), recalls:

We fed them, we loved them, and we hugged them . . . if they were creative and didn't know what to do with it we found someone who could support them in that creative pursuit. If you love somebody, you care about all the parts of them not just one part. (Mary Phillips, personal communication, April 16, 2014, pp. 212–213)

When queried about theories underpinning the school's work, Huggins replied, "We didn't come to our theory because somebody put some books in front of us . . . we looked at history . . . and we decided that we all are worthy of being regarded highly that we are of value" (M. Phillips, personal communication, February 20, 2010, p. 210). An undated informational flyer about the OCS described features of the school:

The school provides . . . students with three meals a day, a full curriculum which includes (Language Arts, Spanish, Mathematics, Science,

Social Science, Environmental Studies, Physical Education, Music, Drama, Dance, and Art), new clothes and shoes, family counseling, healthcare screening and tutoring . . . (para 2)

The school's philosophy is that children should learn <u>how</u> and not <u>what</u> to think. Our approach is that learning should be a full and ongoing educational experience. Instructors do not give opinions and passing in information, instead, facts are shared and some conclusions are reached by the children themselves. (para 4, emphasis in the original, Official Website of the Black Panther Party Worldwide, 2021)

Later, Huggins expanded on the BPP belief that "all human beings are of value whether they go to the academy or not and . . . the Black Panther Party was itself full of scholars if we unpack the word scholar and reframe it" (Phillips, 2015, p. 39). As the director, Huggins believed the school offered students "individual attention in reading, mathematics, writing, and . . . an understanding of themselves and the world" (Huggins quoted in Perlstein, 2005, p. 51). The individualized attention meant that teachers were flexible and they built upon student knowledge. Huggins observed that OCS "was very concerned about children relating to their environment and to this world as it really is" (Huggins quoted in Perlstein, 2005, p. 51). Education was not confined to a school building; there were field trips and programs for students outside the classroom, ranging from assisting the elderly to visiting local museums.

At the onset of the 5th year of OCS, Newton (1975) expounded on the virtues of the school in the *Black Panther* newspaper. And in a letter written to the community, Huggins (1976, as quoted in Wong, 2021) highlighted other unique features of OCS: 16 licensed teachers and 13 volunteers and aides, with a 1:10 teacher-to-student ratio. The language arts curriculum focused on "phonics, parts of speech, syntax, handwriting, library and reference skills, language mechanics, vocabulary, spelling, reading and comprehension, literature, prose, poetry, and speech" (Newton, quoted in Wong, 2012, p. 43). The literature that students read was written by Black authors, philosophers, scientists, and sociologists. According to Wong (2012), "OCS also intricately linked its curriculum with the community and social justice, particularly through poetry, prose, and writing letters" (p. 44). Williamson (2005) notes that the BPP "sought to improve Black education by linking schools to the community, using students' backgrounds as a conduit for learning, infusing Black-centered content and themes in the curriculum, demanding communal control of the schools, and encouraging social action" (p. 153). Robinson (2020) positions their approach as a forerunner to Ladson-Billings's (1994) notion of culturally relevant pedagogy as well as Paris's (2012) notion of culturally sustaining pedagogy.

LITERACY AND JUSTICE: BLACK INDEPENDENT SCHOOLS

As this brief history has demonstrated, many Black people who sought a quality education did not look to the local or state government for support. Black churches and communities created their own Black schools for their children. After the Civil War, the federal government and philanthropic organizations also provided educational access for Black people. Throughout the next half-century, Black people continued to establish faith-based and community schools, the latter known as independent Black institutions (IBIs). A reason for the formation of IBI schools, according to Johnson and Anderson (1992), was so that Black parents could "exert more control over their children's educational destinies . . . ensuring that that control ultimately results in a broad spectrum of successes—academic, social, economic, interpersonal, and otherwise" (p. 121). An example of one type of IBI school is Afrocentric schools, which Asante (1992) characterizes as "placing Africa at the center of any analysis of African phenomena" (p. 2). Among the many Black independent schools were Chicago's New Concept Development Center, established in 1972 by Don and Carol Lee, and the Nairobi Day School in East Palo Alto, California, established in 1966 by Gertrude Dyer Wilks and Mothers for Equal Education. Collectively, these leaders and other Black parents took a stand against educational and racial injustice. The leader of the Nairobi Day School had not planned on being either an activist or a school administrator.

Gertrude Dyer Wilks (1927–2019)

Gertrude Dyer was one of 11 children born to sharecropping parents in Duboc, Louisiana. She had a deep-rooted desire to learn, but she was needed in the fields to help support her family. She explains that this period of her life taught her about "making a way out of no way." According to her granddaughter, LaPira Wilks, Gertrude Dyer was the first person in her family to learn to read and write (Taaffe, 2019). She left the South along with her husband and headed to California, where they found work in a factory. Soon, she became a housewife and took care of their three children by helping to support them as a dressmaker. As a conscientious parent, she was aware that her children were not making sufficient progress, yet when she asked their teachers she was rebuffed by comments meant to "put her in her place" because she was not a teacher, and she was generally discouraged from helping them at home. However, when her oldest child, Otis, was preparing to graduate from high school, she noticed that he could barely read or write.

Wilks, along with several other Black mothers, formed the Mothers for Equal Education (the Mothers) at a local church in 1965. They drew on their religious roots and began each meeting with a simple prayer: "Oh Lord, here we stand, joined together heart and hand, to help provide better education throughout this land" (quoted in Rickford, 2016, p. 106). With support from the Black Power movement, CORE, and the NAACP, they began to protest the school's miseducation of Black students. The Mothers unsuccessfully tried to work with the local White community and the public school administrators. Seemingly out of options, they established the Nairobi Day School as a supplemental (Saturday) tutoring program in a local church. Wilks remembered her angst: "I decided right there that I had to do something about giving a black child some security, by proving that we as black people could build an institution that was as good as anybody's right here in our community" (quoted in Rickford, 2016, p. 110). In her memoir, *Gathering Together: Born to Be a Leader*, she emphasized that "we decided that if our kids were going to be educated, we had to do the educating ourselves. Many of us were afraid of it because we'd always believed that we knew nothing, but we knew that we had to take on this responsibility." Unsurprisingly, for the Black community of East Palo Alto the Nairobi Day School was hugely popular and a much-sought-after alternative and resource.

Sandra Blakeslee (1975), a *New York Times* reporter, revealed that "there is a small private school within this small predominantly black, low-income community that is making an extraordinary offer: The school guarantees to teach black children to read within one school year or it will refund their parents' money" (p. 35). Blakeslee noted that the director of the elementary school, Barbara Mouton, stated that the school "focused entirely on the premise that black children could learn, and it attempted to extend and build on the values in black homes" (p. 35). As such, the school "offered inside a black community at an institution whose survival is based literally on the number of chicken dinners or sweet potato pies cooked in any given period is phenomenal" (p. 35). The community-based school had been influenced by members of the Black Power movement. The staff, according to Mouton, included Black and White teachers, college faculty and students, Black professionals, and volunteers, who "are familiar with modern theories of early childhood development, but, they say, you have to accept a child as he is day to day, not as a textbook says he is. Our theory, a teacher said, is to treat the whole child and the whole family if necessary" (p. 35). By contrast, the reading program at the Nairobi Day School consisted of a mixture of approaches that Wilks (1990) proffered as "an ever-evolving 'home grown' system which is derived from methods which work, plus the first-hand experience of Nairobi Day School staff and parents" (p. 29). She explained that the reading program also used commercial textbooks, and basal readers

> . . . in kindergarten (when) we stress oral skills. The Black language that the students bring to school is respected. They are encouraged through songs, games, poetry, and plays to make use of it. In the meantime, they are adding new words to their vocabulary and gaining language facility in Standard English. In general, we stress a systematic phonics approach to decoding. Learning to comprehend then becomes a life-long endeavor. Initially, the alphabet is mastered by name and sound (one sound for each consonant and only short vowel sounds). (Wilks, 1990, p. 28)

The Nairobi Day School built upon approaches (cultural, personal, synthetic) to teaching reading as espoused by Hilliard (1976) with a focus on students of varying levels of linguistic proficiency in English (Hoover, 1992). Taaffe (2019) confirmed that Wilks "offered a guarantee that children would learn to read within one year or she would give parents a full refund" (n.p.) Wilks amplified the importance of language as well as the support they received from a linguist, Mary Hoover. Hoover (1992) explained that "at Nairobi Day School the use of and respect for Black vernacular language and Standard Black Language [standard grammar enhanced with elements of Black style, speech events, and vocabulary; Taylor, 1971] was encouraged through songs, games, poetry, and drama to make students bidialectal" (Hoover, 1978, p. 205). Given the ill-informed national narrative about Black English/Ebonics, the decision to retain the students' home language as an avenue of communication was unprecedented, as most schools and teachers were encouraged only to use, and, teach Standard English. However, the teachers at Nairobi Day School understood that

African American speech was a language with a rule-governed system. Hoover (1992) suggested that "culturally sensitive approaches were also found to be of practical value in classroom management" (pp. 205–206). The Nairobi Day School expanded to the Nairobi High School. Later, the Day School was renamed the Gertrude Wilks Academy (*Palo Alto Weekly*, 2002, para 6). Her life's work in her community centered on bringing a quality education to Black students, providing them with the knowledge and skills needed to succeed. Another extremely successful IBI school was Westside Preparatory Academy, established by Marva Collins.

Marva Collins (1936–2015)

Marva Knight Collins was born in Monroeville, Alabama, to parents who were considered wealthy because of their material possessions as well as their way of life. Collins adored her father, Henry Knight, who like generations of men before him was a businessman (Collins & Tamarkin, 1982). Marva learned to read before attending school, in part because her grandmother taught her to sound out words and blend sounds. Her grandmother read to her, quoted long poems, and read Bible stories, ideas that Collins used when she taught reading. Collins graduated from Clark College in Atlanta, and then returned to Monroeville, where she taught typing at Monroe County Training School.

In 1959, as a married woman, Marva Collins moved to Chicago and, before starting a family, started teaching in Chicago public schools with a temporary certificate. She recalls trying to follow the curriculum sanctioned by the Board of Education, but she found it below her students' ability, boring, and slow-paced. She drew upon her own success as a phonics reader and began teaching her students phonics, reading fairy tales aloud, and teaching life lessons along the way. She became a strong supporter of the phonics method as a beginning approach to reading, in opposition to the "look-say approach" used in public schools. Collins maintained that "phonics enables a child to decipher words and so allows better reading comprehension. When a child understands the relationship between a series of spoken sounds and the printed word, the child will read for meaning" (Collins & Tamarkin, 1982, p. 118). She was aware of the critiques leveled against a phonics reading approach, especially the many irregularities in the letter-sound relationship, but she countered by revealing that she taught regular and irregular rules (p. 119). Except for the

45-minute silent reading period, all reading in class was read aloud (p. 45), across subject areas. She also believed that it was important for students to comprehend and learn vocabulary. She participated daily in silent reading after lunch with her students. Then students wrote about their reading, and she also read aloud from her book and shared the notes she had written. In addition, students were required to select books to read twice a month for independent reading, and she shared new books with students once a week.

Collins proffered that "my approach was to teach the total child. A teacher should help develop a child's character to help build a positive self-image" (Collins & Tamarkin, 1982, p. 58), suggesting that it was important to let students know how much you care for them. Collins (1991) used several examples of Black students under her tutelage who blossomed as people and as readers, some a few grade levels in a matter of months. She recalled the success she had with children who had been labeled learning-disabled and unable to learn, as well as students who had been expelled from school for minor offenses: "[C]hildren are real, and they can never become unreal once they find someone who really, really loves them for what they are with a genuine respect for what they can become" (p. 138). When queried about why she taught, Collins answered,

> . . . to think that I have given a generation the torch of literacy that can be passed to their heirs is truly the denouement of living. To think that I have been a small part of a miraculous living person is truly God's work here on Earth. (p. 138)

In spite of her love of teaching, after 12 and a half years she grew disgruntled with the public school system's focus on test scores, discipline practices, and labeling of children as disabled, failures, and troubled. She believed that some were not doing their jobs as teachers of reading because they were more focused on test scores than students. In fact, she wondered, "the strange thing was that if a child didn't learn, no one held the teachers responsible" (Collins & Tamarkin, 1982, p. 56), by contrast, she held herself accountable for being an effective teacher.

In 1975, she launched her own school, Daniel Hale Williams Westside Preparatory School. Collins emphasized the importance of making each child feel loved and accepted as well as preparing lessons that were designed to build upon the knowledge they had. Collins and her students' accomplishments quickly gained national recognition and fame. She explained that her pedagogical stance centered on accepting each child, encouraging and praising children's efforts, and setting high standards of excellence. She often began the school year by letting students know that "you are the best and brightest children in the world and there is nothing that you can't do" (Collins & Tamarkin, 1982, p. 83). Collins's philosophy, pedagogy, and instruction were part of her original school, additional schools, and a teacher training program.

OUR TEACHERS

In this chapter, we have pointed to many Black women teachers who reflected an understanding of the values held in the Black community writ large. We also have experienced this form of care by Black women teachers in our own lives who viewed "the success of black students as central to the success of their own teaching" (McKamey, 2020, n.p.). We are grateful to the Black women teachers in our lives, those teachers who believed in us when we were young, helped to form in us a sense of self-worth, and taught us to read and write: Arlette— much love to Mrs. Carter, my 1st-grade teacher; Gwendolyn—I was blessed to have Ms. Wyche, my teacher for preschool, 1st, 2nd, and 3rd grades, for all those years; and Patriann—for the few years that I attended formal school, my favorite teachers were Ms. Kerstin Peter (elementary) and Ms. Beverley Ferguson (secondary).

CONCLUSION

In this chapter, we have contextualized a history of Black readers' access to literacy within narratives of Black women activist teachers. We share their narratives to highlight how their beliefs and commitment to Black people's access to literacy served as catalysts for change, their pedagogy revealed and understood through their actions. Conceptually, the narratives are drawn from historical and contemporaneous sources to demonstrate how Black women have embraced the moral responsibility to extend literacy to Black people.

Historically, members of the Black community have been strong supporters of education in general, and literacy in particular. Black people with very little money offered what they could to ensure that children would have the best education possible. They were willing to break the law to learn to read, and some Black women teachers willingly broke the law to teach reading. And they often went above expectations, holding classes for adults and traveling throughout the community to teach elderly folks to read.

The contributions of Black women to literacy centers on their sense of moral courage and responsibility. Black woman activist teachers conveyed an understanding of the values held in the Black community, the desire for racial uplift, and the need for Black leadership.

Barnett (1993) captures their contributions:

> Sisters in struggle—sharecroppers, domestic and workers, schoolteachers, college professors, housewives, beautician, students, and office secretaries—all shed blood, sweat, and tears in the movement. In their homes, churches, voluntary associations, political organizations, women's clubs, college campus organizations, neighbors, and work groups, southern Black women of differing backgrounds shared common desire for freedom from oppression. (p. 163)

Their acts of care and Othermothering exceeded teaching because they were "not focused on one area of the child's life only, but was a type of caring in which the one who cared was willing to explore the plethora of concerns that could affect performance" (Siddle-Walker & Tompkins, 2004, p. 90). In several narratives, across decades, Black women teachers emphasized how they began the school day by letting students know that they were loved, intelligent, and valued. Teaching reading and writing also included conveying a critical perspective on the world, understanding their cultural and racial heritage as well as local community history. The Black women teachers showcased in this chapter appear to have intuitively understood that learning to read is so much more for Black people than simply learning that letters have sounds, that blending sounds together makes words, and that words convey thoughts. They believed that literacy was needed for the survival of the race; they understood that knowing/thoughts precede actions and that words have the power to change and save lives.

By the mid-20th century, Black women activist teachers made clear their preferences for one reading approach over another: Huggins preferred culturally relevant, Wilks preferred language experience, and Collins preferred phonics. They envisaged literacy in general, and reading in particular, as part of a complex web of communication skills and ideological positions that begins with the ability to comprehend your place in the world as you seek to liberate yourself toward freedom; to be able to read as well as write embodies the enactment of civil and human rights, freedom, liberty, and justice. What is particularly striking is that philosophically, Black women activist teachers expressed both a sense of moral consciousness and responsibility in the role that they were willing to assume for Black people. They theorized that the Black child was central: their life was worthy of their best efforts, Black children were intelligent and eager to learn, and Black children represented hope in the future for the Black race.

During the last 2 decades of the 20th century, Black women teachers were aware of the back-to-basics movement, skills-based instruction, and standardized testing. Intentionally, they adopted, then adapted, commercial approaches to literacy by reframing culturally appropriate and informed pathways to literacy. Black women teachers in this chapter sought change, equity, and justice. Black women teachers also relied on literacy to support racial uplift, predicated on faith, love, and morality. They characterized and described Black students as eager, joyful, intelligent, readers, writers, and learners. Moreover, they maximized connections among the lived realities of Black students and the literacy needed to survive and thrive.

We share a deep appreciation for the Black women teachers featured in this chapter, as well as those who are unnamed, especially their activism and determination to ensure literacy access for Black people. Collectively, these women "walked the talk," as their lives and teaching demonstrate. We are grateful they articulated that an approach to reading begins by acknowledging and appreciating the humanity, intelligence, and value of Black children. Also, they expressed a determination to provide a quality literacy education informed by Black culture, language, and heritage—which is to be treasured. We have a deep and abiding commitment to continue building on their legacy.

CHAPTER 3

The Mis-Education of a High-Performing Black Girl

Shawyn Williams Jenkins (1976–2018) was a daughter, faculty member, friend, mother, sister, and wife. She is remembered for her lifelong desire to be a teacher, from her childhood when she "played teacher" with her siblings to her undergraduate degree in elementary education. Shawyn attended the University of Illinois Urbana-Champaign, for graduate school and earned a master's and a doctorate degree. Following her graduate studies, she accepted a faculty position at her alma mater, Coppin State. While there she taught preservice education courses, served as the coordinator of the master's reading program, and was tenured. She also taught teachers and online technology courses for the University of Maryland, College Park. She was regarded as a gifted teacher and praised for her creativity and commitment to empowering students. She will be remembered by the many people whose lives she touched. She also was Arlette's former doctoral student. Shawyn passed away on July 19, 2018. She is remembered as a brilliant and hardworking young woman whose commitment to the literacy of Black students is part of this book. With her family's permission, we include excerpts from her dissertation in this narrative as the entire text is verbatim. The following excerpts from Shawyn's dissertation center on one focal student and conclusions and recommendations of the study, primarily pages 77, 82–112, 149–168, and 223–228.

SHAWYN'S NARRATIVE: A SUMMARY

I am not a native of the focal community; however, I do share the same racial/ethnic and gender background as the focal participants. I have been teaching or observing in public school classrooms for the last 10 years. I have mentored, tutored, and advocated for public school students in my hometown and within the focal community throughout this 10-year period. My three siblings and I all attended and graduated from public schools. Throughout the duration of this project, I lived, worked, and attended school within the focal community. I bring a wealth of knowledge and experience to this research project regarding the public school system as it relates to the Black community.

My classroom observations, teaching experiences, work with preservice educators, and experience as a reading specialist and now as a research assistant have all allowed me to see and to feel the frustration experienced by many teachers, parents, and students. For instance, I have seen trusting Black families repeatedly let down by their schools; I have observed bright, enthusiastic teachers completely break down upon discovering the realities of teaching within high-poverty communities; and I have witnessed Black students routinely left behind academically despite their teachers' and parents' best intentions. These experiences have left me frustrated with the inertia of our educational bureaucracy, tired of the endless home-teacher blame game played by many adults and horrified by the undereducation and ever-increasing incarceration of our youth. Collectively, these experiences have provided me with considerable knowledge regarding Black schooling, but most importantly, they have helped me to realize that it is my right and responsibility as a Black scholar to speak for and with those in our community who have not been given a platform to voice their objections or concerns.

It is my obligation to disrupt "ideas of neutral relationships and structures" by providing "alternative truths" and using new ways to view reality (Dillard, 2000, p. 662). With this study I seek to disrupt the notion that organizational and structural school conditions are neutral by revealing the manner in which they contribute to the educational neglect of high-performing Black girls. I relied on my view of research as a responsibility to guide the data collection and analysis process (Ladson-Billings, 2000). I utilized my specialized knowledge of Black schooling to "sort" and "sift" the data collected, and to determine "who to trust, what to believe, and why something is true" (Collins, 1990, p. 202). This metaphor of "research as responsibility" (or view of the researcher and the research process as being "responsible and obligated to the very persons and communities being engaged in inquiry") is a contrasting view to the prevalent notion of "research as recipe" (Dillard, 2002, p. 663).

THE STUDY

From the beginning of the project, I viewed the participating parents and teachers as experts regarding their families, homes, schools, and classrooms, and I used the information that they provided (during observations and interviews) to inform each stage and every aspect of the research process. The participants informed the research process in five specific ways by (a) assisting in the identification of the theoretical framework and research questions, (b) shaping the data collected, (c) collecting data, (d) evaluating my data-collection and analysis, and, (e) providing interpretations and recommendations.

As a result, the participating teachers viewed me as both a researcher and a friend of the participating families since I often attended parent-teacher conferences with the families, school open houses, field trips, plays, and school functions, and I maintained regular contact with them through home visits. For the focal students and families, I had observed and videotaped their children, provided them with feedback, and maintained an open line of communication between home and school in a consistent manner. When their child entered kindergarten and first grade, I was able to provide their teachers with background information about the students and their families. I often spoke with the families more often than the school and teachers could. Therefore, teachers and parents confided in me, and used me to maintain contact between the home and school.

This study centered on the girls' reading progress in preschool, kindergarten, and first grade, in part because their experiences represent the most vulnerable targets of colonial school. My research details the experiences of people who are often talked about and for whom decisions are regularly made but who generally possess little power. My participants are rarely in control over the educational decisions that significantly impact their children, and I felt that it was very important to share their stories.

I initially assumed that the focal participants would continue to experience a great deal of school success while in kindergarten and first grade since they completed preschool with high reading skills and interests. However, by November 2001, their classroom reading instruction consistently neglected their reading skills and interests. So, instead of observing their reading growth, I felt compelled to document how their reading skills were neglected. Visits to each focal participant's home were conducted to monitor their reading growth,

document their home reading routines, collect artifacts, and triangu-
late the data gathered from the other data sources. During each home
visit, I engaged in unstructured conversations (Fontana & Frey, 2000)
with the focal participant and their caregivers about their interests,
progress (academically and socially), concerns, perceptions, and reading development. Unstructured conversations allowed the participants
to lead the discussion and to build a level of trust. I allowed the care-
giver to lead conversations with me by dictating the subject matter
discussed. On occasion, however, I would question the parent about
their personal school experiences, their feelings regarding their child's
schooling, and their hopes for their child's future. These conversations
provided background information on each case, and they were generally not recorded. I videotaped the students participating in home
reading activities (elicited and spontaneous) and regularly conducted
formal and informal reading assessments to monitor the students' progress (three times a school year). These assessments were videotaped
and/or audiotaped. During the visits, I engaged in the focal students
typical after school activities with them. I allowed them to direct the
conversation and to dictate the activities that we completed.

AESHA

Aesha was a Black female who was born in the focal community on
August 22, 1996, and lived with both of her parents and three siblings (two sisters, one older and one younger, and an older brother)
in a three-bedroom home in a racially mixed community. Most of her
extended family lives in the community, and she frequently inter-
acted with her aunts, cousins, and grandparents. Her mom completed
her nursing certification and worked as a nurse in a local hospital
during this project. During home visits, Aesha enjoyed showing off
her substantial book collection, self-created stories, and texts she
had written on her bedsheets and bedroom walls. She enjoyed reading, bike riding, and playing basketball during the project. Aesha . . .
constantly studied her older siblings to learn from their cursive writing techniques . . . She is independent by nature and prefers teaching
herself than being taught by others.
       Aesha has an oval-shaped face, smooth brown skin, and bright
eyes. She has a pleasant disposition and can be shy at times. She is
well-liked by her peers and is an eager and curious learner. Aesha's
mom, Nicole, was born in the focal community and graduated from

high school there. When I met Nicole in 2001, she was completing her nursing certification at a local college and worked the late shift as a nurse in a hospital. Nicole planned to move to a large city when she completed her certification to work as an emergency room nurse. Significant changes occurred in Aesha's home throughout the duration of the project. In the 2002 school year, Aesha's parents separated and her father moved to Iowa. Subsequently, Aesha, her mom, and siblings moved in with Nicole's sister, who also had three children, in a three-bedroom home. The following school year, Aesha's mom left the family for several months to get settled in a nearby city while Aesha and her siblings lived with their grandparents. In the summer of 2004, Aesha and her siblings reunited with Nicole, and they all currently live in a large Midwestern city.

Preschool

In 1999–2000, Aesha attended preschool for the first time. She attended the focal preschool center and was taught by Ms. King. In 2000–2001, Aesha returned to preschool and was once again placed in Ms. King's class. Aesha's steady growth and development throughout the school year made her an interesting case. According to Ms. King's assessment history, by age 3 Aesha:

1. enjoyed listening to stories read aloud,
2. liked to look at books in the reading area,
3. knew the front and back of a book,
4. held a book and turned the pages correctly,
5. recognized her name in print,
6. used her left hand to write, and
7. used scribbles to write her name.

By the first half of the focal school year, fall of 2000, Aesha:

8. could answer questions correctly about the story,
9. often looked at books individually,
10. wrote her name the conventional way,
11. could spell her name aloud when we pointed to the letters in her name,
12. used her finger to point to words as she read memorized pattern books,
13. enjoyed listening to stories independently at the listening area,

14. enjoyed playing JumpStart Spanish on the computer, and
15. repeated words in Spanish on the computer.

Aesha's interest in reading, writing, and Spanish grew throughout this school year, and she was one of the highest performing students in her class. During free choice time, she frequently displayed her literacy knowledge by reenacting aspects of Ms. King's morning routine. Throughout these reenactments, Aesha usually "played" Ms. King by leading her classmates in the reading of alphabet cards, the spelling of names in English and Spanish, or the rereading of chart stories. By the end of her second preschool year (2000–2001), she could correctly name all 26 letters of the English alphabet (uppercase and lowercase). Additionally, she could correctly name 21 uppercase letters of the Spanish alphabet and 20 lowercase letters. She also could conventionally write her name, her classmates' names, several sight words, and several phrases. Finally, she could identify all of her classmates' names, and she received 10 out of 12 on her school district's kindergarten version of Concepts About Print. She exuded high levels of confidence in her abilities as a reader, writer, and Spanish speaker.

Preschool Teacher's Perceptions of Focal Student and Family

To obtain a better understanding of Ms. King's perceptions of Aesha and her family, I have summarized data collected throughout our numerous conversations, home visits, research team meetings, and within teacher-created documents. By the end of preschool, Ms. King felt that Aesha had made tremendous gains socially from the previous year. In contrast to the year before, Aesha would initiate conversations with classmates and familiar adults. She expressed her feelings in conflict situations, was beginning to stand up for her rights, was well liked by her classmates, and was a very eager and curious learner. Nicole, Aesha's mom, had known Ms. King for several years, and they had a good relationship. Ms. King also taught Aesha's younger sister in her morning class for 3-year-olds.

Summer 2001 Home Visit

During this visit, Nicole discussed how Aesha enjoyed attending summer school and how she read books and wrote stories often. According to Nicole, Aesha usually initiated the home reading routines by reading to family members, reading independently, or writing stories. Nicole explained how Aesha even wrote on the walls. Aesha was very interested in Spanish, and her parents learned many words from her. Aesha's mom appreciated all of the literacy routines that Ms. King used and her incorporation of Spanish instruction. Nicole valued the Spanish instruction so much that she enrolled Aesha in the only elementary school in the district that offered Spanish foreign language instruction to its K–5 students.

Kindergarten: Interviews and Conversations with Kindergarten Teacher

Ms. King also served as Aesha's teacher during her kindergarten year. This became the third consecutive year that Ms. King was Aesha's teacher. However, it was Ms. King's first year teaching kindergarten and her first year at Lakeside School. Initially, Ms. King was excited about her transfer to Lakeside School because she was told that she would have a one-hour and 50-minute literacy block, an uninterrupted block of time to complete literacy-related tasks. Later, Ms. King was disheartened to learn that during this literacy block, her Spanish-speaking students would be pulled out of her class and lose 25 minutes of the time that had been allotted for foreign language instruction. Unfortunately, Ms. King's attempts to coordinate her literacy instruction with the teacher of the pull-out program did not work. This lack of curriculum alignment contributed to Ms. King's disappointment. Additionally, Ms. King felt constrained by the school's rotating 6-day weekly schedule and pressure from the school district to bring low-performing students to grade level. She was unable to fulfill the hopes of parents because of her lack of control over her Spanish-speaking students' curriculum, and she was helpless to meet the social and emotional needs of many of her students. Furthermore, she was told by a colleague, "If you want to survive here [at Lakeside School] you have to give up your dreams and do like everyone else." These stressors intensified as the school year progressed and caused Ms. King to experience health difficulties.

Kindergarten Literacy Development

Based on audiotaped conversations with Ms. King during the 2001–2002 school year, Aesha's reading, writing, and Spanish development continued to blossom. In addition, Aesha's confidence in her abilities grew as she began to help classmates with their literacy questions. She became the person to ask "how do you spell this?" when the teacher was busy. On Aesha's third-quarter report card, Ms. King wrote, "Aesha is gaining more self-confidence in her reading and writing abilities. She shows pride in her work." By December 2001, Ms. King had begun guided reading lessons for Aesha. Although many of her classmates were not ready for guided reading, Ms. King asked me, "Why should I hold Aesha back?"

a good teacher question

On January 24, 2002, Ms. King reported, during my classroom observation, that "Aesha is really progressing. My running records indicate that she is reading where she should be at the end of the school year." In free choice time, Aesha continued to write notes to Ms. King. When I visited her classroom, Aesha took pride in reading to me all of her guided reading books and journal entries. On my April 12, 2002, classroom visit, she read 14 small books as her classmates watched in awe and I videotaped her. By the end of the school year, Aesha had exceeded the kindergarten literacy expectations for her district, and her teacher wrote these comments on her fourth-quarter report card: "Aesha is an excellent student. She has been a great role model for her classmates."

Kindergarten Teacher's Perceptions of Focal Student and Family

Ms. King and Aesha's family members have known one another for a number of years and they have mutual respect for one another. Nicole respected Ms. King's school instruction and her rapport with her children. Ms. King respected Nicole's hard work as a mother of four, nurse, and student. According to recorded conversations with Ms. King, Aesha was consistently one of the highest-performing students in Ms. King's class and was a source of pride for her. Ms. King had been Aesha's only formal teacher, and Ms. King enjoyed watching Aesha's literacy skills "take off' under her direction.

Kindergarten Home Visits

During home visits, Aesha enjoyed showing off her substantial book collection, self-created stories, and the stories she had written on her bedsheets and bedroom walls. After school she spent a lot of time reading stories independently and writing stories that she shared with family members. She enjoyed reading the "wall and sheet" stories to me and always made a point of reassuring me that her mom didn't mind. Nicole was often at work during my visits (since I conducted them immediately after school; in order to interview her, I had to work around her schedule). Aesha did not frequent the library, but she regularly asked her mom to purchase books from the grocery store.

First Grade: Interviews and Conversations with Aesha's First-Grade Teacher

The 2002–2003 school year was Mr. Hubert's first year teaching at Lakeside School. Mr. Hubert was a White, 20-something newlywed. He held a bachelor's degree and had 2 years of teaching experience at the elementary level. Mr. Hubert was an enthusiastic teacher who wanted "to help all of his students" and "to make a difference." He was hired a month after the 2002–2003 school year began to replace the initially hired teacher, Ms. Johnson, who resigned after one week of teaching at Lakeside School.

Ms. Johnson was a White, 20-something, first-year teacher, who I had previously taught in an undergraduate literature course for preservice teachers. She had previous experience working with children, and based on her work in the course, she had a great deal of creativity. On Friday of the first week of the 2002–2003 school year, I visited her for an initial interview. When I entered the classroom, Ms. Johnson was sitting on the floor sobbing. She explained that she could not "handle this class" and that the students were unruly. She felt "drained." In addition, she had "lost the energy to even think of a new way to arrange the classroom seating" to accommodate all of the personalities in the classroom. Moreover, she could not understand why she could not lead the students through an activity without them hitting one another. Ms. Johnson described an incident that occurred early in the day in which a student threatened another with a pair of scissors. Furthermore, Ms. Johnson felt unsupported by the school's administration. During our lengthy conversation, Ms. King visited Ms. Johnson's classroom. Ms. King had previously taught a majority of Ms. Johnson's current students the previous year.

Ms. King confessed that she experienced similar feelings last year, specifically the anxiety, disappointment, and helplessness that Ms. Johnson was experiencing. Additionally, Ms. Johnson was also coping with a personal family tragedy, which intensified her unhappiness. Later that evening, Ms. Johnson decided to resign from Lakeside

School. After Ms. Johnson's resignation, Aesha's class had a number of substitute teachers; members of Lakeside's staff and even the principal attempted to "deal" with the "unruly class." Ms. King, their kindergarten teacher, was routinely asked to come to the classroom to help staff members manage the class.

Mr. Hubert was inexperienced with reading instruction, so within a few months of his arrival the reading coach provided him with literacy support. To manage his "lively" class, he rotated their seats every four weeks and used table points as rewards. On the comment section of Aesha's report card, Mr. Hubert focused his comments on her behavior and emotions. During our end-of-the-year, Mr. Hubert confessed that he had trouble throughout the school year meeting Aesha's needs because of her high skills. As a result, he had recommended Aesha for gifted and talented testing, and she had recently taken the placement test. However, she missed the cut-off score by a few points. Mr. Hubert felt that Aesha should continue to be tested each year until she was placed in a gifted and talented classroom because she was "very bright."

First-Grade Teacher's Perceptions of Focal Student and Family

To obtain a better understanding of Mr. Hubert's perceptions of Aesha and her family, I have summarized data collected during our February 2003 parent-teacher conference; the June 3, 2003, end-of-the-year meeting; and conversations that occurred during classroom observations that I conducted. During Aesha's February 19, 2003, parent-teacher conference, Mr. Hubert expressed that in the beginning of the school year, his relationship with Aesha's mom was good, and she regularly attended school meetings; however, at this point in the school year she had not been responding to his messages (Nicole did not attend this parent-teacher conference). Mr. Hubert was disappointed that Nicole did not attend the conference because he was worried about Aesha. According to Mr. Hubert, within the last week her stubbornness had "taken a turn for the worst" and she was becoming outright defiant, "folding her arms" and refusing to follow his directions. By the end of the school year (June 3, 2003), the teacher-parent relationship had not been fully healed. Since Nicole had a difficult work schedule, Mr. Hubert had arranged appointments with her beyond the school's allotted time. He also shared with me how he even had to arrange home visits with a few parents because of their refusal to enter the school. Additionally, Mr. Hubert described Aesha as being "older than her years," and he felt she had "to grow up too fast." He also believed that she was developing issues "with males" because she would often retort, "You are not my father," and refuse to comply with his instructions.

First-Grade Home Visits

I present data collected during conversations with parents or caregivers that occurred during the 2002–2003 school year to illustrate parental and familial perceptions of school and discuss the family's home reading routines or the focal student's reading interests. After school, Aesha did not spend as much time reading as she had in the past. During first grade, she spent more time learning bicycle tricks and playing basketball than reading and writing stories. On my October 25, 2002, visit, Nicole explained that Aesha had not warmed up to her classroom teacher and that she did not talk about school much anymore. When asked about her future goals for Aesha, Nicole replied that above all else she wanted her daughter to be happy, "whether that means going to college or not." Nicole reminded me of her plans to move and her hesitancy to put Aesha into gifted and talented classrooms because of her personal experiences with the program. Further, Nicole was not surprised when I explained to her that Aesha's school reading instruction was below her actual grade level. Nicole explained that she knew Aesha was smart and felt that the regular classroom instruction was always going to be easy for Aesha.

Final Interview Responses

On May 10, 2005, I emailed an information packet to Nicole. This packet included (a) a cover letter thanking her for her participation in the study, (b) the aforementioned summary of the major research findings, (c) a copy of Aesha's vignette, and (d) the analysis. I left a message for Nicole on May 18, 2005, and I plan on hearing from her in the near future. Ms. King no longer teaches within the district, and I plan to hear from her in the near future. On May 12, 2005, I placed a summary packet of information in Mr. Hubert's school mailbox (because his class was on a field trip). This packet included (a) a cover letter thanking him for his participation in the study, (b) the aforementioned summary of the major research findings, (c) a copy of Aesha's vignette, (d) the analysis, (e) the Guided Reading and Literacy

Center section (with the corresponding transcripts), and (f) analysis. I followed up with Mr. Hubert on May 19, 2005, to schedule a final interview. Mr. Hubert did not return my phone call.

DISCUSSION

The aforementioned interviews, conversations, and home visits with the participating teachers and parents reveal the pressure created when the conflicting interests of high-performing Black girls, the interests of the school district, and the characteristics of the school (high class size and fragmented classroom instruction) clash within kindergarten and first-grade reading instruction. This study suggests that the intense pressure created between these conflicting interests forces teachers to pick sides. More often than not, the interests of the school and school district are chosen over that of high-performing Black girls. The focal students' experiences indicate that, when teachers have limited instructional time, high-teacher-to-student ratios, and mutual distrust of the parents of high-performing Black girls, the skills of high-performing Black girls are likely to be neglected by their teachers. This is likely to occur because their teachers do not feel a sense of urgency, necessity, or obligation to "fight the system" and work alongside Black parents to meet the needs of these students. Subsequently, by first grade, district mandates, school conditions, and deficit theories of Black students and families have won this battle and these powerful forces work in conjunction to inhibit the teacher's ability to fully recognize or develop the skills of high-performing Black girls.

not boys?

Interviews with participating teachers in this study indicate that the combination of fragmented daily schedules, fragmented instruction from one grade level to the next, large student-to-teacher ratios, intense focus on "closing the achievement gap," and teacher inexperience dramatically decreases a teacher's ability to fully develop the skills of high-performing Black girls. Based on the interview data, this instructional neglect occurred in part because of district mandates, teacher inexperience, and organizational conditions within the school that forced teachers to focus their priorities on managing their large class sizes and closing the so-called achievement gap, rather than focusing on fully assessing and meeting the individual needs of the focal students. In essence, the teachers were made to be more accountable to the school district than the students and families that they served. Below, I list

organizational and structural characteristics that contributed to the focal students' educational neglect:

1. *Fragmentation and inconsistency*: The students' beginning
   reading instruction was (a) not aligned with their
   individual reading levels, (b) not aligned with the previous
   year's instruction, and (c) not aligned with their home
   reading routines. The students' educational process was
   equally fragmented each school year when they were
   assigned a new teacher who had their own set of rules, roles,
   schedules, and classroom procedures that the students had
   to adapt to every school year.
2. *High teacher-to-student ratios*: When classrooms average 22–25
   students with one classroom teacher and a part-time aide (if
   a teacher is lucky), it is extremely difficult to engage in any
   in-depth dialogue with young students in a whole-group
   setting. Additionally, it is difficult to manage the entire
   classroom when teachers use small groups, because the
   remainder of the class is left largely unsupervised. Without
   lower teacher-to-student ratios, teachers are often reduced to
   using very authoritarian techniques to maintain their power
   or simply allow students to misbehave.
3. *Acceptance of the school's organization and structure:* It
   appears that the widespread acceptance of and adaptation
   to the aforementioned organizational and structural school
   conditions is the most difficult characteristic to overcome.
   The teachers and parents in this study largely accepted
   the impositions of high teacher-to-student ratios and
   fragmented daily schedules by adapting their instruction
   to fit into these oppressive models rather than uniting to
   dismantle these structures.

The Effects of Strained Teacher-Parent Relations on the Growth of High-Performing Black Girls: A Case of Divide and Rule

The data from interviews with parents and teachers suggest that the
tension between Black parents and teachers also inhibits the development of high-performing Black girls. Without respectful relationships between parents and teachers, teachers do not feel obligated to

fully assess or develop the needs of high-performing Black girls. For instance, when teachers are disconnected from Black parents and do not possess respectful relationships with them, the constraints and pressure they experience from high class sizes and limited instructional time is greater than the pressure they feel from their relationships with high-performing students and parents. Therefore, teachers are more likely to accept popular deficit theories of Black students and families as an excuse for failing to develop the abilities of high-performing Black girls or develop sympathetic relationships with these students, as opposed to challenging the status quo and fully developing their skills. However, working together they could jointly develop the skills of high-performing Black girls and challenge oppressive school conditions.

The normalization and acceptance of mutual teacher-Black parent distrust creates and perpetuates a cycle of teacher-parent passivity, inaction, and acceptance of oppressive school conditions. For example, while the teacher and parent accept their mutual distrust as normal, the student suffers instructional neglect, is trained to accept the neglect as normal, and learns to accept parent-teacher disconnection as normal. The interviews suggest that when the skills of Black girls are not fully assessed and developed, they misbehave in school, stay home from school, and/or fall behind academically. This provides teachers with evidence to explain why the teacher should not change their instructional practices, critically reflect on their instructional practices, or challenge the school's organizational-structural conditions to develop the skills of high-performing Black girls. Likewise, teachers place the "blame" for the students' underdevelopment on the students' difficult home conditions and use these conditions as a basis to create a sympathetic relationship with the student as opposed to using it as an impetus to "fight the system" and meet their educational needs. Finally, longitudinal home visits reveal that when the skills of high-performing students are ignored, they disconnect from their teachers, disconnect from school teaching and learning, and lose interest in literacy-related tasks.

Mutual parent-teacher distrust is more likely in situations in which the teacher, parent, or student are strangers who have not had extended conversations with one another. Additionally, these distrustful parent-teacher relationships appear more likely to occur in classrooms in which a continuous "socially conscious" effort has not been made to bring the communities and experiences of the students and families into the classroom (Harris, 1995; Sims, 1982). Without these personal connections, people generally form their opinions of "other people's children" based on media stereotypes (Delpit, 1995; Roediger, 2003).

CONCLUSION

This collective case study suggests that the educational neglect of the focal students was not random, accidental, or the result of an overburdened, benevolent system. Instead, it appears that the focal students' educational neglect was the result of a purposefully created institution that successfully maintains the current power structure by eliminating potential opponents to colonialism at the very beginning of their academic careers. It is particularly beneficial to the colonizer when high-performing Black girls' (potential community leaders and future opponents of colonialism) skills are underdeveloped because of the following:

1. When high-performing Black girls' skills remain ignored and underdeveloped, they do not acquire the skills needed for self-defense and community uplift. Instead, they learn to accept passivity and inaction as normal and fail to develop the knowledge or abilities needed to effectively participate in, challenge, or dismantle the oppressive power structure.
2. When Black girls act out in school or stop attending school because their skills are ignored and underdeveloped, it appears to legitimate popular theories of Black students as unmotivated, low performing, and disruptive in relationship to White students and it appears to reinforce the continued need for the current school system (to help Blacks achieve social, political, and economic parity).
3. When teachers and Black parents remain disconnected, they are unable to unite to fully develop the skills of high-performing Black girls, to realize their shared goals, or work together to dismantle oppressive school conditions. Therefore, their disconnection appears to legitimate the need for the current school system to help teachers and help Blacks to achieve academic, social, political, and economic parity.
4. The division between teachers and Black parents directs attention away from the oppressive effects of "colonial spaces" and the motives underlying their use. Instead, this division appears to legitimate deficit theories of Black parents

as uncaring and unsupportive of their children's education, and of teachers as racist and uncaring. These images appear to legitimize the need for the current school system to help teachers and help Blacks to achieve academic, social, political, and economic parity.

IN CONVERSATION

Arlette's Comments

As you can imagine, it is with great sadness that I reread Shawyn's dissertation and formatted the narrative without her. In truth, I love her thoughts on resistance because they detail and show us how an intelligent young Black girl, someone who is a reader, finds herself as a 5-year-old struggling within a dominant and domineering system when she just wants to be herself as a child/student. Aesha, at such a tender age, appears to sense that the world she has known (acceptance, unconditional love, support, warmth) is shifting under her when she begins to attend school (K–1). I find that this narrative captures how this Black girl's sense of self is under attack and how she struggles to survive. Somehow, she seems to know that what she is being asked to do is immoral—that without explicit instruction she is being groomed to take on a persona in school that differs from her "real self," yet appears to confirm her teachers' preconceived and stereotypical notions of what "Black girls are like." Adding to the complexity, Aesha enters a school district, school, and classroom that are ill-prepared to accept her as human, herself, and capable. Her 1st-grade teachers do not build upon the reading behaviors and skills that she possesses. In truth, she becomes an unpaid teaching assistant in the classroom, while simultaneously not being provided the instruction she needs to progress as a reader. In the eyes of her 1st-grade teacher, Aesha's behavior, or at least his perceptions of the root causes of her behavior, appear to overwhelm his assessment of her academic abilities. Finally, I am struck by how often Black parents I know have experienced the same scenario as Nicole and Aesha: allowing your intellectually gifted Black child to undergo a "gifted" intellectual assessment, then learning that she is "only a few points away" from making the cut!

I may be reading more into the study than appears in the text because of recent research that says many of the same things about the treatment of Black girls in our society (Crenshaw, Ocen, & Nanda,

2015). The studies are based on interviews with Black girls and women, and I respect their experiences. For this book, however, the opportunity to learn from Shawyn's longitudinal (3-year) study, when she was a part of the girls' (and their families') lives, is invaluable. It is precisely this type of reading research, however, that is not part of the body of research that is used to inform reading improvements for Black readers.

This situation has me pondering: what happens to a student's sense of dignity, self, and being fully human when they spend nearly 8 hours a day at school and are ignored as unintelligent, and/or used as a tutor? The manner in which reading as an act of liberation is taken from Aesha is inconceivable, but we all know it happens, and that it is happening every day in the lives of Black students. When I step back from this individual account and consider the massive scale on which this occurs among Black students—the youngest ones who are learning, or should be learning to read—I am without words.

Gwen's Comments

I attended predominantly Black schools, and my research has been conducted in predominantly Black schools. Unfortunately, what happened to Aesha in Shawyn's study is a common occurrence. Students are excited when they begin school. They show up with great expectations for themselves, their teachers, and their learning environment—but then "school" happens. Year after year, they are miseducated and undereducated, and their identities are berated by teachers who are not prepared to implement innovative instructional techniques based on students' individual needs and strengths, a curriculum designed to deplete them of their critical thinking skills, and an educational system created to perpetuate institutional racism. I am appalled when teachers describe Black students as unmotivated. Who would not become unmotivated if they were required to go to a place where they are oppressed on a daily basis?

Aesha, like so many young Black children, began school with high expectations. Her first several years were great experiences. She connected with the teacher, and her family life was intact. But when she began 1st grade, everything seemed to change. When her parents separated, a social worker and/or psychologist should have stepped in to support her, and the 1st-grade teacher was very unprepared. She should have never been hired in the first place. Imagine how Aesha must have felt. Her home life changed when her dad moved. I'm sure she missed her father, and at school—her previous home away from home—teachers continued to abandon her.

Shawyn's list of structural and organizational characteristics that contributed to Aesha's educational neglect reminds me, as a Black educator, of my responsibility to advocate for students and families like Aesha. It also challenges me as a teacher educator to ensure that every teacher education student who crosses my path is taught how to connect with all types of students. What Aesha was lacking in her 1st-grade experience was a teacher-student relationship. Many students are relationship-oriented, and if teachers do not know how to build relationships with them, their learning experience will be less than ideal. Remember, we are teaching students, not content. When teachers focus on the content instead of the students, they are setting themselves, and their students, up for failure.

Patriann's Comments

As I read Shawyn's narrative, two elements caught my attention. The first is that this counter narrative interrupts the often implicitly accepted notion that most Black young children come to school with a disconnect between their home and school and is based on differences between the way in which language is deployed across home and school (oral language tends to be referenced here, and written language is also included as a reason for this discrepancy). In Shawyn's narrative, we see the assets brought by Black girls to the school setting and how these are torn from the Black child through a system where the agenda falls short of placing the Black child at the center (see, for instance, Greene, 2016; Henry, 2001). We see these assets through the multiple literacies that Aesha brings to bear in and beyond the classrooms, causing her teacher to refer to her as a "bright child." If schools (and a system) strip "bright" Black girls like Aesha of their capacity to leverage literacies while also rendering them helpless to use their creativity through language, how does this challenge a narrative of teachers being the culprits?

Clearly, the system appears to be more than just teachers who work within it, many of whom think only of their "daily bread." Is there a need for a new kind of teacher who is taught to navigate the systemic structures that fail students such as Aesha so early on in life? For a teacher to want to (and develop) a sense of advocacy for youth, they must feel some sense of shared burden, some togetherness, or perhaps a bond. In this narrative, we see the distancing of teachers from Aesha over time, which creates an us-versus-them scenario that dooms both the teachers who work with Aesha from ever hoping to reach her as well as the Black girl that she is from ever wanting to be the child who cared about school. To me, there is an opportunity here for a "both-and" approach—one that envisions the potential of Aesha's teacher, parent, and mother in the struggle. This both-and approach serves as a pathway to create conversational pathways that are free from blame.

The second element that struck me in Aesha's narrative was her giftedness and its failure to be captured by a school system that premised this categorization solely on a test. The notion that giftedness can be measured merely by an assessment with undue regard to other data points that emerge from interactions, observations, creations of the child, the child's daily language use, and so forth is an area to be challenged. Expecting Aesha—a Black girl who had already begun to endure distancing techniques from those who were responsible for instructing her—to perform more than excellently on a test of giftedness designed through Eurocentric methods clearly creates a situation where she is being doubly affected. The use of other measures in conjunction with the test of giftedness is justified given that it takes a particular skill set to complete a test and to do so excellently. At some point, it would be important to ask, to what degree is the performance on a gifted test a measure of the child's ability to complete tests presented in a specific format as opposed to the child's capacity to reflect and convey informed thought about a given task? This element specifically stood out to me because I remember the same thing happening to my daughter, who, after repeatedly being recommended for gifted testing, kept somehow "falling short of the score."

What happens when you have gifted children kept in a mainstream classroom with undue attention and tasks that challenge them to move forward? They tend to channel this energy elsewhere (in what are often considered to be negative pathways), or they become so disengaged that it is difficult to interest them in literacy tasks. Fortunately for me, I was able to make the sacrifice and enroll my daughter in a private school at different periods of her life where she flourished, engaged in tasks that she enjoyed, honed her critical thinking skills, and, now that she is 17, can clearly explain the difference between instruction geared toward capitalizing on her strengths and instruction that is completely removed from her interest in classrooms.

Unfortunately for Aesha, and for so many of our young Black girls and boys, this privilege is not present. Who, then, suffers the consequences of what often results in so many broken lives? There is a moral imperative, it seems, to ensure that gifted students receive the support they need, particularly when they are Black children who may not always score "well" on gifted measures. By extension, there is a moral imperative here also, to rethink the notion of giftedness as it resides in all Black children. How do we represent giftedness as such? In fact, it would be interesting to see how many Black children "fall short" of reflecting their giftedness on such measures in the early stages of school yet thrive and demonstrate the ability to reach and touch so many as adults.

CRITICAL DISCUSSION QUESTIONS

Black Parents/Caregivers: How can the teachers and school administrators listen to what I know about my daughter? How can the teachers accept her as a fellow human? How can teachers acknowledge my daughter's abilities, strengths, and limitations, and something other than her behavior? What will supporting her reading growth look like?

Teachers: How can I recognize my racial biases associated with young Black girls and acknowledge their innocence? How can I ensure that I am addressing the literacy needs of high-performing Black girls? How can I remove barriers and obstacles to literacy learning for high-performing Black girls?

Educators/Administrators: What professional development is scheduled to address anti-Black racism? Who will facilitate the discussion? How will the academic needs of Black girls be addressed?

Politicians: When will there be an examination of past legislative reading reform and policies that have been barriers to educational justice? Once examined and a report published, when will substantive changes begin and how will they be enforced?

Reading Researchers: How can reading research begin to acknowledge its past response to Blackness? How will reading research be reimagined and reconceptualized to include Black students as valued humans who are equally capable of learning to read?

SUGGESTED READINGS

African American Policy Forum. (2021). *Black girls matter: Pushed out, overpo-liced and underprotected.* https://www.aapf.org/blackgirlsmatter

Anderson, B. N., & Martin, J. A. (2018). What K-12 teachers need to know about teaching gifted black girls. *Gifted Child Today, 41*(3), 117–124.

Andrews, D. J. C., Brown, T., Castro, E., & Id-Deen, E. (2019). The impossibility of being "perfect and White": Black girls' racialized and gendered school-ing experiences. *American Educational Research Journal, 56*(6), 2531–2572.

Epstein, R., Blake, J. J., & Gonzalez, T. (2020). *Girlhood-interrupted. https://gender justiceandopportunity.georgetown*.edu/wp-content/uploads/2020/06/girlhood -interrupted.pdf

Morris, M. W. (2016). *Pushout: The criminalization of black girls in schools.* The New Press.

Patrick, K., Onyeka-Crawford, A., & Duchesneau, N. (2020). *"And they cared": How to create better, safer learning environments for girls of color.* The Education Trust, National Women's Law Center. https://edtrust.org/resource/and -they-cared-how-to-create-better-safer-learning-environments-for-girls-of -color/

Wilmot, J. M., Migliarini, V., & Annamma, S. A. (2021). Policy as punishment and distraction: The double helix of racialized sexual harassment of Black girls. *Educational Policy, 35*(2), 347–367.

CHAPTER 4

Cultural Dissonance in a First-Grade Classroom

I come from very humble beginnings, and I am grateful to view my foundational upbringing as a gift. During the Great Migration, my parents moved to Michigan from the sharecropping South and made many sacrifices for me and my siblings to become first-generation college graduates. My father pastored a Black Baptist church from the time I was 2 years old, and my mother was my first Sunday School teacher. Like Mama, I am a pastor's wife. My husband pastors a Black Baptist church that is located in the neighborhood where we grew up. I see the world with the heart of a Black woman who loves God, my husband, sons, family, church family, and community. A passion for teaching, conducting research in the Black community, and working as a servant-leader was instilled in me throughout my childhood. My educational experiences began at home and church, followed by a predominantly Black pre-K–12 education, and moved abruptly to a predominantly White university where racism reigned freely. Corporate America was the home of my first career as a stockbroker for wealthy clients. After having children, my priorities changed from a focus on finances to a focus on family. I wanted to stay home and invest quality time in my own sons during their formative years, rather than invest money for others. I spent several enjoyable years as a stay-at-home mom and subsequently returned to school to transition to a career in education, after God called me into the teaching ministry. For the past 30 years, I have spent my time teaching and conducting research in formal and informal spaces in school, church, and community-based learning environments.

GWEN'S NARRATIVE: A SUMMARY

I began my journey in the field of education with the goal of identifying the sources of incongruence and possible points of connection for students who are successful in the learning environment of the Black Church but are considered at risk in their classrooms at school. My narrative is an excerpt from a larger study conducted over a 5-month period, during the second semester of the 1999–2000 academic school year (McMillon, 2001). I invite you into the lives of two 1st-grade African American boys, Tony and Travis, who were brilliant students, according to their teacher, principal, reading resource teacher, and parents. In fact, as 1st-graders, both Tony and Travis were reading on a 5th-grade level, according to the reading resource teacher. Despite their exceptional reading ability, Tony and Travis were suspended multiple times during their 1st-grade year. Their teacher believed that Tony and Travis were academically smart but reported that their behavior prevented her from being able to teach them. They spent most of their classroom experience in time-out. Their parents eventually became ambivalent toward the teacher and the school when they were unable to effectively teach their smart 1st-grade sons.

This narrative illuminates the tragic undereducation of Black boys in classrooms with teachers who are unable to develop effective communication practices, implement transparent curricula, and engage in disciplinary actions that are adaptable. In order to successfully teach Black boys, teachers need to (a) build meaningful relationships with students and parents, (b) intentionally work with them to identify cultural clashes, and (c) adapt classroom communication, instruction, and disciplinary policies to meet the unique needs of their students. In this narrative, disciplinary actions such as time-out prevented Tony and Travis from receiving important instructional time. They were frequently denied privileges such as recess and field trips, which led to a cycle of ineffective discipline and learning denied.

SETTING

The setting of my study was Paradise Elementary, located in a well-established inner-city neighborhood in a Midwestern city. Several African American community leaders, including retired teachers, principals, and politicians, lived in the neighborhood. Paradise served 485 students from preschool to 5th grade, and approximately 92 percent of the students were African American. Twenty-two teachers were on staff at Paradise, including four African American females, one African American male, two Hispanic females, and 15 White females. Two African American male 1st-grade students were chosen to participate in the study because they were considered the most at-risk 1st-grade students by their teacher and principal. Both students were in Mrs. Rudolph's class, and she was considered the best 1st-grade teacher at the school by parents, teachers, and the principal.

TONY

Tony was a friendly 7-year-old who lived with his mother and four siblings. Until the birth of his younger brother, he was the baby of the family. In many ways Tony's family life was similar to the stereotypical narrative of African American students in an inner-city neighborhood. His mom, Ms. Donaldson, was a single mother, and his father was incarcerated. Tony rarely heard from his father, but his paternal grandmother, aunt, and uncle stayed in touch with him. One could easily pass judgment upon the Donaldson family based on their family status, but they would be very incorrect in their assessment unless they personally spoke with Ms. Donaldson. She was a very articulate woman in her mid-thirties who was employed full-time at a group home for troubled teens. She owned her home, which was located in a well-established neighborhood two blocks from Paradise Elementary School. Upon entering her house for the parent interview, I immediately noticed that her home was well-furnished with items that would encourage learning. For example, an expensive set of Britannica encyclopedias was neatly placed on a beautiful wooden bookshelf, with many other books in sight, including several spiritually based self-help books. The big-screen television set was on one side of the living room, and a few educational toys were on the floor. Ms. Donaldson mentioned that the family owned a computer, and her oldest son wanted to show me the similarities and differences between their video camera and the one that I was using to collect data.

Ms. Donaldson felt that Tony was an exceptionally bright child because he benefited from having older siblings. She required her children to read every day after school. Before he became a reader, Tony's older siblings were required to read to him. His mother also explained that she began reading to Tony when he was an infant and was intrigued by his keen interest in books. To her surprise, however, Tony did not necessarily choose books that one would expect a 1st-grader to read. For example, while at the doctor's office a few days before the interview, Tony picked up a *National Geographic* and started reading aloud to his mother. She was amazed at the words that he was reading and double-checked the article to make sure he was reading the words in the magazine and not making up words. To her amazement, he had read every word in the article correctly, and was able to engage her in a conversation about it.

Ms. Donaldson stated that Tony has always been an exceptional child. He walked and talked early, and carried on detailed conversations with adults as a very young child. According to Ms. Donaldson, Tony could recognize and say the letters of the alphabet at the age of one, and he continued to advance at a fast pace until his kindergarten experience.

Several years ago, Ms. Donaldson was married to Tony's father, Tony Sr. They moved the family from their current locale to a larger metropolitan area to find better jobs. Initially, her children excelled while attending schools in the first school district in which they lived. However, after a few months they moved into a predominantly White apartment complex in a different neighborhood. Her older children, ages 11, 9, and 7, were constantly harassed by White teenagers who called them "niggers" and warned them that they were not welcome in the neighborhood. The Donaldson family's toys were often destroyed, and their family car was also vandalized. Ms. Donaldson tried to talk with the parents of some of the teenagers whom her children accused of harassment, only to be harassed herself.

Tony's older siblings were able to find some refuge in their classrooms at school because they had good teachers who did not allow them to be harassed by other children, but Tony was not as fortunate. His mother explained:

> Tony's kindergarten teacher was extremely prejudiced. She would do little things in the classroom to hurt Tony, like intentionally ignore him. I complained to the principal, who asked me for concrete evidence. It was difficult for me to prove that the teacher was not treating Tony equally until their Valentine's Day celebration. I stayed up all night cooking cupcakes so all four of the kids could have a special Valentine treat for their classmates.
>
> That was a lot of work, but I wanted them to have something nice. When Tony and I arrived in his class, he was excited and immediately began to pass out his Valentine cards and prepare his treat. The teacher told him that they would pass out the cards and treats a little later. When I arrived at the school to pick Tony up, he met me at the door, tears in his eyes with the cards and the cupcakes. I was so angry that I immediately went to talk with the principal. I knew that I had the evidence I needed

to confront the teacher. When asked, the teacher claimed that she didn't know Tony had Valentine cards and treats. (Parent Interview, March 7, 2000)

It took a long time for Tony and his family to recuperate from the damages that occurred during that time in their lives. In fact, Ms. Donaldson stated that she was still trying to help her children rectify some of the effects of those traumatic experiences. She noticed that Tony's whole personality changed during his negative kindergarten experience. At first, he loved school, but after several weeks he did not like it anymore. His conversation also changed. Ms. Donaldson noticed that he began to describe people based on their race, specifically detailing if they were Black or White.

After returning to his hometown, Tony began his 1st-grade experience. His teacher, Mrs. Rudolph, described him as "an introvert who carried a lot of bottled-up anger." He cried every day when his mother dropped him off at school, insisting that his mother let him stay home with her. Mrs. Rudolph explained that Tony would not interact with her or his classmates during the first month of school. Ms. Donaldson shared information about Tony's negative kindergarten experience with Mrs. Rudolph, who patiently waited for an opportunity to connect with him. Mrs. Rudolph stated:

> I remember one day after about a month of not talking to me or anyone else in the class, we were doing some type of activity and the students were having fun—laughing and enjoying themselves. Tony looked at us and I kindly invited him to join us, just as I had done every day from the beginning of school. But this time he slowly got up and sat with the group. He didn't say much that day, but when he got ready to leave he gave me the biggest hug. It absolutely made my day. I knew then, that he would be all right. You know that's why he received the "Hug Award" this year. No matter what happened between us during the day, he never left school without first giving me a hug. He's a very special child. (Teacher Interview, April 6, 2000)

According to school records, Tony did not know all the letters of the alphabet when he began 1st grade. However, during the parent interview with Ms. Donaldson, it was discovered that Tony had known all the letters of the alphabet since he was only one year old. His mother felt that Tony did not do well during the initial testing because he was still suffering from the terrible kindergarten experience. She also explained that she was having a hard time coping with life circumstances resulting from the relocation, and perhaps her feelings were affecting his interest in school. Whatever the reason, Tony's test scores showed that he only knew 18 of the 26 letters of the alphabet.

Not only did Tony do poorly on his test scores, but he remained on the retention list for two marking periods. Mrs. Rudolph expressed her concerns about Tony to Ms. Donaldson during a parent-teacher conference early in the school year. She felt that Tony was not working up to his potential and that he should not be on the retention list. She requested that his mother work with him more diligently at home. Ms. Donaldson assured Mrs. Rudolph that she would follow her instructions for the plan devised specifically to bring Tony's skills up to par.

After the conference, Mrs. Rudolph immediately saw improvement in Tony's work. He got off the retention list, passed the students in his first reading group, and was placed in the next group, where he soon passed the students, ultimately ending up in the top reading group with two other students. At the end of 1st grade, Tony was reading at a 5th-grade level, according to the reading resource teacher. Mrs. Rudolph attributes Tony's success to his mother:

> I wish I had more mothers like Tony's mother. I told her what she needed to do to help her son, and she followed through. Tony often told me that he was required to read every night. I believe him because the proof can be seen in the way he progressed. I couldn't have done it without her. I just don't have the time during class to give individual students everything they need. I need more parental support. (Teacher Interview, April 6, 2000)

Tony became successful academically because his mother and teacher approached his literacy learning as a team effort. However, within the social norms frame, Tony was not nearly as successful in his classroom at school.

TRAVIS

Travis was an interesting 6-year-old, 1st-grader who lived with his father, mother, and two older brothers. Travis always had very advanced motor skills and was an avid basketball player. According to his mother, Mrs. Cunningham, who was a teacher education student at the local university, learning always came easy for Travis. He walked at 10 months old and spoke in complete sentences at an early age.

As young children, all of the Cunninghams were read to by their parents and grandparents. The importance of receiving a good education was often stressed in the Cunningham home. Mr. Cunningham, who was also a student and full-time employee, decided that he would "put school on hold for a little while" until his wife finished. He felt that having both parents working and in school was causing too much stress for the family. Mr. and Mrs. Cunningham participated wholeheartedly in their children's educational activities, and the father wanted to ensure that their sons did not suffer in any way. Therefore, he voluntarily postponed his pursuit of a degree "to focus on the kids," while his wife focused on finishing up her college program. Both parents believe that their attending school had a positive impact on their sons' ideas about schooling. Travis liked the idea of his parents having to do homework. Mrs. Cunningham challenged her sons by competing with them for good grades. This competition seemed to motivate the two oldest sons, but Travis was a "different type of child." He was strong-willed and decided when he would make a genuine or a half-hearted effort. He got good grades in school and was the "top student in his class," according to Mrs. Rudolph, who told them that Travis did not have to give his best in order to get good grades. She felt that he was naturally talented in reading and math. He "zooms through the work and then has too much free time on his hands while waiting for other students to catch up," according to Mrs. Cunningham, based on comments from Mrs. Rudolph.

All of the people interviewed in this study agreed that Travis was an exceptional child. Mr. Cunningham stated that "As a young child Travis always seemed to notice things that children don't usually pay attention to. You would think he's playing with the other children, and a few days later he'd say something to let you know that he was fully aware of what was going on." During data collection, Travis displayed this unique ability. He was very relaxed during videotaping and rarely looked directly at the camera, although he was aware that he was one of the subjects of the study. After taping, he would often ask his mother questions about the study. He was especially interested in knowing how his classroom experiences would be utilized to help other children like himself. Mrs. Cunningham made a special effort to thoroughly explain the study to Travis and make him feel comfortable about participating.

Having in-depth conversations was a routine practice in the Cunningham home. Mrs. Cunningham believed that parents should allow their children to ask questions about anything. She wanted her sons to feel comfortable expressing their feelings and articulating their beliefs. Travis's contributions to these conversations often took the Cunninghams by surprise. Mrs. Cunningham stated that:

> Travis will just be sitting around while his brothers are talking to me about something . . . acting like he's not even listening. Then all of a sudden he'll just chime in and say something that he's too young to say. He's just so deep, sometimes we don't even know how to respond to him. (Parent Interview, March 23, 2000)

These spurts of maturity displayed by Travis made it difficult for the Cunningham family because from day to day they were never quite sure if Travis was going to be a "6-year-old" or a "60-year-old." When he was not dazzling his family with his brilliance, Travis acted like most 6-year-olds who are the youngest in the family. His brothers tended to cater to his needs because he was their baby brother. "He always gets his way," stated Mrs. Cunningham. "He's so spoiled!" She continued, "He has everybody's number. He knows just what to say and do to get us to do whatever he wants. He's a good child and we love him."

When their children were younger, Mr. and Mrs. Cunningham took them to the public library often. They would read to their sons and let them explore on the library computers. During the interview, I learned that they had their own computer, and their sons preferred to utilize the one at home. Although they encouraged Travis to read, they admitted that he was very strong-willed and that it was difficult to get him to do something that he did not want to do. "Travis has to be interested in a book to read it. If he's not interested, you can forget it," explained Mrs. Cunningham.

Travis's educational experiences had been positive until he entered 1st grade. For some reason, he and Mrs. Rudolph were unable to get along for an extended period of time. Travis had been suspended eight times when the study began, and he was suspended twice during the data collection period.

Mr. Cunningham was disappointed with the ineffective discipline methods being used at Paradise. He stated:

> I can't understand what they think a kid can learn if they're constantly sending him home. I think Mrs. Rudolph overreacts to Travis. Once she let him see that he could frustrate her, it was over. He will win every time in his mind, because she doesn't know how to deal with him. I've spanked him several times as a last resort, trying to get him to act right

at school, but Mrs. Rudolph has let it go too far. He'll never listen to her now because she tries to force herself on him. (Parent Interview, March 23, 2000)

Mrs. Cunningham agreed with her husband:

That's right. Travis has a very strong personality for a child and you have to let him think he's in control. He'll shut down every time when someone tries to "make" him do something that he doesn't want to do. (Parent Interview, March 23, 2000)

Unfortunately, Mrs. Rudolph was unable to develop effective strategies to convince Travis to change his behavior. She tried several ideas but to no avail. For example, she implemented a positive-behavior lunch program. If a student finished a day without any major behavior problems, they would get a star. After a certain amount of stars were accumulated, she would take them to McDonald's for lunch. Several times Travis almost made it, but he would get into trouble with one or two stars to go. Mrs. Rudolph decided to give him one more chance. Mrs. Chamberlain, the principal, described what happened:

It seemed that everybody in the whole school was pulling for Travis, trying to motivate him to win a trip to McDonald's. The office secretaries and I would encourage him every day to "be good" so he could win his McDonald's lunch. Mr. Adams, the janitor, would also remind him to be a "mannerable young man" in class. The day finally came that would determine if he would go. Mrs. Rudolph ran into the office and announced, "He made it!" All of us started jumping and clapping . . . rejoicing! We were so happy for him! (Principal Interview, April 12, 2000)

Travis went to McDonald's and got into trouble again the next day. Although Travis was exceptionally successful academically and his parents were involved in school activities, he was incredibly unsuccessful socially in his classroom at school.

A CLOSER LOOK INSIDE MRS. RUDOLPH'S
FIRST-GRADE CLASSROOM

Mrs. Rudolph's class was very stimulating. When I first entered the classroom, I saw about 15 cloud mobiles hanging from the ceiling. On one side of the room a Word Wall covered an entire wall, filled with colorful words in alphabetical order. In one corner, an overhead projector and flip chart were neatly stored. On the other side of the room were several neat shelves of books on top of a colorful, large rug. A computer and other learning tools were organized in various parts of the room. Next to the sink was a large orange sheet of paper on the wall with a Handwashing Rap printed on it. The individual student desks were arranged in groups of twos or fours, with the exception of three desks, which were about 3 feet away from the groups of desks. Two round tables with chairs were near the sink, which students used when they needed to work alone away from their groups.

Prior to this study, I developed a conceptual framework that highlighted specific areas of concern when examining learning environments for Black students (see McMillon & Edwards, 2000). Those areas were (a) discourse patterns or communication styles within the classroom, (b) pedagogical issues such as instructional practices and how they aligned or did not align with students' learning styles and cultural mindsets, and (c) social norms that focused on disciplinary practices, how they were enacted, and how they influenced the actions and interactions of the teacher and students. I will use this same framework to share my narrative.

Discourse Patterns/Communication Styles

After 12 years of teaching experience in urban schools, Mrs. Rudolph considered herself an expert in African American language and culture. Although she used Academic English in her class, most of her students utilized Black Vernacular English. During classroom observations, it was apparent that she did not degrade or devalue the discourse patterns that her students used. Her response to them was not ridiculing or demeaning in any way. Instead, she carefully, and almost unnoticeably, scaffolded their language-acquisition skills through revoicing methods (O'Connor & Michaels, 1996). For example, during a classroom discussion about antlers (Classroom Observation, February 17, 2000), Mrs. Rudolph asked the students:

Ms. R.: Boys and girls, what are antlers? Okay, Lorisa.
Lorisa: 'Dey lit'le sticks up on his head.
Ms. R.: They look like sticks on the moose's head. Very good, Lorisa. And what are they used for?
Mark: 'Dey grow big!

Ms. R.: Yes, Mark. Some antlers are very large. But what are they used for?

Tony: I know, Mrs. Rudolph! (waving his hand in the air). They're used for protection.

Ms. R.: That's right, Tony. Antlers are used for protection.

Because of her way of genuinely valuing the home language of her students, and naturally scaffolding their oral language development, some students were able to develop code-switching skills. Specifically, I observed that students in the class utilized Black Vernacular English; however, Tony and Travis were able to negotiate cultural language patterns within the classroom setting. During observations, it became apparent that some students, such as Tony and Travis, used words that displayed a much broader vocabulary, as indicated by Tony's response in the above example when he stated, "Antlers are used for protection." During formal instructional time, question-and-answer periods, or when talking directly to the teacher, Tony and Travis often used Academic English, and frequently used words from the teacher-talk register (Cazden, 1988), indicating strong language skills and an advanced comprehension level. However, during playtime or whenever addressing their peers, they would code-switch to Black vernacular language patterns.

While talking to the students seated near his desk, Travis speaks one way, but when asking Mrs. Rudolph a question he uses teacher talk:

Travis: I ain't go say nothin' else 'til 'um done with dis' stuff.

Miranda: Mrs. Rudolph said we gotta get done.

Travis: We got gym today. 'Um ready to be done.

Tiffany: You almost done, ain't chu (you)?

Travis: Uh huh. Almost. I gotta question. . . . Mrs. Rudolph, can I ask you something?

Ms. R.: Yes, Travis?

Travis: I wrote a two in the ten's place and a three in the one's place, which makes 23, right?

Mrs. R.: That's right, Travis. Are you finished?

Travis: Yes, I'm finished now. That was my last problem. (Looks at Miranda and Tiffany). 'Um done. I told yall 'um ready to be done and 'um done. Yall slow (jokingly). 'Um ready to go to gym.

(Classroom Observation, February 22, 2000)

Pedagogical Issues

In addition to helping her students with oral language development by valuing their usage of Black Vernacular English and code-switching skills, Mrs. Rudolph worked hard to develop applicable teaching strategies in response to the varied learning styles of her students. She continuously adjusted her instructional methods and used various approaches and tools to appeal to students with different learning styles, such as (a) lecture, (b) overhead projectors, (c) hands-on projects, (d) peer tutoring, (e) collaborative learning, (f) field trips, (g) exposure to different types of literature, and (h) playing soft background music while students completed assignments. She provided creative opportunities to learn, such as Word Wall Bingo and writing sentences on desks with shaving cream. Also, reading groups based on ability allowed more individualized attention. A member of the Grandmother's Tutoring Group, the reading resource teacher, and sometimes a teacher's aide were available to assist with focused reading activities.

Like many teachers, Mrs. Rudolph believed that the most successful students were the ones with parental support. She had higher academic expectations for students with parental support, and they thrived academically. Mrs. Rudolph tried to connect with students' parents in several ways, including weekly letters and parent meetings to recommend specific home literacy activities that could help improve their child's academic success. She had high academic expectations for Tony and Travis because their parents were very involved in their sons' learning in and out of school. They responded by becoming the two top 1st-grade readers.

Social Norms: Cultural Clashes Lead to Exclusionary Practices

Mrs. Rudolph lived up to her reputation as the best 1st-grade teacher when I observed her instructional practices; however, Mrs. Rudolph, whom I believe had the best of intentions, was utilizing several debilitating methods to establish social norms within her classroom.

Mrs. Rudolph had low behavioral expectations for Tony and Travis, and they acted accordingly. Although Tony and Travis were the two top 1st-grade students academically, they were considered at risk because they were often disciplined for not obeying classroom rules. Tony was suspended eight times and Travis was suspended 12 times during the school year for negative behavior, which left the teacher and parents quite frustrated. The parents' frustration eventually became ambivalence, after receiving numerous negative reports without being given effective strategies for helping improve their sons' experience at school.

During my first classroom observation, I noticed that Mrs. Rudolph utilized several different classroom control and disciplinary methods, including using cue cards to indicate when students should raise their hands or speak out, writing names on the board, and excluding students from activities and participation in small-group interactions.

Based on her interview, Mrs. Rudolph explained that certain students had been given ample warnings over the course of the school year, and by the time data collection began for this study, she had become frustrated with their continued misbehavior. Whatever the reason, it became immediately evident to me that certain students were disciplined excessively more than others. Their names seemed to remain on the board throughout my observations.

For example, Tony's name was on the board every time classroom observations were made. He was a very social student and often conversed with other students. The classroom was set up with individual desks pushed together to make small groups. Tony and two other students were not in groups. Their individual desks were placed on the periphery of the small groups. Tony often got into trouble for trying to get a friend's attention across the aisle or for getting caught talking to another student when he should have been listening to the teacher. Unfortunately, it seemed that Tony was being disciplined excessively for doing things that might not have happened if he had been placed in a group with other students. Students who were in groups were able to communicate with one another during times when they were not supposed to be talking. They would whisper or gesture and would not be disciplined.

Not only was Tony excluded from being a part of a small group like some of the other students, but he was often placed in time-out, which required him to sit on the floor on the other side of the room, farther away from students. During one classroom observation, the students were completing a math assignment and Tony was in time-out. Mrs. Rudolph was walking around answering questions for students as they worked on the assignment. Tony held up his hand several times without a response from Mrs. Rudolph. He tried to get her attention by shaking his hand fiercely, but she still did not respond. Finally, two students who had been watching him got up out of their seats, went over to the time-out section of the room, and started playing with Tony. For a while Tony would look up to see if Mrs. Rudolph was looking, but she seemed to be absorbed in the math activity. Finally, she told the two students to sit down in their seats or their name would be placed on the board. Tony asked if she could check his paper, and she told him to raise his hand and wait his turn. He responded by saying that he had his hand raised for a long time. She cut him off with "You have to wait your turn." He dropped his head and started checking over his paper. When he raised his hand again, Mrs. Rudolph told him that it was time for gym and he would just have to complete the assignment later.

This missed opportunity could have been detrimental to Tony. He was being disciplined for his behavior and the discipline was not working. In this case and many others, methods of exclusion go beyond social discipline and extend to academic exclusion as well. Tony's experience above is a case in point. However, it was not the only time that I observed this type of action. Tony was the type of student who raised his hand often, but he was not called on as much as some of the other, better-behaved students. The more behaved girls were given the most opportunities to answer questions. After watching Tony, I observed that it did not seem to bother him that he was rarely called on because he continued to raise his hand, and whenever he was given a chance his answers were usually correct.

Travis's classroom behavior was different from Tony's. Tony seemed to get into trouble over little things continuously throughout the day, but Travis would get into trouble over things that escalated into a major standoff between him and Mrs. Rudolph. Travis sat in a group with three girls who were mild-mannered and highly regarded by the teacher. Mrs. Rudolph explained that she was unable to sit Travis next to anyone other than Miranda. She stated, "For some reason, I don't understand it, but Miranda really likes Travis, and he doesn't get along with anybody but Miranda." By being a part of a group, Travis was able to quietly communicate with his group members all the time, unlike Tony. During my observations, Travis's name was placed on the board two times for misbehavior, and he was suspended twice. As indicated above, the observations were made toward the end of the school year; therefore, it is evident that Mrs. Rudolph had decided that she was not going to allow certain types of behavior any more. She was understandably quite frustrated with student behavior in her class. However, as discussed earlier, she seemed to respond to negative behavior from some students differently than others.

For example, once during observations (Classroom Observation, February 24, 2000), I noticed that Miranda, Travis's group member, was passing licks (hitting). She tapped his shoulder several times, and he smiled at her. Finally, he returned the lick (hit), smiling. Mrs. Rudolph rushed over to him, placed her hand on his shoulder, and sternly said:

Ms. R.: You apologize to her right now this instant!
Travis: She hit me first!
Ms. R.: Don't you lie on her. You apologize!
Travis: (Speaking a little louder) I didn't do anything.
Ms. R.: Apologize now!
Travis: (A little louder, shaking her hand off his shoulder) No! I didn't do anything.
Ms. R.: Either apologize or go to the office.
Travis: (Frowns angrily, twisting his body out the chair, and walks slowly to the door).

After this episode in class, Travis was eventually sent home because he became so upset. He continued to say that he did not do anything, but nobody believed him because of the low expectations that they had for his behavior. Miranda was never questioned concerning the incident, and she never voluntarily told that they were just playing.

Later during the day, I asked Mrs. Rudolph if she thought Travis could have been telling the truth this time. She responded, "No way. Miranda is a perfect student. She never does anything wrong. I know that she did not hit Travis. He needs to learn to keep his hands to himself." Mrs. Rudolph had high behavioral expectations for Miranda, and Miranda always lived up to those expectations. On the other hand, she had low behavioral expectations for Travis and Tony, and they always seemed to live up to those expectations as well. Students tend to live up to the self-fulfilling prophecies that their teachers establish for them. Travis, Tony, and Miranda were not exceptions to this rule.

Although Ms. Donaldson and the Cunninghams were very supportive of Mrs. Rudolph's academic curriculum, they were not supportive of her disciplinary techniques, and their ambivalence influenced their sons.

Tony and Travis were very perceptive and understood that their parents were quite frustrated with the social norm issues occurring in the classroom. During classroom observations, Tony and another student (Tony's cousin) had a disagreement, which escalated into a pushing match. This altercation occurred 2 days before the class's final field trip. I was planning to videotape during the field trip to gain insight by studying the subjects in a more relaxed setting. When I asked the teacher for permission to make observations during the field trip, she told me that she did not expect Tony and Travis to attend the field trip. Tony had not been allowed to go on any field trips all year because of his behavior, and Travis had been sent home from the last field trip. Although Travis's parents were chaperones, he refused to follow the rules of conduct on the field trip and his parents were asked to take him home. She expressed her low expectations of their behavior by telling me that she would be surprised if Tony and Travis were not suspended before the field trip. Tony and his cousin, Marquis, began arguing in class and were sent to the office. I followed them to the office to continue the observation (Classroom Observation, May 18, 2000). The following conversation took place in the office lobby while they were waiting to see the principal:

Mrs. McM: Do you realize that you may not be able to go on the field trip?

Marquis: I can't go no-way. I don't care.

Mrs. McM: Do you think that it was nice to get Tony in trouble and prevent him from going to the picnic, just because you can't go? (Tony had been sitting there with a terribly angry expression on his face, as if he might burst at any moment. He immediately chimed in when he thought I was "scolding" Marquis.)

Tony: That's okay, Mrs. McMillon. I-ain't wanna go no-way. Mama told me that we goin' on our own picnic if Mrs. Rudolph won't let me go. We gonna have barbecue and everything! Mrs. Rudolph just go have sack lunch. I want some barbecue and stuff.

Marquis: Yea, barbecue is way better than some old sack lunch. (Grins)

Mrs. McM: Tony, don't you think that you would enjoy hanging out with the kids from your class at the picnic?

Tony: They don't like me no way. They think I'm too bad.

Mrs. McM: Are you bad, Tony?

Tony: Nope.

Mrs. McM: What will your mother say about you getting suspended again? Won't you get in trouble and maybe be put on punishment or something?

> *Tony:* Nope. Mama usta' ground me when I got kicked out. But
> now she just say, "oh well," and tell me to go play.
> *Mrs. McM:* Why?
> *Tony:* Cuz she said that she tired of Mrs. Rudolph putting me out.
> She say they don't know what they doin' up here.
> *Mrs. McM:* What do you play at home when you've been
> suspended?
> *Tony:* Nintendo, PlayStation, and Game Boy.
> *Mrs. McM:* Your mom lets you play games when you're
> suspended?
> *Tony:* Yep! She just say, "Well I guess you got another vacation."
> *Mrs. McM:* Do you read or do other schoolwork while you're
> kicked out?
> *Tony:* Mama read to me every day . . . when I'm kicked out and
> when I ain't. Then I have to read to her. Then we done.
> Then I just go play.

Although she tried not to negatively influence her son's education-al experiences, Ms. Donaldson's frustration had turned into ambiva-lence, and her conversations with Tony were indicative of her feelings.

The expectations that Mrs. Rudolph had for her students seemed quite simple at first, such as raise your hand before joining the conver-sation, walk in a straight line in the hallway, and pay attention during classroom lessons. However, after careful analysis it became apparent that Mrs. Rudolph, Tony, Travis, and their parents were operating from different cultural frames of reference concerning issues of student be-havior and discipline. Mrs. Rudolph was implementing implicit rules of conduct that Tony, Travis, and their parents did not agree with. These invisible rules were debilitating to both Tony and Travis because they were based on cultural values that they did not have in common with their White, middle-class teacher. In their homes and other settings, such as their churches, they were taught to speak out, be assertive and energetic, and openly share their opinions. Mrs. Rudolph valued stu-dents who were passive and did not challenge her authority. Students who challenge their teacher's authority are often considered behavior problems. Unfortunately, these issues were not resolved early in the school year, and the entire year was spent in a power struggle be-tween the teacher and Tony and Travis. Because Mrs. Rudolph made such an impact on Tony by helping him through his difficult time, he seemed to be more willing to give in and let her have control from time to time. Their student-teacher relationship seemed to influence

Tony's actions in a positive way. But Travis never allowed her to control him, nor did they develop a wholesome teacher-student relationship. He fought all year and refused to let her reach him. During one of her interviews (Teacher Interview, May 29, 2020), her words provided support for this belief: "I could never reach Travis. I feel as if I've failed him. I didn't teach him anything all year." Cultural clashes in classrooms can debilitate teaching and learning.

The reading resource teacher and Travis's parents wanted Travis to get into the gifted program in the school district, but Mrs. Rudolph refused to refer him because she said that students in the gifted program needed to be able to work independently and Travis's behavior would be a problem for the teacher. Travis's parents and the reading resource teacher were disappointed with Mrs. Rudolph because they felt that part of the reason for Travis's behavior was because he was bored. He would finish his assignments before everyone else and have time to get into trouble. Mrs. Rudolph's refusal to refer Travis placed limitations on his future educational experiences.

CONCLUSION

Although Mrs. Rudolph was considered the best 1st-grade teacher at Paradise Elementary, and I believe she had good intentions, she was unable to identify the source(s) of cultural dissonance in her classroom. Her limited ability to recognize cultural clashes and adapt her practices accordingly resulted in an academic year of power struggles, frustration, and excessive suspensions. Why didn't she listen to the parents of Tony and Travis? They understood their sons and tried to explain their idiosyncrasies, but Mrs. Rudolph didn't listen to the parents.

Unfortunately, the pain of their 1st-grade experience, as with many other Black boys, would not be left behind. Instead, Tony and Travis had to go to the 2nd grade with the same group of students—students who had come to believe that Tony and Travis were bad and who didn't like them because of the reputation that had been nurtured by their teacher. Travis was also unable to switch to another, possibly more suitable learning environment, because Mrs. Rudolph prevented him from advancing to an academically rigorous program, thus using her power to extend her 1st-grade exclusionary practices beyond her classroom to place limitations on his educational potential.

IN CONVERSATION

Arlette's Comments

There is a lot for me to unpack in large part because growing up, I had my father, grandfathers, 13 uncles, four brothers, and lots of male cousins. As an adult, beside my husband and seven brothers-in-law, I have three sons and three grandsons. What I know is that, unlike the stereotypical depiction of Black males in the media, each of these Black males is a different and unique human being.

Much like the parents in the narrative, I was aware of my sons' strengths and limitations as communicators, learners, readers, thinkers, and writers. And, as with the parents in the narrative, my sons entered school able to complete 1st-grade requirements. They, too, were often bored in school. Teaching my sons to read was not something a 1st-grade teacher had to struggle with, but they seemed to want to struggle with something regarding my Black sons. My husband and I had done all the things we thought parents should: reading and writing at home with purpose; lots of books and educational toys; many excursions to historic places of interest, libraries, movies, museums, zoos, and so forth; and lots of talks and discussions about issues. We attended school conferences, programs, and volunteered; we were not strangers. And our sons arrived at school ready to learn and with broad interests; they spoke Academic English, but they were often seen as "Black boys," with little regard for what they knew or their abilities. Comments about their in-school behaviors included the terms abrupt, chatty, and social, but seldom included the terms academically prepared, intelligent, kind, thoughtful, or polite. This happened even though the teachers knew I was a teacher education professor at a local Tier 1 university.

Unsurprisingly, most teachers had little knowledge or regard for Black culture, history, language, or worldviews. And as parents, we were struck by how each school conference with our sons' teachers began with a conversation about their behavior, in large part because they were well-behaved. My husband and I would smile politely and thank the teacher as we pushed the conversation for more information about their academic progress. This is when the conversation often became bogged down with descriptions of curriculum and not academic progress. In short, our experiences with teachers' outreach to Black boys and their lack of understanding of Black culture and language patterns mirrored those of the Cunninghams and Ms. Donaldson, although our sons had attended elementary schools in a number of different states. It was as if there were some invisible force that would not permit teachers (Black and White) to see these young boys as brilliant, capable, intelligent, knowledgeable, and wise. As a former classroom teacher, it was hard to reconcile this assessment with every White teacher colleague; however, sadly it was true for far too many.

Much like the parents in the narrative, I have known Black boys who arrive at school as readers, writers, thinkers, and learners, who were dismissed and turned off to school.

Moreover, their parents' demand for challenging educational engagement and improved and responsive reading materials, as well as respectful attendance to Black history, are often ignored. Or there is lip service about the need to change, and requests for parents to "be patient and wait; change is on the way."

What I find amazing about this narrative is that the same problems exist for Black boys across class, geography, and time. The singular characteristic is that the boys are Black and thus encounter invisible and unexpected barriers to quality education that meets their academic needs. There are laws that prohibit racial discrimination, but there are no laws that outlaw anti-Black attitudes and behaviors of school administrators or teachers. Nonetheless, clearly there are patterns of behavior exercised by classroom teachers and school administrators that suggest that something far more insidious is at play: a malaise and an ideological misunderstanding of Black boys as human and capable communicators, learners, readers, thinkers, and writers. The history of reading research is replete with examples of deficit language and mischaracterizations about Black boys' cultures, behaviors, languages, and ways of knowing—examples that are promoted and perpetuated.

As a teacher educator, I decided change would start with me, especially when one of my White female undergraduate English majors made a reference to a "large, scary, muscular, Black male" in her classroom. How was it possible that someone who had been under my tutelage could form her thoughts around the stereotypical image of people who looked like the men and boys that I loved? At that point, I made an unapologetic commitment to address issues of anti-Blackness, diversity, inclusivity, and multiculturalism, and to dispel the false narrative about Black male students as learners, readers, thinkers, and writers.

Gwen's Comments

Unfortunately, in a situation like this the students are labeled *at risk*, but my question is: *Who is really at risk—the students or the teacher?* How can we blame 6-year-olds for having a teacher who did not know how to establish social norms that worked for all of her students? On the other hand, how can we blame teachers who are not prepared to teach students with varied academic and social needs? I do not believe in teacher-bashing, but I am appalled by an education system that refuses to take responsibility for miseducating and/or under-educating an entire population of students. Yet this same education system continues to double down and perpetuate ineffective, debilitating instructional and disciplinary practices for Black boys. It's time for a change. Teachers like Mrs. Rudolph will welcome an opportunity to receive assistance. Most teachers genuinely want to make a difference in the lives of their students, their families, and even their communities, but they simply don't know what to do. We have a dire situation that must be addressed. The traditional story that is told talks about how Black boys struggle in their classrooms at school. This shouldn't be surprising if the majority of the teaching population are White, middle-class females. Cultural clashes are bound to happen when students and teachers have multiple positionalities that differ, but when these clashes occur, who is responsible for adapting? Should it be a 6-year-old, or a college-educated adult who has chosen a career in teaching? Another popular accusation is that parents don't care, but both Tony and Travis had parents who *did* care. I've never met a parent who simply doesn't care; they may not know or understand, but they care. Rather than continue blaming others, we should all look in the mirror and reflect upon what we can do to improve the education of Black boys. The first step is to admit to yourself that you don't know what to do, if that's the case. Arlette, Patriann, and I are here to help.

Like Arlette, I have sons and brothers who experienced the anti-Black persecution of Black boys in school—the place where they were supposed to receive a quality education from nurturing, caring, prepared teachers. My sons were fortunate to have several excellent elementary teachers who connected with them. In fact, they are still in contact with several of their teachers. But many of their teachers implemented instructional and social practices that manifested their anti-Black boy beliefs. For example, one of my son's teachers was very unorganized, and had a habit of blaming her students and parents, rather than addressing her inadequacies. During a parent-teacher conference, when she shared that my son received a B in reading, I asked her to explain the criteria for moving to an A. She was shocked that I asked the question and could not clearly articulate a response to my simple question. I finally received the criteria after a couple of weeks, and learned that students were expected to read and take the quizzes for a certain number of accelerated reader (AR) books in order to get an A. Students and parents were unaware of this requirement. My son was reading at an advanced level and we let him read whatever he wanted to read at home every night. After learning about her requirement, we encouraged him to read AR books before reading for pleasure every night. We also shared the information with other parents.

Unfortunately, rather than embracing the idea of having a student whose parents were very involved in their child's education, she chose to retaliate. My husband and I were the kind of parents who volunteered for school activities. Vince was PTA president, soccer coach, and field trip chaperone. I coached the spelling team and a Battle of the Books team, helped with popcorn sales, and chaperoned field trips. In other words, one of us was in the school almost daily. After we finally received the criteria for getting an A in reading, we noticed that our son started "getting into trouble" in his class, and it seemed that he was always in a seat far away from the other students. When we asked about it, the teacher said that he couldn't focus and do his work. This eventually became the "song that she sang" over and over again. I told her that my son does best in a structured, organized environment. After a series of meetings with the principal, we finally demanded that the school psychologist assess him to determine if the teacher had legitimate concerns. When we met to receive the report, the psychologist began the discussion by stating that he had never assessed such a brilliant student. He said our son was extremely intelligent and had an exceptional personality. The psychologist provided a list of things that we should do at home. I looked at the list and shared the extensive educational activities that he participated in at home, church, in the community, and at the local university. I ended by saying, "if the assessment shows that there is nothing going on with my son, and his home life is intact, the only thing left to consider is the classroom." I asked the psychologist to make recommendations to the teacher to ensure that my son received the kind of instruction that would meet his needs as an advanced student. The teacher was visibly annoyed. We spent the rest of the school year watching her closely. Several parents were experiencing the same thing, and we teamed up to support our children. We were unable to move our son to the other class because the other teacher already had 32 students. The teacher left the school after that year, and we were glad that she did. She had damaged enough Black boys.

Patriann's Comments

My first thought as I read this narrative was the refreshing use of the word *paradise*, signaling beauty, purity, light, love, and everything good. To me, reading the word paradise as used to describe an elementary school that supported African American boys portrayed the power of labels for redefining deficit notions of who Black children are and how we come to them and their experiences positively as researchers and as educators.

As I read on, the label *at risk* caught my attention, a clear reminder of the use of the label *underperforming* that I had problematized in the study from which I drew excerpts for my narrative in this book. Seeing *at risk* juxtaposed against *paradise* signaled for me a symbolic indication of the work to be done in schools, with the eradication of language that serves as a detriment to youth's beliefs about who they are and how they can engage as readers in classrooms. I liked seeing the use of the term as one that we should problematize, and I have since been thinking about how we might use our scholarship to introduce new labels that counter the deficit ones we problematize in our work.

From my impression of Tony, there is just so much sadness with which he tries to reconcile as he grapples with the school as a site of trauma. Clearly, the immediate or visible action on the part of the teacher, through an act of omission, reinforces Tony's previous trauma, and he immediately appears to develop a negative connotation of a school that he once loved. From Tony's perspective, I am sensing that this seemingly innocuous act by the teacher, one that she may believe can be overlooked, creates a lasting impact, one that causes Tony to identify the school as an unsafe space. It is no surprise, then, that he withdraws. This affective element that is often overlooked in favor of academic norms for children at such a young age, who need to feel comfortable in order to feel psychologically safe and comfortable enough to learn, is clearly one that stands out as critical for teachers who work with young Black males. As pointed out in the narrative, Tony did seem to "catch up" academically, but he shouldn't have had to "catch up." And what happens to the rest of the mind and body when the site of trauma remains a space with which they have to grapple daily? As I read the narrative, I see even more clearly that the affective elements of Black males' progress as young readers seem to need to be more highly regarded as a part of "progress" and "success."

Reading about Tony reminded me of a Black student who I taught years ago as a novice in the Caribbean. It seems that instead of reacting to behaviors displayed by Travis, Mrs. Rudolph instead reacted to Travis, creating a dynamic of exclusion that escalated (rather than defused) the tensions arising. Much like we have heard about the interactions between police officers and Black men where situations were escalated and individuals shot (sometimes killed), in classroom situations where a very young child such as Travis is not responded to strategically, the situation becomes worse, and the very act of rejection of the child in the classroom via suspension represents a "killing" of the self. To reject and exclude this young Black male from the time he is in a 1st-grade classroom is to say to him, "We do not want you in the classroom and in school."

For me, such a message has a powerful impact on the mind and body of a young child, creating the perception, in children's minds, of schools as a site of trauma. Again here, just as was done with Tony, the affective element appears to be entirely disregarded from this equation with Travis. In the minds of the authoritative figures, Travis is apparently seen as Black and male, both of which connote premises for fear, rejection, refusal, and ostracization. (We see the effect of this site of trauma effect again when the narrative talks of Tony's exclusion from small groups in the classroom.) I ask the question here: "What if Travis were viewed as a child, someone who needs care, and a human being who can be reasoned with to arrive at a plan for how he can support his teacher and peers in the classroom?" Immediately, Travis would notice that there are positive expectations for him, and he would recognize that his brilliance is being acknowledged as part of the solution. I notice this was touched on later in the narrative, and I was happy to see this. Beyond this, I also believe that the approaches used to support Travis appeared to address the symptoms of the problem and not the basis of the problem. Measures were taken against Travis as opposed to with him in consultation with expert others regarding his affect. This situation reinforces the importance of affect in supporting the reading performance of young Black males.

Toward the end of your narrative, I thought that the power of the difference between parent and teacher norms was well reflected. Here you have parents teaching their kids to be normal kids and a school teaching the same children in ways that undo those normal behaviors of the child. One wonders about the principles of early childhood education here, by and large, but also the ways in which a lack of understanding about how being vocal, active, energetic, and questioning rules and regulations can be easily seen as a sign of resistance when these are enacted by Black males. Even as young Black males, these acts appeared to create a threat with which the teacher grappled daily. In a situation such as the one with Mrs. Rudolph and Travis, as a parent I would have transferred the child to another classroom or even another school. But many parents do not have such a luxury, and their advocacy can go only so far. Thus, it is schools that do not intervene in such cases that cause a lasting and adverse effect on young Black males such as Tony and Travis. There is so much learning to gain from this narrative—and so much more that we can do to show that young Black male readers are just children.

CRITICAL DISCUSSION QUESTIONS

Parents/Caregivers: Black parents and caregivers of Black boys may ponder: How can teachers and school administrators listen to what I know about my son? How can they accept him as a fellow human? Why do they feel obligated to surveil his behavior but not equally empowered to improve his reading? How can I position myself to provide the support needed for my son? Which literacy educators can I speak to for help as I serve as an advocate for my son?

Teachers: Teachers of Black boys may ponder: How can teachers acknowledge Black boys' intellectual abilities as well as their strengths and limitations as learners and readers? How will supporting the reading growth of Black boys differ from current instruction?

Educators and Administrators: What professional development is scheduled to address anti-Black racism? Who will facilitate the discussion, and how will the academic needs of Black boys be addressed? How can teachers attend to the affective domains of young Black male readers in reading and literacy instruction? What modules in early childhood education devote time and effort to preservice teacher preparation for teaching young Black males in ways that align with their cultural, linguistic, behavioral, racial, and other differences? What provisions are made for in-service teachers in the elementary grades to receive support when working with young Black male readers whose behavioral, cultural, linguistic, and other ways of being appear to be contrary to their own?

Politicians: How have federal, state, and local government educational agencies addressed systemic racism in reading policies and programs, as required by President Biden's Executive Order 13985? In what ways will proposed and new reading reform legislation be informed by anti-Black racism? The bulk of reading reforms and policies have had a disparate impact on the reading performance of Black boys—what substantive changes are needed, and how will they be enforced?

Reading Researchers: How can reading researchers begin to make institutional and structural reforms in how reading is conceptualized to transform over a century of anti-Black racism in reading research?

SUGGESTED READINGS

Bryan, N. (2020). Shaking the bad boys: Troubling the criminalization of black boys' childhood play, hegemonic white masculinity and femininity, and the school playground-to-prison pipeline. *Race Ethnicity and Education, 23*(5), 673–692.

Gershenson, S., Holt, S. B., & Papageorge, N. W. (2016). Who believes in me? The effect of student–teacher demographic match on teacher expectations. *Economics of Education Review, 52*, 209–224.

Hilliard, A. (1991). Do we have the will to educate all children? *Educational Leadership, 49*(1), 31–36.

Iruka, I. U., Curenton, S. M., & Durden, T. R. (Ed.). (2017). *African American children in early childhood education: Making the case for policy investments in families, schools, and communities.* Emerald Publishing Ltd.

Sullivan, D. R. (2016). *Cultivating the genius of black children: Strategies to close the achievement gap in the early years.* Redleaf Press.

Tatum, A. (2021). *Teaching elementary Black boys in the elementary grades: Advanced disciplinary reading and writing to secure their futures.* Teacher College Press.

Tatum, A. W., Johnson, A., & McMillon, D. B. (2021). *The state of Black males in literacy research, 1999–2020.* Literacy Research Report.

Wright, B. L., & Counsell, S. L. (2018). *The brilliance of black boys.* Teachers College Press.

CHAPTER 5

Transcending (Dis)Belief: Black (Immigrant) Youth Literacies

As an emerging scholar who focuses on Englishes (multiple Englishes) (see Kachru, 1992), Black immigrant literacies (Smith, 2020a), and anti-racist language teacher education (Baker-Bell, 2020), spaces to freely engage in discussions about how Black youth develop overall, and particularly with regard to their literacies and languages, bring joy to me. Much like the Black immigrant women scholars who have come before me, I straddle multiple identities as a French Creole speaker, an Afro-Caribbean/West Indian multilingual immigrant mother, a teacher educator, and a researcher focused on diversity. Emerging from a childhood where religious and agricultural literacies played a major role, I have come to be grounded in the spiritual and in nature as an adult and mother of a Black girl. In my role as a Black literacy and language educator, I have been fortunate to teach at the K–12 level as well as guide students in higher education primarily with regard to English language arts, literacy, and diversity, in the Caribbean and in the United States. It is always a joy to serve students and colleagues as well as mentor and connect with scholars of color who, like me, advocate for Black (immigrant) youth and teachers of Black students.

PATRIANN'S NARRATIVE: A SUMMARY

In the narrative that follows, I organize my story about my role in the lives of Black children and youth so that you can easily come along this journey with me. First, I provide some information about who I was as a Black writer coming into the role of supporting Black children's writing in schools in the United States. Second, I present insights from my teaching of a Black/Latinx immigrant student, Jorge, followed by excerpts from the conversations of Black American youth who became dear to my heart as I worked with them to develop their reading through developing their sense of self as writers. Toward the end of the chapter, I briefly share what I learned about race, language, literacies, and learning that are necessary to believe that Black children can read and write. Extending beyond my then dean at the College of Education in Texas who was very much expecting improved literacy results and outcomes with Black students from my efforts, when you've read this story, I will ask: "How will you show our Black children that you believe they can read and write?"

AN INVITATION FROM A BLACK IMMIGRANT EDUCATOR

This story comes from the joint decision by my literacy sisters and I to write from our hearts for our children—Black children who are often thought of in ways that cause many to think that they are unable to read or reluctant to write. As an elementary teacher in St. Lucia and Trinidad and Tobago, I worked with Black children, all of whom cared about books but differed in how they reflected this. And as a Black literacy educator in Illinois, Texas, and Florida, I have seen Black children care about sharing their thoughts as they discuss and write stories about issues in the United States and across the globe. I insist that Black children can and do read and write—boys and girls alike. I choose to write this story because, as my sisters and I agreed, if not now, when? If not now, when our Black children continue to be disproportionately placed in special education classes, when? If not now, when our Black children continue to be viewed as adults while the innocence of their childhoods is stripped away, when? If not now, when our Black children continue to be seen as "free and reduced lunch" cases in "underperforming" schools where resources are allocated only when they "fail" to meet "standards," when? If not now, when our Black immigrant children find out for the first time that their Blackness, "foreignness," and language matter more than their humanity, when?

Our now is for us—past, present, and future. To write this story now is to honor all our Black children who have grown into adults and will never have a chance to be seen or treated as a child who can read. To write this story now is to tell our Black children who continue to wonder about how to show that they can write, that we believe they are writers. To write this story now is to tell our Black children of the future, "We see you and we care enough to write our stories so that you can read this and believe in yourselves when we are long gone." For us, all the academic writing we do in journals that Black children and their parents will never get to see or read is not enough. We want to give to our Black children and their parents this gift from our hearts that tells them we, teachers who believe, are here, though they may not see us . . . are here, though they may think the ivory tower confines us . . . that we are here and care enough to share.

As you can imagine, I debated quite a bit about what I would present as my story. Would it be about the horrible mess I made out of teaching in my 1st year as a teacher in St. Lucia when I was so young and so unaware of the differences between my intellectual and privileged academic background as a home-schooled child to even understand how culturally removed I was from the day-to-day experiences of my Black students? I am sure I have some students who will still attest to that! Would it be about the poetic eloquence of this lovely Black girl called Wanda (pseudonym) in my 5th-grade class in St. Lucia who had migrated from Britain to the Caribbean with her mother and whose mannerisms had been so rehearsed because of how she had been socialized to act in Britain as a Black child? Would it be about the completely loving and respectful Black girl, Naila (pseudonym), whom I had spent hours trying to find one afternoon in Trinidad because she was so anxious about an exam that she wouldn't come to school and therefore was missing my class? In the end, I decided to draw from experiences of my teaching during my earlier years in the United States as a Black immigrant educator working with the Black/Latinx/White immigrant youth, Jorge, and from previously conducted research completed in what was designated as a "significantly underperforming" school. There, I worked with Black American youth—Barack, Nelson, Imani, and Cornell, among others (all pseudonyms).

I had supported the literacies of the Black, Latinx, and White American youth by co-guiding their reading and writing practices while visiting their middle school on a weekly basis in Texas. I chose to share my story from this experience through which I helped students to connect reading and writing because when I signed up to assume a faculty position in Texas, part of the challenge that I accepted from my then-dean, who has since departed this world, was a responsibility for working with my district, school, and university partners to some-how "save" this school. Now, though I did, you and I both know that Black kids don't need another "savior" who claims to be able to protect them from all the anti-Blackness in the world when it is virtually impossible to do so. They already spend all their lives working to save themselves by acting "right," speaking "right," wondering if they look "right," drive "right," play "right," and making sure they stay in the "right" places at the "right" time. So while I did not feel like I was saving Black children in that role, I did feel the need to advocate for Black students in ways that empowered them, empowered them to know that there was someone on whom they could rely for support as they navigated an anti-Black world while I worked intentionally to dismantle anti-Black practices in their schools.

So I did something I hadn't done before—*I put my butt on the line*—taking up the challenge of this White dean of mine who believed that change would come. I chose to understand what the Black children and parents in this school lived, felt, believed, and wanted. I also felt that I could work with the children and their community around these needs to see how best they could be addressed in numerous situations where the needs of the school, district, and university were entirely different. I tell my story here about this experience because who I was when I came into this role from the ivory tower was transformed into who I wanted to be by the time I left.

Who I was: a scholar who wrote about diversity in literacy and teacher education. Who I wanted to be: a scholar-educator who understood what it meant to write about diversity in literacy for people of color and for Black children. Because of this story, and as I increasingly saw the world through the lens of my daughter, I learned to write about the beautiful Blackness of our children, about how this beauty becomes burdensome when doing literacy and languaging while migrating and being Black (Smith & Warrican, 2022), and about how, even in the midst of it all, our Black children's languaging transcends this burdensome beauty. It is through this story, which continues today, that I learned to advocate for changing literacy standards while addressing anti-Blackness in language education, both in schools and at the university (Smith, 2020b). It is through this story that I learned to create spaces for the beauty and complexity across languages and literacies of the Black child. But first, it is important to understand who I was, coming to this space and to Black children and youth as a Black scholar-educator of literacy.

BLACK IMMIGRANT EDUCATOR LITERACIES

To know the other as literacy educators seeking to undo anti-Blackness, we must first know the self (Smith & Warrican, 2021). Writing about and researching my work in Texas helped with that process. (Re)writing this story now, as it were, gives me an opportunity to revisit and understand my fears, anxieties, and joy about writing, as well as my concerns, thoughts, and strategies for supporting writing as a Black scholar. It is almost as if I can again see myself through the eyes of a now more evolved Black scholar-educator (i.e., me) (see Smith, Warrican, & Kumi-Yeboah, 2016, for a discussion) and through the vivid lenses of Black children whose excitement about me visiting their school never faded. You will see, in the stories of my Black sisters and mine, that just as no Black child is the same as another, no two Black educators are the same.

As mentioned earlier, I was a mostly home-schooled child who enrolled in the university as a teacher trainee at the age of 16. Learning how to teach curriculum for 2 years, I focused on 14 subject areas in a program that could be described as nothing but extremely rigorous. I took courses such as "Principles and Methods of Education." I also focused on other content subjects such as science, math, reading and literacy, English language arts, music, agricultural science, and art methods. There was a wide range of possibilities in terms of thinking about how curriculum works, what theories inform this curriculum, how we teach, and so forth. I was assigned to many internships working in specific schools in different areas in Trinidad and Tobago where I studied at the time, learning how to teach.

During my internships, I began to understand the real science of teaching. As I began to understand how the theory in my coursework informed my teaching, I learned how to integrate this theory into my practice. I did this first with students in grade 1 and then students in grade 5. For the most part I worked with elementary students at that time. In terms of writing, I don't recall specifically working to support students' writing per se during my teacher training program. But I do recall that I took many classes later that focused on developing as a writer. For example, one of the four writing classes in which I enrolled when I moved on to earn my bachelor's degree focused on how writing works for students. Unfortunately, because I was not teaching in a classroom during that time, I was not able to make the connections between the theory that I was learning about writing instruction and how experiences become the basis for students' writing in classrooms.

Given the absence of a context for transferring my learning to practice, I created a number of varied genre products. My then writing instructor in the undergraduate program required students to write many poems and short stories. I remember enjoying the process of creating these poems and stories. I also remember that one of my then-professors, who was herself Black and a Caribbean national like me, seemed not to be satisfied with a lot of what I felt was my creativity and my written products. Unlike this teacher, I also had another professor whose course was focused on thesis writing. I absolutely enjoyed this professor. She believed in my writing and supported me, providing iterative feedback every time I missed the mark. Although she was not one to dole out compliments, the expectation for a "high level of writing" was present, and I met this mark. A third instructor, also Black and Caribbean, taught me about writing focused on literature. Like the fourth instructor, who taught English language arts methods, this literature instructor was less worried about technicalities and products involved in writing and more focused on the creative writing process. So, in terms of writing, you could say that as a Black young adult, I had seen varied approaches to writing across four different Black female professors' courses. Notwithstanding, there was never any reference to the nuances of being a Black child or on how coloniality or race situated the Black child as a reader and writer in the local or global landscape (Smith, 2021a, 2021b).

Fast-forward to the United States in 2009 when I began working on my master's degree, moving into a predominantly Black-White racialized context, as I migrated from the largely Indo-African country of Trinidad. It was only then, after teaching for 5 years, that I began to realize how different writing was from what I had originally thought. For one, I realized I had engaged in a lot of didactic teaching back home in the Caribbean such as simply telling my students what a prompt was and having them sit down and write, a practice that, I believe, still occurs in the United States but that also seemed to be challenged in the U.S. graduate literacy courses where I was enrolled. Thinking back on it then, I realized that I had never really *taught* writing as a teacher. And so, it dawned on me in my master's program that I didn't really know then that I had to *actually* teach children how to write, nor had I known exactly *how* to teach children to write. I had simply thought, "Okay, fine, let them practice writing about things; then they would automatically become wonderful writers." After all, it was what had been modeled to me as a budding teacher. And so, I came to the United States after teaching in the Caribbean across all the subject areas and realized there was so much more to literacy pedagogy than I had previously thought. Needless to say, I began to wonder about all the elements to this piece that I was missing.

One of the things that immediately struck me is that the U.S. system, at least from the schools that I had visited, seemed to be very different in terms of how they encouraged students to write and how they encouraged students to engage more openly in thinking and learning. It seemed to me then that the student-centered classroom reflected a big difference compared to what often happened in the Caribbean, where the teacher was almost always the "sage on the stage," telling students what to do. And yet, notwithstanding, while I did encounter a level of attention to diversity in courses such as literature in my master's program in the United States, there seemed to be no courses focused on anti-Blackness nor did the courses appear to be focused on how pervasive anti-Blackness was in literacy (see Willis et al., 2021). This discrepancy created quite a bit of dissonance for me because I wanted to be a teacher who could teach writing and be excellent at literacy instruction, but I did not know then about the ways in which anti-Blackness functioned within and beyond literacy teaching and learning.

JORGE: A BLACK IMMIGRANT LATINX YOUTH

Fortunately for me, the dream of being a teacher who could teach literacy excellently would come true. I soon enrolled in a course specifically on writing within my master's reading program in the U.S., where I was required to complete a case study to support a student with writing over a period of 6 to 8 weeks. Working with this immigrant student weekly was probably the most insightful experience for me in my master's program. Remembering the student, Jorge (pseudonym), now, I think I do still have the written products that he created with me. Jorge was mixed-race but identified as Black sometimes and Latinx in other instances. He had three brothers and a sister, was quite articulate in his speech, loved cars, cared about the weather, and had a passion for space travel. His mother was caring, sincere, and wanted Jorge to be a great reader and writer even though she could not often communicate with me because she spoke primarily Spanish and I know very little of the language.

Working with Jorge, I began to realize that he had all these rich linguistic and literate experiences as a Black immigrant Spanish-speaking student from Mexico even while speaking the African American Language while living in the United States. He seemed very shy but had so much to bring to the table that I needed to "tap into" so that we could complete the writing product he was creating to reflect his experiences. And so, Jorge and I talked a lot about his ideas, about how he could put these ideas on paper, about how we wanted to showcase these ideas, and about how he would use a multimodal product in the form of a book to present his thoughts. He wanted to write a poem and put music to this. Jorge also had a chance to complete many wonderful journal entries about these reactions to events that extended beyond school and about which he was concerned.

I guided Jorge to journal informally and simply share his experiences every time he came to visit me, responding to these in his journal. I guided him also to work on a specific topic, documenting the ways that he felt about certain experiences that he had had and how they affected his feelings about school. Jorge worked with me to create a multimodal fictional text (i.e., book) while at the same time freely expressing his personal experiences in writing. He also created a poem about his migration from Mexico to the United States and later wrote a poem as a basis for producing a rap video through which to present the poem to his audience at home. At that time, I began to realize that writing was not something that was static. Instead, much like I had been reading in the writing course in which I was enrolled, I realized that writing was iterative. Though there were rules for the technical elements, I needed to be the teacher who made room for the ideas as well as the process of flexibility, allowing students to feel that their authentic writing mattered. For Jorge, who had migrated to the United States and who had shared many personal stories of loss, discrimination, fear, anxiety, and hope for his future, I learned that writing about what a student cared about, particularly when they were not White, mattered in defining who they were as readers.

It was during this time that I also began to realize that "Okay, there's a lot to this that has to do with the humanizing of Black students, so that they begin to feel that they matter and that this writing is an extension of themselves." I thought to myself, "I have to be careful as a teacher about how I react to this writing or else this student gets damaged, and it can prevent him from wanting to express himself further." I completed this project with Jorge, and it changed me. As a newly immigrated Black teacher, it changed me because I began to look back at my teaching experience in the Caribbean and see how I almost never focused as much on the literate identities, or Blackness, of students in the classroom and that I had perhaps inadvertently stripped students so much of their identities that they couldn't share things about themselves or things about their writing in ways that would lead to a use of their unique Black voices. Back then, it was the teacher's identity that seemed to matter most.

As Jorge's use of Black American English occurred simultaneously with his use of Spanish, I also related this to my daughter's background as a Black child speaking the Trinidadian English dialect, as well as my background as a Black child speaking vernacular English and French Creole in St. Lucia, both of which were very different from the academic writing that was expected in schools and universities. I recalled, for example, being a Black youth completing the culminating regional secondary English Language Arts test in the Caribbean, which served as a basis for transitioning into college, and then getting a "C" for expression. Though not always front and center, this "C" remained a permanent fixture in the back of my mind. I realized I had always wondered why I did get a "C" on writing expression. I later noted how I partitioned the expectations required of me when writing so that they fit academic writing to the extent that my natural and expressive ways of speaking remained completely divorced from academic writing tasks. For me, such a huge disparity existed then between how I was talking (in the English vernacular mostly) at home and what was being expected of me when I wrote in academic contexts to reflect learning. And so that "C" on expression always stayed with me, for a very long time. I thought, "Well, maybe I'm not so good at writing."

As I worked with Jorge, I thought in many ways about how the "C" had affected my writing identity and how my feedback on his writing could affect him as a Black, Spanish, African American Language reader and writer. As a Black emerging scholar-mother, I wanted for Jorge what I would want for my Black child: to affirm him so that he would never have a "C" etched in the back of his mind, causing him to question his literate capacity. Coming to the United States, enrolling in literacy courses, working with Jorge, and seeing how Jorge spoke the African American Language while also speaking Spanish as he was expected to write in standardized English, I noticed how he would draw from his Spanish-speaking background to write, even as he used his Black American English, working to merge who he was on the page with who he was in person. Jorge's translanguaging practices (García & Wei, 2014) as a Black immigrant student (Smith, 2020b),

We need to take race out we are All humans ✗

through which he reflected his unique and individual linguistic repertoire, allowed him to reflect his whole self, though racialized. I noticed that if I did not support students like Jorge to use their writing to consolidate their raciolinguicized identities across contexts, what could result were separate and distinct identities, only some of which would be presented in classrooms while others remained suppressed. This, to me, seemed then to be important to prevent the emergence of children with empty selves, presenting themselves on a page with an absent soul. It also seemed critical to preventing students from being subjected to the institutional schizophrenia that was often reflected in school spaces where they were rewarded for speaking and writing in ways determined by Whiteness, while at the same time rejected when they tried to bring their full selves into classrooms (Smith, Lee, & Chang, 2022, advance online publication).

I took this learning about Jorge—writing, and creating room for students' self-expression—from my master's program into the doctoral program that I joined soon after. At the time I worked predominantly with White monolingual preservice teachers, supporting them as they completed literacy internships with students. We had a cohort model, so I was responsible for certain groups of teachers. While teaching writing instruction to the cohort of teachers focused on special education, I learned so much. Not only did the preservice and in-service teachers in this class have to do what I had done as a graduate student to create a range of writing products, they also had to examine the various ways in which writing pedagogies could work for students with a range of backgrounds and disabilities and, specifically, Black students.

BLACK AMERICAN YOUTH LITERACIES

My trajectory as a Black immigrant educator in the United States would later allow me to develop even more concrete understandings about what it meant to teach literacy to Black youth. I now share what Black American youth taught me more recently, about believing in their literacies. Before I do so, I would like to provide a background for understanding the context in which I worked with these youth.

I began my role as a faculty member in Texas in 2015. As I mentioned earlier, getting to Texas was interesting because my then-dean had shared, before I got hired, "I am doing outreach work and I need people who can work in schools. Can you do that stuff?" And I had answered, "Yes, I can." He responded, "Well, you haven't done it before." And I said, "Well, I've worked with University of South Florida (USF) teachers in partnership development schools, I have worked to coordinate the University of Illinois at Urbana-Champaign (UIUC) reading clinic, and I have worked with certain schools in the district, not to the degree that I think you're expecting here, but I do have some background experience that I can bring to this work and I'm pretty confident that I can learn." I began my work as a "Literacy Champion" in Texas, in a district that was very open at that time to the structure of our work. In the 1st year, I worked with the district and, specifically, in a school with predominantly Black students, focusing on reading interest, reading motivation, and improving students' literacy outcomes by supporting teachers in the schools. I developed relationships with principals and teachers, being in classrooms every week for at least 6 to 8 hours a week. I visited my assigned school and organize read-alouds, book giveaways, centers for students to work independently on reading, and systems for helping students set goals for themselves to monitor and improve in reading.

In the 2nd year, there was more structure and I worked with stakeholders to focus primarily on writing. I also coordinated the entire writing effort and structure with specific goals and outcomes based on the agreement between multiple schools in the district and our then-College of Education. I collaborated and planned with coaches, teachers, and principals to set aside time for journal writing. I wanted to give Black children in our classrooms the freedom to love writing, generate ideas, organize these ideas, show that they could write, read what they wrote, review each other's writing, prepare their writing for presentation, and share their ideas with us. I also worked with them, because of the concern about their "underperformance" on developed mechanisms and protocols, to support the enhancement of students' writing, to identify the specific and corresponding reading and writing outcomes that were emerging, and to focus on self-efficacy and on students' achievement. I wanted to improve students' self-efficacy with writing, and worked with middle-school teachers weekly in a professional learning community (PLC) to reflect on and identify patterns from student data, and plan, based on that data, to provide specific kinds of instruction that would allow students to improve. For more information about the data, classroom and school context, please see Smith (2020c).

EXCERPTS FROM BLACK AMERICAN YOUTH

identify

The data from which I draw here were part of focus group interviews conducted with youth who identified as Black from the broader study described above. I chose excerpts from the focus group interviews to demonstrate instances through which Black American youth reflected their unique abilities to read and write. Specifically, in the excerpts that follow, I share part of my focus group conversation with the Black youth that occurred in their conversation with White and Latinx peers about a writing project in which we had engaged for a duration of 1 year. All names below are pseudonyms.

Excerpt 1: Black Youth Speak About Conferencing During Writing: *"We Just Put Our Thoughts Together to Make a Sound"*

Patriann: Okay, now I'd like us to talk a little bit about working with your peers or students in your class. What is the most exciting thing that you like to do with them while writing? *(Cornell, Imani, Deandre, Sabrina raise their hands.)* Let's start off with Sabrina.

Sabrina: Oh, I like sharing my ideas and talking about it, like, I compare my writing to theirs and see what we both need help with.

Patriann: How does that make you feel? What does that do for you?

Aliyah: I don't know.

Patriann: Okay. Yes, Cornell?

Cornell: Mines is like, mines is disagreeing, because when we both share ideas and we don't really agree with each other, we can have a conversation and talk about which one would fit best with our writing or what we're talking about.

Patriann: That's really smart. I do the same thing too. Sometimes we don't always have to agree on everything.

Nelson: Well, in our groups, Ms. Lovell, she will do, like, how to get along in a group. We'll talk and discuss, and we'll probably go back and forth about things we messed up on, things we got right. If I can compare my paper to his or hers and see what we both messed up on. Like, what I got wrong, and she got right.

Patriann: (Four hands up) So the comparing piece is a big deal. Yes?

Barack: I'll say, hearing others' opinions and then sharing my
opinion, because like even if we have different opinions we
can see how we can make my opinion and their opinions
work together to collaborate on. That's like when I don't
know how to put them in words. Their opinions and mines.

Patriann: Okay. Would you like to add something? *(Focuses on
Cornell)*

Cornell: I like to argue with everyone. Like if we're writing a story,
we're talking back and forth. Like right now we're writing a
story in our reading class and me and my friend, we're arguing
about what should be in our story, what shouldn't. And I think
that's probably one of the funniest parts, because then it makes
us have to go back and look at some more things. So that we
can get along with each other about it.

Patriann: Do you ever get really upset with your peer because
you're arguing against his or her perspective? Tell me about
that.

Nelson: Like he said, my partner, we do a book and we go
like back and forth, and he tries to tell me that this is what
should go there. But we go back and forth about how
we should write it and put a thought, like put it down on
the book for it to make more sense. And try to figure out
how the books end and start.

Patriann: How did you resolve the differences sometimes? How do
you get on the same page?

Jacobe: We just put our thoughts together to make a sound, to
make it sound better, try to make sense. [May 4, 2017]

Perspective

An assumption often made about Black youth is that they cannot discuss cordially about reading and writing, or that they might descend
into chaos if given the opportunity to engage in peer conferencing
about their work. This excerpt was an excellent illustration of how
Black youth show that they do value the conferencing time and use
this time to make meaningful writing progress in literacy. Being able
to talk about how peer conferencing leads to shared consensus for developing a piece was impressive because writing is a social process, a
key part of how Black youth make sense of their authentic languages

All Students need and worlds. My takeaway: Black youth need time to talk to each other in literacy classrooms.

Excerpt 2: Black Youth Speak About Audience and Writing: *"We Be Textin'"*

Patriann: How do you feel about the way you speak and write at home and school? How do you think the way you speak affects how you write?

Aliyah: Like some words we say like, they are the real words but when you write them on paper and they'll be like, you can't write this word, use like a more proper word.

Patriann: Okay.

Cornell: I think so too. Because like sometimes, I like, talk how I text.

Patriann: Give me an example of how you talk.

Martin: Eh . . . ummm . . . *(Laughs)*

Patriann: No, it's just who you are, it's okay to talk.

Martin: I don't know. Don't like to give examples of how I talk.

Patriann: Okay, that's okay.

Juan: What's up, dude?

Patriann: Right, here you go.

Martin: Yeah, so like that. *(Indicates that Juan's speech is an example of what he means)*

Patriann: And then you do that, so you are in the class and you speak like that in your writing. Talk to me about that.

Martin: Stuff like that, but like when you got to write, like they'd be like, you can't spell it like this, my thing is like I when I start writing, like I'm writing, like if I was texting somebody back or responding something. Like I want to use like instead of saying "Y-O-U.," I probably just put "U" or I just don't want to like, use proper syntax or anything.

Patriann: Talk to me about syntax. Do you want to go ahead? *(Multiple hands up for this question in excitement to share opinions)*

Martin: Whenever I'm writing, my teacher will always look at my passage when I'm done because I'll use like abbreviations instead of using like real words like Y-O-U, instead, I'll put "u." And I'll just make it, because whenever you put the full word it's taking up a lot more space. And whenever you're just doing abbreviation, it's a lot more smaller and you got a lot more space to write.

Patriann: You told me earlier that you do have a lot of detail. All right. Tell me about the whole speaking and writing piece.

Barack: Okay. I agree with what Martin said, 'cause like sometimes we say words that's a word and we put [them] in our story and then our teachers don't know [what] we are talking about, they'll be confused. But I don't like to abbreviate. Because I don't know, I just don't like doing it.

Patriann: So you don't normally use language from the way you speak in your writing. You just try to write it "proper"?

Barack: I try to write it like my teacher hoped.

Patriann: So you think about how your teacher's going to want it. Okay.

Damian: Like how we be texting.

Patriann: I like how you said "how we be texting." Tell me more about that.

Nelson: How we be texting? Instead of putting like, "a-r-e," we just put the letter "r." We can't write like that.

Patriann: Why can't you write like that?

Damian: Because the people who are going to be reading going to be thinking you are lazy.

Patriann: Why would they think you are lazy?

Nelson: Because they think that we don't like to take the time to actually write the full word and actually help ourselves to be better. They just want us to, they just think we want to get it over with.

Patriann: But if that's who you are, shouldn't you be writing that down on paper? *(Many students immediately respond simultaneously.)*

Damian: I don't think they want us [to]. I think they want us to change ourselves and actually be like serious and professional instead of just being who we were actually are.

Patriann: Why do you think somebody would want you to do that?

Nelson: Because the world is not just about being silly. We need to take time to be serious.

Imani: Because you never know who would read your paper.

Deandre: Because some people get offended.

Patriann: Some people get offended. Tell me something about that. Why would some people get offended because you're being yourself on your paper?

Jacobe: That's part of like, "They was raised how they talk." So they think, "Oh, they didn't get no discipline." They want us to be like them.

Patriann: Who is they?

Students in unison: (All respond at the same time; they seem united in their response) The people who read our paper.

Patriann: What do they look like? Are they people who look like you or me? Or?

Students: They are elderly. They are old. They are White and elderly.

Patriann: Oh, they might be older and wiser?

Imani: They are White. The people that read our stories (*Nelson:* Are old people.) Our teacher said that they are White people.

Patriann: So let's say that the people, some of them are probably Black like me or professors. How would they want you to write? *(Nelson, Barack, Imani, Damian, and Deandre raise their hands.)*

Jacobe: Professional.

Damian: Because you can't write how you always used to write it. You have to change. You have to write in a different way someday, because if [you] still write how you're writing and say you have to write something important, like for work and stuff and your boss can't understand anything you say. You have to by changing your writing into a different type.

Patriann: So you think sometimes the person that you're writing to might be affected and I know someone said they might be offended?

Imani: Maybe that Black professor, how Black people are recognized these days are terrible. Or maybe he just wants the best for us. Some people think that we talk just crazy. (*Nelson:* Ghetto.) But if we write professional then it changes. (*Sabrina:* It will change the perspective.) How we act and how we write. It makes us, not make us look better but it helps us to feel smarter about ourselves and helps us to go a long way in writing.

Patriann: Whether it's a Black professor or White elderly lady, do you think that's going to change the perspective, the perception?

Cornell: Yes.

Imani: No.

Patriann: Okay, Imani said no. Tell me more about that. I just want you guys to be honest with me. This is a safe space, talk about your writing and I really want to understand what you're thinking. Go ahead.

Imani: They want us to be like them. They want us to like, 'cause like, everybody know how our school is represented.

Patriann: How is the school represented?

Nelson: It's dumb.

Cornell: Dumb.

Barack: They feel like we dumb.

Cornell: They want us to prove them right, basically.

Nelson: That's why our teachers be trying to get us to do all this stuff, because they want us to prove that White people are wrong.

Cornell: We are really smart. It's just the way we react.

Barack: But it's not just White people, some Black too. I guess.

Patriann: You said that they want to prove White people wrong. Talk to me about that.

Cornell: It's not just White people, it's some Black people too, they live on the other side, [don't] live [in] our hood, basically.

Imani: The Black people they went to colleges.

Aliyah: They feel like we can't make it.

Patriann: Okay. How do you feel about me as a Black person being a professor, and when you see me and you hear me talk. What is the first thing that comes to your mind? Do you feel like "Oh, if I write for her and she looks at my writing, she's gonna feel a certain way about my writing?" How do you feel about that?

Imani: You believe in us.

Patriann: She said I believe in you. What do you think about that?

Cornell: I think if like you said, if we were writing to you, I will feel kind of nervous because if like I'm writing how I write, it's like words I say I'll put on a paper. From my perspective, how I think, I can't, like my words are just different from other people's. [May 4, 2017]

Perspective

We often claim that Black youth simply disregard the norms of language imposed on them by schools. This excerpt clearly indicated

they have a thought process around this that reflects their recognition of audience in a way that really influences what they write and
how they write with intention and purpose. It also reflects how they
read the world critically (Luke, 2012) even while they make decisions about writing. By describing these thoughts, and demonstrating
in some cases a shared understanding about how audience works to
influence their writing process, the Black youth illustrated the brilliant approach to navigating what they believe are societal expectations over which they believe they have no control. Operating, as it
were, at the mercy of a system that they believe is not geared toward
helping them and based on the perceptions and expectations of both
Black and White people who want to make them somehow better
versions of themselves through literacy, the Black youth reflected a
complex understanding of how using literacy placed them in a position of power based on European norms or deprived them of agency
based on the same. My takeaway: Black youth need schools, spaces,
and assessments in which they believe their literacies are accepted,
honored, valued and fairly evaluated.

CONCLUSION

I began my story by sharing that Black children can and do read and
write. I then provided a picture of how I developed as a Black (immigrant) teacher, writer, scholar, and educator and how I evolved
through that process. I wanted to demonstrate that it is my experiences as a Black teacher-scholar-educator over the years that brought me
to this point. By subsequently presenting the story of Jorge, a Black/
Latinx immigrant youth in Florida, and excerpts from Black American
youth with whom I worked in a middle school in Texas, I illustrated
the thought processes central to how Black youth connect reading
and writing. I ask you now, having read my story, "What can you do
to demonstrate your belief that Black children and youth can inherently read and write?" To ask this of you is to trust that you are willing
enough to acknowledge how ordinary it is to see brilliance manifested
in the literacies of Black kids and, thus, to join me on this journey.
As I've shown, I have not always been the perfect advocate for Black
youth. And perhaps I never will be. But none of us will do this per-
fectly. It is in our attempts to engage with the process that we learn to
become more of what we choose to believe in.

IN CONVERSATION

Arlette's Comments

I appreciate your coming-to-teaching portion of this narrative. In my response, I have followed your lead. Much like you, very early in my life, I realized that I wanted to be a teacher, and, perhaps sadly, so did my three younger brothers! I grew up in a small town and attended local public schools. Most of the town's neighborhoods and schools were integrated, and there were students from varying socioeconomic backgrounds, and while our small town had few options, some families elected to send their children to Catholic schools. All students were encouraged to work hard and to do well in school. I attended school with my brothers and several different sets of cousins, so we were all very competitive when it came to—well, everything from academics to athletics, to dreams and goals.

All of our parents had southern roots, so there was often talk of Black accomplishments and history. We always rooted for the teams that had the most Black people on them; whether it was a scholastic bowl, football, or basketball, we wanted to see people who looked like us as winners. We took a great deal of pride in our local Black heroes and joined our churches, communities, and family in celebrating Black excellence. We did not envisage their accomplishments as examples of exceptionalism but as examples that could be emulated and expanded.

While we were aware of racial prejudice and discrimination, we did not dwell on it; we learned, or at least tried to learn, to work around it and move forward. This is not to suggest we did not experience painful instances of outright discrimination or attempts to assuage a matter that was clearly racial; we were determined not to allow other people's prejudices to stop us from our goals. As many young Black women elected much more grand-sounding career paths, in venues that were unusual for Black women, I followed a path trod by many members of my family into education. After receiving my undergraduate degree in elementary education, I pursued graduate degrees in reading (life span). While in graduate school, I realized that an undergraduate education does not prepare you well to teach reading.

As a public school teacher, I have taught a 2nd/3rd-grade split and grades 6 through 12. All of my teaching focused on teaching literacy, although at the elementary level classes also included everything from art, to music, to physical education. I enjoyed teaching literacy, reading, speaking, and writing, and often used art, drama, music, and technology to extend notions of text. My students ranged from children who lived in poverty to children born with silver spoons, and spaces in between.

The journey to finding my voice as a Black scholar-educator was filled with unforeseen events: I did not understand why someone would invite me to apply for a job they had no intention of hiring me for, nor did I realize that I could be "interviewed" for a job that I had not applied for, merely to fill an affirmative action quota. Those were difficult lessons, and once I was hired, the hits kept coming: being informed of a pecking order for all decisions as a faculty member or being asked to "share your thoughts" on a committee only to hear your words repeated without acknowledgment as the "committee's work." Besides committee work, as a university instructor, I had many tense conversations with colleagues about their definitions for terms like *community* and *culture* (whose), language (all languages or Standardized English), literacy (whose body of work—fiction/nonfiction), and students (they are not generic, which ones). These were not welcomed queries, as they challenged the way of doing things, and the status quo, and pushed for clarifications and commitments to diversity.

As a Black scholar-educator, I was informed on numerous occasions that journals had published their multicultural article (for the year) and my work was not needed. And several other manuscripts were returned because the reviewers felt that I had not cited the most salient (White researchers') body of literature. With three sons in public school, and living through their experiences, I realized the importance of prayer and the need to be a voice for the educational needs of Black male students. One way I like to share that information is through personal narratives, and doing so became a favorite way of relaying my research interests and inquiries. Among my earliest publications is an article about my youngest son, Jacob, and his school experience of writing for a state competition. I encouraged him to write about things that were familiar to him, and as a 3rd-grader he told me that school was not a place where he could be his "real self." As a parent, that stings. Sadly, my grandson is experiencing similar dismissiveness of his thoughts and understandings as a young Black male writer. Another way that I convey information on literacy is by focusing on issues that are important to Black people. For example, I have documented the history of literacy practices at a Black school, Calhoun Colored School, as well as looked closely at the historical and ideological barriers to reading reform for Black students in the

United States. It is important to fill in the gaps of missing or ignored information about the accomplishments of Black people, as well as the hardships they have endured. This is where I believe my voice can be heard and that I can add to what is known.

Gwen's Comments

As I mentioned previously, I view my foundational learning experiences as a gift. For the first 11 years of my life, I had Black teachers and principals who took an interest in me and told me that I was a brilliant student. They told me I was an exceptional reader and writer and speaker and singer. They said I was smart in math, social studies, and science, and they bragged about my test scores. By the time I went to junior high school and experienced several teachers who did not go above and beyond to support, motivate, and challenge their students, my level of confidence was established, and they didn't impact my thinking. In fact, I remember thinking that I didn't care what they thought. As I reflect on your chapter, Patriann, I immediately think about the importance of relationship-building.

You took the time to build relationships with your students, especially the students you interviewed. Young people do not take the time to talk and be honest with someone who isn't genuine. If they like you, they'll respond to you. They want to meet your expectations, because they realize that you really care about them. That's why they said you believe in them, because teaching is a heart-to-heart experience, and they recognized that you were sharing your heart with them. They wanted to open up to you and meet your expectations, because you established a relationship with them.

Not only did you have a relationship with the students from the excerpts, but you also had a relationship with your dean. You accepted his challenge and bought into his vision of "putting your butt on the line" because you believed that he was genuine in his request. I didn't know him, but I imagine that he was the kind of dean who practiced what he preached.

This relationship-building issue is also connected to Aesha in Shawyn's study, Tony and Travis in my study, and Arlette's experience with her sons in school, as well as my experience with my sons in school. It's a difficult thing to say, but until teachers can view our Black children as *human* with love and respect, it will remain next to impossible for them to teach them. Unfortunately, it's not just one race of people who view Black children as less than human. Many people have trouble viewing children as fully human, which is why there is such poverty among children.

Thank you, Patriann, for reminding us that all of us were once children, and we are still developing into what God wants us to become. He's not finished with us yet.

CRITICAL DISCUSSION QUESTIONS

Parents/Caregivers: What can I do to ensure that my child has opportunities to write about what matters to them? How can I discuss with my child's teacher how to create opportunities for youth to write personal narratives as they attend each grade? How can I help my child talk about what they are reading with others? What opportunities can I create for my child to use writing to respond to what they have read? How can I talk with my child about what it means to be an immigrant who is Black and who "sounds different"?

Teachers: Are my Black students free to discuss and use their various languages to talk about text as they read or while they write in the way that the students above have done in this excerpt? How do I create a classroom atmosphere where Black children converse about high-quality texts using their critical thinking skills in the same way that the students did in the excerpt above with no fear of the teacher's critique? How can I reflect how race, language, and immigration are all a part of the literacies of many of my students?

Educators/Administrators: How am I preparing teachers to engage with the languages of Black children in their reading and writing? How am I preparing them to validate the literacies of Black children in tangible ways? How do my evaluations of teachers incorporate their inclusion of the languages and literacies of Black children in their reading processes, writing processes, and writing products? How do I educate up, providing district administrators with opportunities to address anti-Blackness in curriculum adopted, professional development, and school-community partnerships?

Politicians: How am I engaging with and developing policies that require schools to use literacy and English language arts curriculum that addresses anti-Blackness? How am

I developing legislation that requires all teachers to address anti-Blackness in literacy and language teaching?

Reading Researchers: How am I designing research studies based on ways of examining literacies of students that are designed to center their Blackness in literacy products and practices? How am I rethinking epistemologies that erase the Blackness of children in literacy classrooms? How am I interrogating assessment practices in literacy that punish students when they use their Black Englishes and that cause them to feel so uncomfortable that they hardly speak and write in schools? How am I informing language policies that push back against anti-Blackness and that are informed by anti-racism in literacy research?

SUGGESTED READINGS

Agyepong, M. (2013). Seeking to be heard: An African-born, American raised child's tale of struggle, invisibility, and invincibility. In I. I. Harushimana, C. Ikpeze, & S. Mthethwa-Sommers (Eds.), *Reprocessing race, language and ability: African-born educators and students in transnational America* (pp. 155–168). Peter Lang Publishing Inc.

Anya, U. (2020). African Americans in World Language Study: The forged path and future directions. *Annual Review of Applied Linguistics, 40,* 97–112.

Bauer, E. B., Colomer, S. E., & Wiemelt, J. (2018). Biliteracy of African American and Latinx kindergarten students in a dual-language program: Understanding students' translanguaging practices across informal assessments. *Urban Education, 55*(3), 1–31.

Charity, A. H., Scarborough, H. S., & Griffin, D. M. (2004). Familiarity with school English in African American children and its relation to early reading achievement. *Child Development, 75,* 1340–1356.

Jackson, D. (2020). Relationship building in a Black space: Partnering in solidarity. *Journal of Literacy Research, 52*(4), 432–455.

Kelly, L. L. (2020). Exploring Black girls' subversive literacies as acts of freedom. *Journal of Literacy Research, 52*(4), 456–481.

Rogers, R., & McMillon, G. T. (2019). Racial literacy. Critical Race Theory in teacher education: Informing classroom culture and practice. In K. T. Han & J. Laughter (Eds.), *Critical Race Theory in teacher education: Informing classroom culture and practice* (pp. 46–58). Teachers College Press.

Skerrett, A., & Omogun, L. (2020). When racial, transnational, and immigrant identities, literacies, and languages meet: Black youth of Caribbean origin speak. *Teachers College Record, 122*(13), 1–24.

Smith, P., Lee, J., & Chang, R. (2022). Characterizing competing tensions in Black immigrant literacies: Beyond partial representations of success. *Reading Research Quarterly*. Advance online publication. https://doi.org/10.1002/rrq.375

Wandera, D. B. (2020). Resisting epistemic blackout: Illustrating Afrocentric methodology in a Kenyan classroom. *Reading Research Quarterly, 55*(4), 643–662.

Willis, A. I. (2017). Re-positioning race in English language arts research. In D. Lapp & D. Fisher (Eds.), *Handbook of research on teaching the English language arts* (pp. 30–56). Routledge.

Wynter-Hoyte, K., & Smith, M. (2020). "Hey, Black child. Do you know who you are?" Using African diaspora literacy to humanize Blackness in early childhood education. *Journal of Literacy Research, 52*(4), 406–431.

CHAPTER 6

It's Never Too Late

I welcome this opportunity to converse about a topic I know well, as someone who has lived and researched the literacy education of Black people in the United States. As a wife, mother, grandmother, teacher, and researcher, I bring my experiences and insights about nurturing and shaping the lives of Black children, in and out of school settings. Faith anchors my life. As a child, my parents made sure that we attended weekly Sunday school and morning services at an African Methodist Episcopal Church, and that we participated in church ceremonies and rituals. My early religious experiences and teachings were a foundation on which I later built as I departed from rigid doxology and embraced faith not bound by man-made rules and regulations. My knowledge is based on believing in, loving, and working with Black children/learners/students not as subjects but as people who are cherished, loved, and valued. In this conversation, I add my voice to the experiences and insights shared by my colleagues. As an educator, I have taught preschool, grades 2 through 12, and graduate and undergraduate classes. These varied experiences include teaching English language arts in a variety of settings: in impoverished and wealthy communities, in urban and suburban areas, in several states, and when opening a Christian preschool. For the last two decades, I have taught and conducted research at a Research I university. My scholarship includes critiques of reading research and the invisibility of Black excellence, a history of Black people seeking literacy, and studies about preservice teacher education. I also have served as an official and unofficial mentor to numerous students of color and women while in the academy. In these endeavors, I often share how important I believe teachers are to the future of our nation and their importance in the lives of individual students as well as within communities.

ARLETTE'S NARRATIVE: A SUMMARY

My narrative rests at the intersection of theory and praxis. I share the story of a young Black boy who was focal student in a research project that I conducted. The student was charming and engaging and his postsecondary plans were uncertain when I met him during the last semester of his senior year in high school. In the study, we enacted culturally responsive teaching and used Black literature. Two decades later, I received an email from him that details his life since the research project and how he believes his participation changed his life.

IT IS NEVER TOO LATE . . .

My narrative grows out of a research study that I conducted, with the help of a graduate research assistant, over 2 decades ago. I mention the fact that the people and events were part of a research project, not because they are somehow more valid because they were part of a study. Given the ethos and purpose of this book, however, herein I have a far more personal understanding of meeting a young man whom I have named Clemente (a pseudonym), in honor of the memory of Clementa C. Pinckney, because that is how we honor those we have lost. I share this narrative to also challenge the commonplace, contrived, deceptive, false, worn-out narrative about Black students' motivation and reading habits in secondary education—specifically, preconceived notions that Black males do not read, don't want to read, or are struggling readers. Although there are some Black males that fit each category, the reading interests and habits of Black males are not monolithic. They are as different as each individual. – As in any race!

    Let me begin by stating—unequivocally—that I had not met nor known of Clemente before entering the classroom. The White female classroom teacher mentioned, "It's so good having y'all here, I haven't gained trust" (translation: as a Black woman you have walked into this classroom and students automatically trust you). Of course, this was not totally true—all Black people do not instantly get along—but it was true that Clemente knew two of my sons, as they also attended SmallTown High (a pseudonym). More importantly, it was true that I walked into the classroom with the expectation that all students were worthy of my time and that I was willing to lend my expertise, knowledge, and talents to meet their needs. The Black students knew, or I sensed they knew, that I was old enough to be their mom, and that I probably was not "gonna put up with a lot of foolishness." I was not alone. My graduate research assistant, a biracial young woman, held similar beliefs, and together we instructed students in one English class for a semester (15 weeks). The course, "Minority Authors," was an elective course listed under the subtitle of English, but it was generally considered a course focused on African American literature, as the classroom teacher had successfully challenged the lack of African American literature in the curriculum.

A BRIEF BACKSTORY

For years I had taught secondary English methods courses at my university: two courses over an academic year—a pedagogical course in the fall and a student teaching seminar in the spring. I focused on students developing an understanding of culturally relevant pedagogy and reader response theory. To do so, they were required to read multicultural/multiethnic literature and respond to each text using a writer's workshop approach. Yes, that is a lot going on simultaneously, but it worked! Students developed a sense of each theory as they read select literature within a limited choice format. That is, they self-selected the texts they wanted to read (within limits—I constructed the reading lists). After having experienced the instructional approach during the fall semester, students were encouraged to implement the approach during student teaching—encouraged, because they worked under cooperating teachers within high school English departments who had their own agendas, and very seldom were my students permitted to construct their own curriculum or to select the books high school students were assigned to read. As pleased as I was about the success of the instructional approach, I had not used it with high school students and had only used it with university students, most of whom had been in Advanced Placement classes as high school students, and I wondered how well the approach would work with students who represented varying levels of academic performance in high school.

After receiving a small university grant, I hired my graduate students (both of whom had completed the two-course series with me) and found a local high school English teacher who was willing to collaborate with us to implement the instructional approach in her classroom. Together, in the summer of 1998, we read a number of novels and settled on one for the project, Ernest Gaines's (1993) *A*

Lesson Before Dying. It was not my first choice; although I enjoyed the content, I desperately wanted to move away from novels that traumatized the Black experience, and I wanted students (and their teachers) to read something that told a story of Black life with loving families, and good times—not abject poverty, incarceration, and racial injustice. Collectively, however, we agreed to teach Gaines's novel.

We conducted a semester-long qualitative research study in which we critically framed the teaching of a work of African-American literature, highlighting issues of social justice. We specifically wanted to focus on how sociohistorical information informs students' reading of a text and how the use of multiple forms of reader response supports students' ways of knowing and communicating their understanding of text. "We critically framed reader response theory by supplying readers with sociohistorical information not found in the text but important to understanding it and extended the forms of reader response beyond individual written response and shared dialogue to include performance (e.g., artistic, dramatic, and oral interpretative responses), (Willis and Johnson, 2000, p. 356)." We wanted to augment what they already knew about the intersection of literature, history, and politics in their reading of a novel by providing additional sociohistorical information. In so doing, we created spaces for students to respond in multiple ways to the historical, cultural, social, and political nature of the text, of their world, and of society.

Working with the high school teacher, we taught "Minority Authors" for the spring semester (January 25 through May 11, 1999). The English teacher was a White female who had taught the minority literature class at the school for 10 years. I am Black and my graduate research assistant identifies as biracial (White/Black); we are female and certified teachers. I (Willis) am a professor at a university near the high school, and my graduate research assistant was a doctoral student.

We began and ended our data collection by audiotaping student interviews, collected all artifacts produced by the instructors and students, met daily to review each lesson and gather materials, and met weekly with the classroom teacher to discuss our progress. Importantly, four guest speakers from the community were invited to participate in our study. The guest speakers were Judge DeLaMar, who had recently been appointed to a panel to review the death penalty laws in the state of Illinois; Professor Anderson, a distinguished scholar of African American history and education in the South; Dr. Fowler, who holds a doctorate in political science and is pursuing a second in law, and who is an advocate for social justice; and Dr. Roithmayr, an instructor at the University of Illinois College of Law and an advocate against the death penalty.

MEETING CLEMENTE

The participants were 13 12th-graders and 12 11th-graders at a high school located in a university town in the American Midwest. Demographically, the class included 10 European Americans (6 males, 4 females), 12 African Americans (7 males, 5 females), 1 Asian American (male), and 2 African-American/European-American biracial students (1 male, 1 female). Although the minority literature course is officially "untracked," it is taught at the mid- or average level. Clemente was one of the 25 students. He was enrolled in this course during his final year, and his final semester, at SmallTown High School. It bears repeating the fact that we met Clemente during the final grading period, of his final semester, of his final year at SmallTown High. His participation in the course has impacted his life and future.

Like all students, Clemente engaged in pre/post-interviews, completed course assignments, and was a vocal participant in class whole-group discussions. He was a slender young man who loved to brush his hair and carried cocoa butter to moisturize his skin. He was charming, engaging, funny, and ever-present. He was in the moment and so much smarter than anyone gave him credit for. From the pre-interview we learned about his home life as well as his out-of-school interests "playing video games, reading comic books, fiction, poetry," as well as watching movies and TV. He mentioned that his faith also was important to him—that is, he was committed to "being part of the church" (Connor and Willis, 2009, p. 86). When discussing his future goals, he looked forward to getting a job to support himself and attending a local community college.

Clemente positioned himself within the classroom as the cool Black male student—that is, he was cool enough that other Black kids didn't think of teasing him for acting White or being a "sellout"; yet he was not so cool that the White kids were threatened by his swagger. He was a popular student: president of the African American club and a sports enthusiast, though he did not play on a school team. When asked to describe his best friend, he elected to describe two friends who he claimed had been "through thick and thin" with him. He was comfortable in himself, with his Blackness and all that it entails. He code-switched between African American Language (AAL) and standard English with ease. Clemente was a delight in class. He was always prepared, completed his assignments with aplomb, and asked questions constantly.

Clemente, like most students in the school—self-identified by their academic placement whether high or low—and took on that mantle. During the pre-interview conducted by the graduate research assistant in response to queries about classwork, discussions, reading, and writing, he (along with others) was quick to respond: "not in our classes." When asked about our research project, the classroom teacher responded: "It is going so well, they just teach and discuss things with them, and plow ahead not wondering which kids are in upper tracks." The students were aware that creative writing, open discussions, and the selection of reading materials were freedoms of expression and opportunities experienced by students placed in higher tracks (of course, they were right). The self-deprecation of students not in the high tracks was especially jarring. It was a custom at SmallTown High to differentiate student abilities and talk about it openly, in large part, as if the placements were academic identity markers of students. Once, for instance, we informed the students that a four-page essay was due and they were in disbelief, comparing the request to an assignment of an Advanced Placement course.

As with so many Black male students, especially those not placed in Advanced Placement or high-track classes in secondary schools, Clemente's intellect was underestimated. In fact, all the Black males performed well in our class, academically and in terms of their behavior. Others may have sought to place "phantom" labels of "at risk," "below average," or "special needs" upon them, but these young men thrived. Clemente had been placed in mid-level classes throughout high school. He was "into" this class; in fact, he enjoyed the ancillary materials best. He mentioned that the multiple documentaries and historically significant videos helped to clarify history. He articulated his thoughts about the guest speakers: "It got real at that point. When you spoke to the judge, you kinda realized that this kind of thing does happen," (Connor & Willis, 2009, p. 93). During the post-interview, Clemente also expressed his disappointment as we concluded the research project. He went on to describe his participation in the course as enlightening.

There are two examples of our interactions with Clemente that left an indelible impression on me. I share these as examples to illustrate Clemente's level of engagement in the class. First, in the novel Gaines creates a scene in which Grant is chastised by two aunts who are Othermothers and fighting to save the life of the main character, with an interpretation after each exchange in parentheses and italics (Connor & Willis, 2009, p. 93):

> "Ain't you gon'n speak to Miss Emma?" she said.
>
> (*Generally, African-American folk know that you are obligated to speak to an elder when you know he or she is in the house, especially if you can see them physically.*)
>
> "I was goint to. I was just looking over some papers."
>
> "She want talk to you."
>
> (. . . *she wants to talk to you about something important and you should move now to see what that might be.*)
>
> "Sit down Grant," my aunt said.
>
> "I can stand, Tante Lou."
>
> (*Grant is uneasy . . . trying to remain respectful to his aunt's commands*).
>
> "Sit down," she said.
>
> (. . . *Grant is not too grown to be told what to do and to do it immediately with no backtalk or excuses*). (Gaines, 1997, pp. 11, 12).

We were reading the scene aloud in class, and I asked the students what they thought of his behavior. There were responses about the importance of speaking up for oneself, to which I offered a response about Southern African American culture: both my parents were raised in the South and they raised my brothers and me to never think about talking back to family members who were adults. My husband and I raised our sons the same way. Clemente, however, found it difficult to believe. He asked, "If Lenny [a hometown athlete] was here and you told him to sit down, he would do it?"

"Yes," I replied.

Then I went on to explain that my son might not like doing what I asked, but out of respect for me, as his mother, he would do it and not say a word in protest. Clemente's face appeared to marvel at this idea as he shook his head in familiar agreement (although this also is a biblical admonition from 1 Timothy 5: 1–2, I did not share scriptural references).

The second example is drawn from Clemente's final class project. Students were given the opportunity to create a final project of their choosing. He elected to audiotape a reading of the text, selecting a few pages to read for the assignment. His reading, using African American Language, was filled with rich tones and precise inflection; he conveyed the story much better than the mass market audiotaped version we used in class on occasion. He led the class in a cheer when we announced that our research project was over: "I don't want you to go. Stay. Why do you have to go?" (Connor and Willis, 2009, p. 93). Clemente earned a letter grade of "A" in the class, but he earned much more than a grade. He became more confident in his abilities as a learner while drawing on multiple sources of knowledge and sense-making in the course: cultural, experiential, linguistic, racial, and religious. Who he was and what he knew were appreciated, important, and valued.

TWENTY YEARS LATER

One warm June morning I checked my email. I was surprised to find an email from Clemente, and it brought me to tears. Well, at first I welled up with tears, had to stop reading, and then restart, because I was again overwhelmed with weeping. Since then, we have corresponded, and below are excerpts from his emails.

June 11, 2018
Dr. Willis,
Wow, this is amazing. Until right now I didn't know you were a Professor of Curriculum and Instruction at the U of I. I knew vaguely that you were a professor, but never actually took the time to do a simple Google search. Tonight, I did and I'm so happy that I did. I get to tell you something I've wanted to do for years.
Thank you. Thank you. Thank you, Dr. Willis, for teaching *A Lesson Before Dying* to my class in 1999!
Back in 1999 at SmallTown High School, I was a 17 year old kid not knowing what I wanted to do with my life. When you came to SmallTown High School that semester of '99 to teach *A Lesson Before Dying*, that book, your teaching, they triggered something in me.
Before that semester at SmallTown High, the majority of the content presented to me especially in my reading classes (even before SmallTown High) were culturally irrelevant. Some of it was good in other ways, but not like your class, Dr. Willis.
You brought culturally relevant and rich content (Black content!) to me, and it lit a fire in me that I had no idea was there. Your curriculum and your instruction spoke to me like nothing else had before. Not only was the content right for me, but the way you spoke to us, to me. You supported me. You affirmed me. You encouraged me. I felt like when you spoke to me I could do

anything. I could be a director or writer or actor or whatever I wanted. I could tell that you valued me. I loved it. There was also this pretty preservice teacher . . . that was your co-teacher; which didn't hurt any of our motivation to be in class every day. But in all seriousness for me, she was cool, but the words of Ernest J. Gaines is what got me excited. Your curriculum and instruction was the cake and ice cream and I was culturally nourished. I am forever grateful to you and of course to your research assistant.

     . . . I'd love to introduce you to my wife . . . (also a PhD student in Curriculum and Instruction, Early Childhood Education emphasis). She can tell you I talk about that class all the time. I'd like to tell you all about my research and plans to follow your footsteps one day into the academy.

July 22, 2018
I was in Illinois for about 21 years, but never once reached out to you! I stayed in SmallTown four years after SmallTown High. I graduated from a community college with my Associates degree, transferred to UIC (graduated in 2005), and graduated from the University of Chicago (2008) with my masters' in Social Work. I have no excuse for why it took so long to tell you how much of an impact you and your class had on my social, intellectual, and cultural development. Charge it to my young and distracted head and not my heart. But yes ma'am, your impact for me continues to this day and I'm glad you know now . . .
For this dept., we were required to take a Curriculum Theory class our first year. The professor assigned the movie *A Lesson Before Dying*. As a father the movie touched my heart in ways I wasn't expecting.

May 4, 2020
I am an official doctoral candidate (ABD)! My IRB was approved and I'm collecting data right now. The plan is to graduate in the spring of 2021 and secure a faculty position/Post-Doc/Research Associate (or something!) come fall 2021. The budget cuts, hiring freezes, and uncertainty, in general, are taking a toll, but we remain positive and hopeful for our future.

December 12, 2021
Lastly, Dr. Willis, you must know that I think your pedagogy is consistent. It's as strong or maybe stronger than when I was in

high school. I'm at a different place in my life, . . . even though it's only email exchanges now, you continue to bring the same level of care and attention to me as a doctoral student that you did when I was a senior in high school. You still encourage me. You're still supporting me. And now, your scholarship inspires me to be the best educator-scholar-activist I can be.

PERSPECTIVE

My response to Clemente's initial email took me over a month to write, as I was left speechless by his unsolicited letter and kind words. I was both overwhelmed and delighted. How does one respond to such a lovely letter? I shared with Clemente my sincere appreciation that he took the time to write and share with me the impact the class had on his life. I also reminded him that he was an amazing student.

There were other thoughts that I shared with him. Importantly, I wanted him to know the impact that his participation in the class had on me: (1) I have included his audio reading of the text *A Lesson Before Dying* in my preservice class lectures as an exemplary culturally and linguistically nuanced reading of the novel; (2) during a workshop at Bard College, I also shared his reading with the audience (anonymously), and his reading was well-received; and (3) the novel is still part of the English curriculum at SmallTown High. Significantly, I told him that I recently saw the classroom's teacher and shared the gist of his letter as well as his current endeavors. She too was excited to hear about all that he has been doing since graduating from SmallTown High.

In closing, I return to comments that I made at the outset of this narrative, as I reluctantly note that sharing this narrative as part of a research project was a moment of angst, because my world outside of academia does not consist of, nor is validated by, how many schools of thought I use, or whose philosophy I'm supporting, or whose theories are substantiated or contested, nor how many researchers I can cite whose work is similar to my own and its findings. None of that really matters. The cachet that is of the most value when working with Black students is how much I do care about them as fellow human beings and about their future; whether I am authentic, genuine, honest; and most importantly, how I can help improve their literacy. Like the other narratives in this book, we offer insights and understandings that are not visible. The intangibles matter because they can change lives.

CONCLUSION

What I have learned, what we all know but seldom say, is: it is never too late to make a difference in the life of a student. For far too long, Black male readers have been characterized as possessing "phantom" reading disabilities—that is, they are not reading up to grade level based on standardized tests and need remediation, remediation that begins early in their lives and is repeated year after year, with little to no substantive progress. When Black males enter secondary schools, some administrators and teachers appear to give up on them as learners and readers. To set the record straight: We reaffirm our belief and commitment to authentic and caring support of some of our favorite people, Black males, without romanticizing or patronizing their individual and personal lives and experiences in K–12 reading situations. Not only are they readers, but they also are strong thinkers and writers; however, few administrators and teachers expect much from them once they are in high school.

I read Clemente's initial email to each of my fall preservice Secondary English methods classes, filled as they are with predominately English-dominant, female, middle-to-upper-middle-class White students. Many of these students are well-intentioned—that is, they voice concern about the history of racial inequality in our country, they seek and have read books written by authors of color, and they are beginning to understand their privilege and Whiteness, and the history of White supremacy. It's a start, but I take it further intentionally, ensuring that 99 percent of the texts they read and the videos they watch present concepts, ideas, and strategies generated and promoted by authors, researchers, and writers of color.

Clemente's letter unearthed a number of what I call *truth claims*: (a) it is so essential that teachers show up, be present, demonstrate care, and offer encouragement; and (b) too many Black males do not see themselves as learners, and certainly not academically successful learners; this is especially true by the time they are in secondary school. In this narrative, Clemente, who at the time was preparing to graduate from high school to an uncertain future, finally had found the support (care for his emotional and intellectual performance, cultural knowledge and insight, linguistic acceptance and understanding, valuing his humanity as sufficient and worthwhile) in our course that he needed. Why is that so, and what can be done to change it? How can we encourage each student to perform to their best abilities? What had Clemente discerned or sensed the first day that allowed him to be so open to us?

Here's my takeaway from this narrative: Our Black students matter, their experiences matter, their histories matter, their resources of knowledge matter, their languages matter, and we cannot be silent any longer about how important they are to our survival.

IN CONVERSATION

Gwen's Comments

Narratives like these are what keeps us going, Arlette. Deep down inside, we believe that we're making a difference and that lives are changed when we make sacrifices, implement innovative practices, and go the extra mile trying to share our cultural capital with students and their families. When someone actually takes time to say, "Thank you, you've made a difference in my life," we have to pause and inhale the smell of the metaphoric bouquet of roses. In my heart, I pause to celebrate you, Arlette, a mentor to many, including me. Your staunch leadership and prayerful guidance have blessed the lives of many. You deserve to receive accolades for your selfless commitment to your students and mentees who dare to carry the torch after you've lit the flame.

Your narrative also highlights the fact that teachers are role models. They can model despair, disillusionment, pessimism, and failure, or they can model confidence, cultural pride, optimism, and a good work ethic. My high school College Writing teacher, Mr. Pratt, taught me a lesson that I've never forgotten. He was known as the toughest teacher in the school, and every student who wanted to go to college was told to take his course, because he would prepare his students to ace their freshman comp courses in college. After going through the process of teaching us how to write a research paper (including using 3×5 cards to collect information from primary sources and other nitpicky requirements), he gave us a reasonable deadline to submit our final research papers. I procrastinated, because I knew that I could write the paper in a couple of days. Some students turned their papers in early, and I asked several friends to let me see their papers. Glancing over their work, I knew that I could write my paper quickly, so I started on the paper 2 days before the due date. I showed up in class and handed him my paper. After about 15 minutes, Mr. Pratt walked up to my desk, with his usual smile, and placed my paper on my desk. I looked down at the paper, picked it up, and asked, "Are you done grading it already, Mr. Pratt?" He smiled and said, "No, I won't accept it. It's not your best work." I was stunned. I had never had a teacher refuse to accept my work. I followed him back to his desk and told him that the paper met all of the requirements. In fact, I had more primary sources than any of the other papers that I read. He kept smiling as he replied, "Gwen, that's the problem. You read other papers and tried to match those. I'm not looking for a paper like the others. I'm looking for your best work, and this isn't it. Do it over. You have until Friday to get it done. Now that will be all." I knew I couldn't win, because he taught all of my siblings, and my parents loved him, so I went home and got to work. Friday morning, I turned the paper back in, after spending at least 10 more hours on it. Mr. Pratt glanced over it quickly and said, "Thank you. This will be my weekend reading. I look forward to it."

I've never forgotten Mr. Pratt's words the day he refused to accept my paper, because it wasn't my best work. Since then, I've challenged myself and asked many times, "Is this my best work?" If the answer was not "yes," I made more revisions. If the answer was "yes," I was confident that the reader would enjoy my writing. Mr. Pratt wasn't saying that I wasn't good enough. He was saying that he believed in me and knew that I was capable of writing something exceptional. Then he complimented me by saying that he was going to enjoy reading it during his leisure time.

Like me, I'm sure Clemente didn't necessarily see any value in engaging in the activities that you offered, Arlette. But in time, as he matured, he recognized the impact that your teaching had on him. How awesome! This is the kind of relationship that teachers need to have with all students. We can be the one who holds the ladder while our students climb to greater heights, or we can choose to be the one who pushes them off the ladder and watches them fall. I choose the former—holding the ladder while our students soar.

Patriann's Comments

It was heartwarming to read this narrative of hope, joy, and care of a Black boy who became a man because he found himself through a Black teacher who cared. I was happy to see you challenge the false but overarching narrative, Arlette, which often suggests a lack of motivation on the part of Black male students in secondary classrooms. I saw this in the Caribbean as a teacher and I see it here as well. This untruth and the faulty assumptions that accompany it, despite evidence, continue to undergird much reading research undertaken to "fix" Black males.

I was excited to "hear" your voice in the beginning of the narrative, and again toward the end when you "got out of scholar mode," so authentic, so warm, *so Arlette*. You were writing exactly as you normally speak when we see each other at the Literacy Research Association conference. I could even see the intermittent winks and half-smiles as I heard you while reading. This experience was quite telling, so moving and very powerful. It reminded me of how I felt when I read the work of Black males who had taken a semester to believe that their voice was a legitimate part of the classroom and deserved to be on a page.

When you mentioned the decision to avoid any further traumatization of the Black experience, I was reminded of my daughter's constant tirade about movies and books on Black people and their tendency to be so focused on slavery. Since she was a child, she avoided these books and was elated to have seen *Black Panther* as an adolescent, which enabled her to finally imagine herself as someone who was not a slave. This traumatization piece is one that I do not think we are often attending to sufficiently as we present readings and work on instruction with Black students in classrooms. How do we inadvertently (re)traumatize Black children when we are not aware of this important nugget?

As I came upon this excerpt from the teacher: "It is going so well, they just teach and discuss things with them, and plow ahead not wondering which kids are in upper tracks," I chuckled, knowing fully well what she meant. Black children who are thinking and talking and sharing in a classroom where they are challenged to read and write based on their God-given potential are never disgruntled or lack interest in what is going on. It was delightful to see that students seemed to have found their voices when you all were in that classroom. In many cases where I visit classrooms, I am often taken aback by how long it takes for me to build students' confidence that I am eager to hear their voices, that their thoughts about text matters, that their writing these thoughts on paper is a legitimate process, and that there is value in their sharing. It is heartrending to notice, each and every time, that Black students in many of the schools designated as "underperforming" have to be taught how to *bring their words to the table* simply because they are not sure that it is okay to use their own words and their own thoughts to write.

Clemente seemed to be an exception, thankfully. Reading about Clemente made me think of the many Black kids with whom I had worked in the Caribbean as well as the United States, who were initially afraid to share, read, and write in class because they were positioned as *uncool* and struggled because of this inability to socially adapt. Many of these students did eventually feel comfortable sharing, reading, and writing in class, but initially they were afraid to do so. In many ways, Clemente had *figured out* how to read his worlds and create a version of himself that fit both in the Black and White spaces across which he moved back and forth daily. Many Black students don't know how to do this.

As I move on from the social piece, I also want to touch on the emotional aspect. When I read the line, "I don't want you to go. Stay," I thought how rare it was for the Black students I taught, no matter where, to feel that way about the teachers with whom they were often familiar in schools. There was something about the trust built with Clemente that came through in his ability to share these simple yet powerful words. In the moment of vulnerability where this Black male youth felt comfortable saying that he wished you would not leave, I saw all the other Black males, and females, in my past whom I hated to leave behind in schools when I had to move on to another country, town, or city.

And now, reading Clemente's email is making me cry for all our babies who never had a Dr. Willis. I, too, feel like Clemente does, grateful as a Black immigrant coming into the racialized spaces of the United States, to have had Black mentors like you and Dr. McMillon provide *translations* of the world as I learned what it means to be, feel, and learn to be oppress(ed). I am sure it is how our Black girls also feel when they find their Dr. Willis. Your closing comments are exactly *me* when I write beyond academia: unjudged, uncut, and free.

CRITICAL DISCUSSION QUESTIONS

Parents/Caregivers: What opportunities does my child have to be validated by a person or teacher of color in a teaching and learning setting who is not a part of my family? What opportunities does my Black child have to develop their confidence, and how can I work with teachers to build this confidence during each grade? What books can I give my child to read that allow them to see Black people in positions of confidence, joy, and power?

Teachers: What internal and external factors caused Clemente to be so comfortable with his literacy practices in this classroom? How was the focus on social, emotional, and historical interwoven into the skills-based instruction required and highlighted by the teacher in the classroom? What literacy strategies were used to build on Clemente's strengths?

Educators/Administrators: How can administrators help teachers learn to affirm each student's humanity? How can administrators support emotional, historical, and social learning in literacy instruction? How can district administrators create opportunities to recruit Black teachers for each of the schools in the district?

Politicians: How can I ensure that policies are in place that support the literacy development of all students from a global perspective? How can I mandate that teachers utilize culturally responsive materials in all disciplinary areas to provide a quality education that includes a broadened perspective of the world in which we live?

Reading Researchers: What am I doing to dismantle the stereotypes of minoritized students in general, and Black boys in particular? Does my research perpetuate racism or support racial justice, with the understanding that there is no middle ground?

SUGGESTED READINGS

Dyson, M.E. (2020). *Long time coming: Reckoning with race in America.* St. Martin's Publishing Group.

Everett, S. (2016). "I just started writing": Toward addressing invisibility, silence, and mortality among academically high-achieving Black male secondary students. *Literacy Research: Theory, Method, and Practice, 65*(1), 316–333.

Husband, T., & Kang, G. (2020). Identifying promising literacy practices for black males in P–12 classrooms: An integrative review. *Journal of Language and Literacy Education, 16*(1), 1–34.

Johnson, A. M. (2019). *A walk in their kicks: Literacy, identity, and the schooling of young Black males.* Teachers College Press.

McKinney de Royston, M. M., Madkins, T. C., Givens, J. R., & Nasir, N. S. (2020). "I'm a teacher, I'm gonna always protect you": Understanding Black educators' protection of Black children. *American Educational Research Journal, 58*(1), 68–106.

West, C. (2017). *Race matters—The 25th anniversary.* Beacon Press.

CHAPTER 7

C
A
R
E
T
O

Conceptual Framework:
Toward a Standard of CARE

R
E
A
D

We demonstrate in this book a parallel, yet unacknowledged, litera-cy historical narrative of reading and reading research. This histori-cal narrative reflects a history of Black people cherishing, loving, and valuing Black lives and literacies. This book also honors how, for Black people, literacy has always meant more than the ability to read and write as a set of discrete skills. Literacy represents a pathway to free-dom, liberation, and power. We write in part to ensure that the cur-rent focus on Black lives includes an authentic and informed focus on Black literacy and to ensure that the current focus does not become appropriated and re-messaged by others. We acknowledge silence about the history and legacy of racism within the literacy community as well as federal government funding agencies that support literacy assessments. As poet Mari Evans (1994) admonishes:

> Speak the truth to the people
> Talk sense to the people
> Free them with reason
> Free them with honesty
> Free the people with Love and Courage and Care for their Being
> Spare them the fantasy
> > Fantasy enslaves

FOUNDATIONS

As we state in the Introduction, ideologically and theoretically we draw on Blackness (Black Feminist Theory, Black Liberation Theology, the Black Radical Tradition) as well as Critical Race Theory and Decolonial Theory. Black women's (counter)narratives, for example, are steeped in a persistence toward access to literacy, accomplished by unteaching anti-Blackness through extending, believing, learning, sharing, and humanizing, all of which support a reimagination of literate Blackness and develop a Black joyful child. Based on our indications in this book, we envisaged literacy that includes the following:

1. (Counter)narratives of Black women scholars;
2. These (counter)narratives steeped in access to literacy;
3. Access to literacy based on unteaching anti-Blackness via:
    a. Moral Responsibility: Extending literacy privileges to Black people;
    b. Liberation Theology: Believing through faith in Black people's ability to contest and eradicate legal limits placed on literacy;
    c. Black Feminism: Black women and activist teachers, Othermothering, extending care to Black people;
    d. Black Radical Tradition: Sharing with other Black people through economic and other means the knowledge of reading and writing via care and love;
    e. Decolonization: Humanizing Black peoples through normalizing excellence based on historical and contemporary truths about the literate excellence of Black peoples;
4. Journeying toward joy: the joyful Black child.

A visual of this reimagination is presented in Figure 7.1. Reimagining Literate Blackness.

There is a long history of the intersection of Black literacy, anti-literacy laws, and White supremacy. As Crenshaw (2021a) expresses, "the chronic failure to confront the master monsters of our past is not destiny; it is a daily choice to accept the American myth in the face of countervailing evidence" (n.p.). She continues, observing that "reckoning with race, on the other hand, means understanding white supremacy as a foundational form of social power . . . [and] how our national mythology continues to naturalize and defend immense racial and democratic inequalities" (n.p.). We believe these foundations support a way forward, and we submit that structural racism exists along with other oppressions that affect the lives of Black students: from the assumptions and biases that underpin White supremacy and its "legitimacy," to those that frame literacy research and undergird literacy assessment, curriculum, and instruction. We believe it is imperative

Figure 7.1. Reimagining Literate Blackness

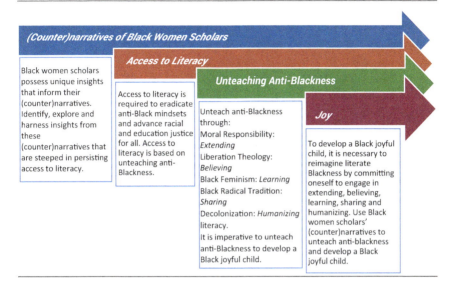

(Counter)narratives of Black Women Scholars

Black women scholars possess unique insights that inform their (counter)narratives. Identify, explore and harness insights from these (counter)narratives that are steeped in persisting access to literacy.

Access to Literacy

Access to literacy is required to eradicate anti-Black mindsets and advance racial and education justice for all. Access to literacy is based on unteaching anti-Blackness.

Unteaching Anti-Blackness

Unteach anti-Blackness through: Moral Responsibility: *Extending* Liberation Theology: *Believing* Black Feminism: *Learning* Black Radical Tradition: *Sharing* Decolonization: *Humanizing* literacy. It is imperative to unteach anti-Blackness to develop a Black joyful child.

Joy

To develop a Black joyful child, it is necessary to reimagine literate Blackness by committing oneself to engage in extending, believing, learning, sharing and humanizing. Use Black women scholars' (counter)narratives to unteach anti-blackness and develop a Black joyful child.

to acknowledge the need for critical racial justice reform in literacy: assessment, funding, instruction, and research through a dismantling of the structures that permit the status quo to be sustained. In doing so, we acknowledge the efforts by many scholars, particularly Black scholars who were forerunners and paved the way for us to unapologetically name race and center Blackness as a basis for moving toward racial justice in literacy research, practice, and assessment.

RACE AND CULTURE

In education research, socially constructed concepts of culture and race are used as if synonymous, although they are not. Educational research often conflates culture and race, and uses the term *culture* to obfuscate discussions of race and racism in education. There is much debate around the use of each term. On the one hand, sociologist Bonilla-Silva (2003) proffers that race has "a social reality . . . it produces real effects on the actors racialized as 'black' or 'white'" (p. 35). On the other hand, Nasir, Lee, Pea, and McKinney de Royston (2020)

> . . . view learning as fundamentally cultural, unfolding through multiple pathways that occur in relation to shifting social and contextual conditions,

to which humans are constantly adapting. We view attention to cultural processes undergirding learning in expansive ways as their requisite subject of scientific investigation not solely an object of political and ideological debate. (p. xvii)

In this book, we endorse a deliberate and intentional focus on Blackness as we reinsert race—Blackness—into education research in general, and literacy in particular. Our willingness to unambiguously endorse Blackness is a political choice to make clear our commitment to Black students. Other students also may benefit from our philosophical and conceptual framework.

We acknowledge the historic and contemporary roles of race and racism in the acquisition of literacy for Black people, while understanding that there is no singular or monolithic Black experience. We also acknowledge that intersections of oppression may be experienced by and influence how Blackness is lived. We are mindful that "whiteness—not a simplistic racial categorization, but a deeply structured relationship to social coercion and group entitlement—remains a vibrant dimension of power in America" (Crenshaw, 2021b, n.p.). Also, Harris (1993) theorizes that the sustainability of these ideas is premised on believing that "whiteness meets the functional criteria of property" (p. 1731). She submits that Whiteness has value and that the reality of Whiteness is tangible. Crenshaw (2021b) extends this idea, noting that "it ties wildly conflicting cross-class interests into a political stranglehold denying any sustainable and actionable sort of racial or socioeconomic equality" (n.p.). We find that all these ideas coalesce in literacy where the concept of culture (usually undefined) and the concept of race (as a lived experience) are avoided. Bonilla-Silva (2012) suggests that discourse that sidesteps race is a form of racial grammar, "a distillate of racial ideology and, hence, of white supremacy" (p. 1). We note people often work around discussions of race and racism, using coded language or dog-whistles, in classrooms, on school boards, at district offices, at state assemblies, and in federal policy deliberations. Avoiding forthright discussions about race in the present is predicated on the assumption that there will be discussions in an unknown future (Bonilla-Silva, 2015). We submit that the future is now.

Agreeably, the constructs of race and culture intertwine, literacy exists within and through both, and to varying degrees, scholars emphasize one aspect or another. Initially, the dehumanization of Black people, for example, was overtly used to bar us from access to literacy. Three hundred years later, in the mid-1900s, race was expressed more covertly as Black culture that was labeled, erroneously, as cultural deprivation, cultural language (e.g., African American Language), and a culture of poverty, and became pseudonyms for redirected discussions of race in literacy. In literacy research and instruction, the concept of culture retains a tacit association, commingling poverty and race. However, we are part of, and inescapable from, varied beliefs, cultures, histories, and languages. It is unnecessary to wrestle with trying to disentangle or debate the influence of culture versus race that defines the experiences of Black people. Culture does not explain race, nor does race explain culture. Each construct represents multiple perspectives, conveying myriad meanings depending on the context in which they are used. We submit that our literate lives are framed, in large part, by the history of systemic racism woven into the institutions and laws of this nation, which is a truth that is unavoidable.

Within the history of literacy research are multiple branches rooted in White supremacy and structured to narrowly define literacy within White frames of reference: (a) research seeking to "fit" Black people into White frameworks while holding them accountable for not being White, and (b) research that "Others" all non-White students and seeks to normalize perceptions of Black students as at risk, challenges, inferior, problems, and struggling. By contrast, we have shown that there also is a body of literacy research that replaces skewed characterizations with understandings about Black students informed by lived experiences and praxis: that consistently reframes "Black students as children who are made vulnerable by the racialized conditions of society, rather than by the child's moral, pathological, or intellectual inadequacies" (McKinney de Royston et. al, 2021, p. 31). Black students deserve the best literacy research has to offer, not the second best, not the "more research is needed" excuses to extend a legacy of lackluster progress, or the "any other time but now" postponement. Change begins, in part, by understanding that Black students do not lack intellectual prowess.

Black students should enter schools and classrooms with an expectation that the school administrators and classroom teachers are caring and prepared to engage with them as fellow humans, while also being knowledgeable and respectful of their cultural, economic, ethnic, gender, linguistic, racial, religious, and sexual differences. Unfortunately, in 2021, Black students continue to be attacked by systemic racism, as demonstrated in a recent incident in a North Carolina school. In a local newspaper, *The Charlotte Observer,* Marusak (2021) reported that the school district shared a collection of mock tweets from 4th-graders containing racist remarks as part of a Civil War assignment. According to the news report, "The students were instructed to write tweets from the point of view of a historical figure." As a result of several racist tweets posted by students, the school system claimed to be "developing training sessions for all employees to address diversity, equity and inclusion. We are committed to working with teachers to discuss best practices for instruction" (n.p.).

Not surprisingly, about 20 years ago, I wrote about a similar assignment my son was given in middle school: pretend you were alive during the time of the Civil War and write a letter to an important person (Willis, 2002). And recently, I (Smith) was forced to ask my daughter to resign from a school initiative where the very podcasts that she was designing to support the Black Lives Matter movement were used as a vehicle by individuals at her school to have her consider the "other side of racism." At the same time, my daughter continued to attend a regularly held weekly meeting and course at the same school where coded language persisted touting White supremacist views, suggesting the innocence of the then-president despite what had just been a recent attack on the U.S. capitol.

There are no quick fixes, no three steps or four tiers to effective literacy instruction. Change—radical, substantive, transformational—must begin long before student/teacher classroom interactions. Since the beginning of this century, there have been calls by politicians and stakeholders to provide all students with an equal and equitable education. The rhetoric behind the messaging notwithstanding, we focus on Blackness, on all that Blackness is, which includes but is not limited to race, as it includes gender, language, social class, and religion. Crenshaw (2021b) observes that an intersectional approach is best to address the multiple intersecting oppressions that affect students: culture/ethnicity/race, genders and sexualities, languages other than Standard English, multiple social economic classes, and religious beliefs. We submit that teaching literacy to Black students requires knowing and understanding Blackness as cultural, gendered, linguistic, and racial, as well as knowing how to provide Black students with effective, high-quality literacy instruction. Addressing both culture and race is important and part of our conceptual framework.

EQUITY PEDAGOGIES

Our work is inspired by equity scholarship: the work of Banks and Banks (1983–2019) on multiculturalism; Ladson-Billings's (1994) work on culturally relevant pedagogy; Gay's (2000) culturally responsive teaching strategies; and the work of Paris and Alim (2017) on culturally sustaining pedagogy. As well, we are inspired by more recent research on anti-Blackness, antiracism, Black excellence, and racial justice that values Blackness and herein moves Black theorizing to the center of reading instruction. Addressing both culture and race is important and part of our conceptual framework—one that serves as a counternarrative to Eurocentric ideologies while simultaneously extending broadly defined notions of cultural and equity pedagogies. We know that debates over culture and race, however, have served as a distraction from the real issue: power (Morrison, 1975), the power to control the narrative about People of Color, and in this case, their literacy. In a stunningly public admission, the American Psychological Association (APA) acknowledged its support of scientific racism and white supremacy and how that support has harmed People of Color. The organization also chronicled its history and pattern of dismissive actions toward Black achievement and Black scholarship, as well as their actions taken in self-interest. On October 29, 2021, APA apologized for the harm it has committed and chronicled the organization's history, noting "one of the central issues for U.S. psychology, both past and present, is its strong ties to hegemonic science and practice" (para 19.) APA also stated:

> This chronology demonstrates ways in which research and practice have focused on White culture and used it as a global standard. This culture, evident from the very beginnings of the field, is inseparable from the social and political landscape of the United States at the end of the nineteenth century. Organized psychology grew up in these conditions, helped to create and sustain them, and continues to bear their indelible imprint. (para 21)

Moreover, APA summarized many, but not all, of the organization's actions that informed their narrative about People of Color:

- Established and participated in scientific models and approaches rooted in scientific racism;
- Created, sustained, and promulgated ideas of human hierarchy through the construction, study, and interpretation of racial difference;
- Promoted the idea that racial difference is biologically based and fixed;
- Used psychological science and practice to support segregated and subpar education for people of color;

- Created and promoted widespread use of psychological tests and instruments that discriminated against people of color;
- Failed to take concerted action in response to calls for an end to testing and psychometric racism;
- Supported the widespread use of educational assessments and interventions that were lucrative for the field of psychology, but harmed people of color;
- Provided ideological support for and failed to speak out against the colonial framework of the boarding and day school systems for First Peoples of the Americas;
- Created, sustained, and promoted a view of people of color as deficient or damaged;
- Applied psychological science and practice to oppose "race-mixing" and to support segregation, sterilization, and anti-marriage laws, using the ideas of early 20th century eugenics;
- Failed to represent the approaches, practices, voices, and concerns of people of color within the field of psychology and within society;
- Failed to respond or responded too slowly in the face clear social harms to people of color. (para 22)

In alignment with the recent apology and resolution of the APA, our philosophical and conceptual framework is unapologetically informed by Blackness and a history of Black literacy acquisition and scholarship. Our framework, CARE, is **C**entered on students, requires **A**wareness, focuses on **R**acial equity/justice, and outlines **E**xpectations.

CARE

We draw on medical and legal definitions of the concept "standard of care" to anchor our conceptual framework for literacy. A common medical definition of the concept suggests "the ordinary level of skill and care that any health care practitioner would be expected to observe in caring for patients" (*Medical Dictionary for Health Professions and Nursing*, 2012, n.p.). Kinney (2004) provides a deeper understanding of the origins and history of the concept and differentiates how the term is used in the field, leading her to remark that "standards of care should not be thought of as a single, uniform whole" (p. 574). Likewise, Moffett and Moore (2011) cite case law in medical malpractice lawsuits used to establish a legal understanding and shifting definitions of the term and medical use, noting that the modern definition of *standard of care* includes "that which a minimally competent physician in the same field would do under similar circumstances" (n.p.). Another medical and legal definition, by Goguen (2021), states:

> The "medical standard of care" is typically defined as the level and type of care that a *reasonably competent* and skilled health care professional, with a similar background and in the same medical community, would have provided under the circumstances that led to the alleged malpractice. (n.p., emphasis added)

We draw on these definitions and shades or meaning as CARE is not singular; there can be variety in application and implementation.

Our use of CARE invokes literacy teachers to be reasonably competent in their ability, knowledge, and skill. We believe reasonably competent teachers and school personnel (literacy coaches or interventionist) should be required to meet "minimal expectations"—that is, provide every student with appropriate, culturally, linguistically, and racially informed, high-quality instruction. Our conceptual framework also is inspired by the ethic of care expressed by Black women teachers and approaches to literacy instruction of Black students: (a) understanding and accepting Black people as human and in search of freedom, liberation, and justice; (b) believing in hope, moral responsibility, sacrifice, and spiritual groundedness; and (c) drawing on creativity, courage, conviction, and resourcefulness to teach literacy. The women we discussed earlier in this book were disruptors of colonization and provided a foundational premise in the way we decide to tell our truths. They sought independence, with a strong sense of self and purpose, and willingly prepared the next generation of literacy learners. Admittedly, we are not the first scholars to call for CARE. Gay (2000), for example, grounds culturally responsive pedagogy in the notion of care, emphasizing how care "is manifested in the forms of teacher attitudes, expectations, and behaviors about students' human value, intellectual capability, and performance responsibilities. Teachers demonstrate caring for children as *student*s and as *people*" (italics in original, p. 44). Gay also observes that

> Caring, interpersonal relationships are characterized by patience, persistence, facilitation, validation, and empowerment for the participants. Uncaring ones are distinguished by impatience, intolerance, dictations, and control. The power of these kinds of relationships in instructional

effectiveness is expressed in a variety of ways by educators, but invariably the message is the same. Teachers who genuinely care about students generate higher levels of all kinds of success than those who do not. (p. 47)

Descriptions of the ethics of care embrace the adoption of moral responsibility, engaging with fellow humans as real people: teaching the students in front of you without questioning their humanity. Ladson-Billings (1995) recalls an oft-repeated comment: "Well, that's just good teaching" (p. 195). In an interview, she extended her response as follows: "Right. It's just good teaching!" . . . "How come so little of it is going on in the classrooms with children who look like me? If it's just good teaching, why are we having such difficulty making it happen?" (Willis, Lewis, and Ladson-Billings, 1998, p. 64). More than two decades later, educators are asking the same question and argue that acknowledging and centering Blackness in literacy functions as a basis for moving this conversation forward.

We suggest that Black students, like all students, should be accepted as fully human and worthy of an appropriate, high-quality, and informed (culturally, linguistically, racially) literacy education. In the next section, we explicate how to implement CARE for Black literacy learners, supplying applicable background knowledge and practical suggestions. In this example, CARE is aimed at improving the educational experience of Black student literacy learners.

Knowledge, Insights, and Understandings Inform the CARE Framework for Black Students

    C Centered on Black Students
    A Awareness of Anti-Blackness—Historical Knowledge and
       Political Knowledge
    R Racial Equity/Justice
    E Expectations of Personnel in School Districts, Schools, and
       Classrooms

[handwritten margin note: how about of students and families too?]

C—Centered on Black Students

It is reasonable to minimally expect that adults in authority (school administrators, classroom teachers, and auxiliary personnel) will care for Black students under their tutelage in ways that are authentic, empathetic, honest, genuine, life-affirming, and positive. Although educators cannot be mandated to love students, they should project an

Figure 7.2. A Framework of CARE

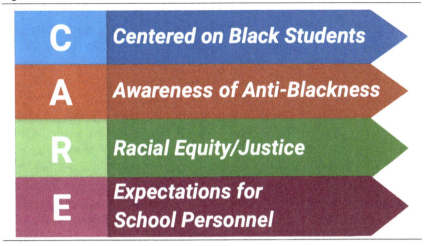

ethic of care—to care for, be interested in, be attentive to the needs of, and be protective of Black students. Adults in positions of power have a moral responsibility to accept Black students, to value them as fellow humans, and to respect and treat with dignity the Black child who is in front of them, the whole child. Moreover, adults, schools, systems, and administrators should be held accountable for Black students' literacy learning, using accurate, appropriate, and informed literacy research and instructional strategies to create a learning program.

We believe Black students are worthy of high-quality literacy instruction based on research conducted among other Black students, not based on the culture, language, and lived experiences of White students, nor the racist research and instruction that frames Black students as a problem in need of fixing. There is no monolithic or singular Black experience, yet there are common experiences that many Black people living—and attending school—in the United States have experienced. Knowledge of global Black history, African and diasporic genius, and Black history in the United States; understanding of the roots and contemporaneous expressions of Black culture and the roots of African American Language; and appreciation of Black culture and language all inform one's learning of accurate racial and political knowledge about the founding of the nation's educational systems as well as the structural racism upholding the status quo.

Critical multiracial awareness in literacy. Given the history of racial tension in the United States, a radical shift is needed beyond generic depictions of diversity that foreground language and culture, to an explicit focus on race and anti-Black racism, specifically, how these ideas undergird engagement with linguistic and cultural diversity in literacy teacher preparation (Haddix, 2017; Willis, 2017). Teachers and school administrators are well positioned to explicitly focus on critical racial awareness (Tanghe, 2016) in literacy research, teaching, and assessment in conjunction with critical multilingual (García, 2015) and critical multicultural awareness (Roxas, Dade, & Rios, 2017), by allowing literacy teachers and educators to revisit how race positions all elements of the self as a precursor for responsiveness. This is particularly useful for White teachers in the United States, the majority of whom are monolingual and often seek to understand how to interact with racialized learners (e.g., Black students) and the associated cultural and linguistic representations in classrooms (see Chin, Quinn, Dhaliwal, & Lovison, 2020). However, it is also true for many racialized and linguicized (Skutnabb-Kangas, 1988) literacy educators and teachers in and beyond the United States. There is often a potential to overlook how predispositions toward thinking about the intersection of race, language, and culture intersect, creating responsiveness that is not always aligned with the needs of Black students in classrooms (e.g., Smith, Karkar, Varner, Nigam, & Finch, 2020). As Smith and Warrican (2021) have observed,

> . . . [we envisage that] literacy teachers and educators, as they enter classrooms and relate to the "Other", will begin to foreground critical awareness as a basis for developing responsiveness. We imagine literacy teachers and educators becoming so self-aware that they develop a critical edge in their personal ways of being, knowing, doing and living together with others which inevitably leads them to action. . . . Critical multicultural, critical multilingual awareness and critical racial awareness, . . . should enable literacy teachers and educators not merely to adjust their approach to teaching diverse groups but to also actively seek to change their own lives as a precursor to, as well as through, actions such as advocacy. Such critical awareness allows teachers and educators to connect with the self and exude care and caring so they focus on the body and how it feels when interacting with the "Other" while they also focus on learning which engages the mind . . . (p. 12)

It is assumed that such an approach will allow for closer attention to the role of race in language and culture when enacting literacy responsiveness to Black students (Louis, Michel, Deranek, & Louis,

2018; McMillon & Rogers, 2019; Smith & Hajek, 2021). This approach raises the question, "What does it look like for teachers (preservice and in-service) as well as educators to arrive at the critical point of awareness where they are moved to respond to Black learners based on the intersection of race, culture, and language?"

A—Awareness of Anti-Blackness: Historical Knowledge and Political Knowledge

It is imperative that teachers and school administrators possess a deep, unvarnished knowledge of our nation's history. Change cannot begin by preferring to address an undefined Black culture while simultaneously ignoring anti-Black racism and Black people as racialized in our society. The process begins by recognizing the history of anti-Black racism in this country, expanding the epistemological bases of knowledge and literacy, as well as changing educational policies to be more equitable. For example, the accomplishments of Black people are underaddressed and undervalued, with the exceptionalism extended to Martin Luther King Jr., and Rosa Parks. Crenshaw (2021c) proffers:

> to build a nation that is a better reflection of our expressed ideals, we have to imagine a different baseline from which conceptions of justice and democracy flow—a baseline not beholden to the legacies of genocide and slavery but one of a republic reborn as a multiracial democracy. (n.p.)

The history of Black lives, from their African homelands to our current positioning, should be part of the history of education in all preservice programs, and learning about Black history and the Black lives currently should be continued throughout in-service teaching. This can be accomplished by interweaving several key tenets that center Blackness in teacher preparation and in-service teacher learning as well as in research about teacher preparation. It also can be done by equipping teachers to support the identities of Black students in ways that help them to define themselves and use their literacies to navigate power, authority, and oppression (Muhammad, 2020).

Pursuing historical knowledge of anti-racism for racially just literacy also means attending to the many varied global depictions of anti-Blackness and the ways in which they coalesce in the United States as Black immigrants (Afro-Caribbean and Caribbean) and African Americans function in a visibly White-dominant society. It means attending to the anti-Black literacies of White supremacy that are used to divide Black populations to uphold and maintain Whiteness under the guise of a supposedly acceptable Black immigrant model minority juxtaposed against what many have been inaccurately taught to believe are an incapable Black American underperforming youth (Smith, Lee, & Chang, 2022). It means attending also to the ways in which literacy assessment, as a function of Blackness positions certain Black students (e.g., Black immigrants) as supposedly exceptional while repeatedly relaying what many have come to believe is somehow an academic brokenness of others (e.g., African American) (see Alim & Smitherman, 2020, on raciolinguistic exceptionalism). It means acknowledging how, through this veil, the literacy assessment scores of all Black youth (immigrant and African American) in certain cases (i.e., the Program for International Student Assessment) appear to fall short of the White established Eurocentric norm, as all Black students together "underperform" (see Smith, Kumi-Yeboah, Chang, Lee, & Frazier, 2019). Accurate and complete histories of literacy are critical if the challenge is to be taken up to identify how literacy often functions as a tool of White supremacy, disrupting how Black people learn to "read the world and word" (Freire, 1970) in ways that reinforce the supposed inferiority of some while touting the seeming brilliance of others. Such historical knowledge will lay bare the raciolinguistic exceptionalism (Alim & Smitherman, 2020) that has been engendered in the past and that persists in the present, fueling dehumanization of Black people, and extending to the inadvertent and resultant policing of Black people, by the self.

R—Racial Justice

Racial justice in literacy demands a multipronged approach to addressing a history of racial injustice in literacy. People in general do not live lives disconnected from the texts that they read, and Black students are no exception. We bring our entire selves to each literacy task, including the historical, linguistic, political, and racial contexts in which we produce literacy. In the United States, however, too few school texts provide accurate accounts of Black contributions to literacy, politics, and society; the history of Black lives prior to our arrival and since in the United States is either missing or inaccurate, and current social movements addressing the national history of Black racial injustice are being redirected so White students will not feel bad, guilty, or sad. It is incumbent upon school district administrators, classroom teachers, and auxiliary school personnel to make available to all students, and particularly to Black students, accurate and appropriate assessment and curricular materials.

Addressing racial justice for Black people, while acknowledging and addressing its variations in literacy instruction and assessment, can be infused foundationally into what teachers and schools do, thereby functioning as a foundation of all teacher preparation programs. First, it is important to prepare teachers and school administrators with a history of the ways in which ancestors of Black students were forced from their homelands. Doing so is possible by centering Blackness in courses and professional development programs that explore "diaspora literacy," demonstrating how Black people "read a variety of cultural signs of the lives of Africa's children at home and in the New World" and as they develop an understanding of their "story" of "cultural dispossession" (Busia, 1989, p. 197; King, 1992, 2015). Second, it is also critical to prepare teachers and school administrators who are racially literate, capable of recognizing how race (and specifically, anti-Blackness) operates contextually as opposed to universally, who are able to identify relationships between race and power, and who recognize how racism operates based on its intersections with numerous social factors (Guinier, 2004; Sealey-Ruiz, 2021).

Third, there is a need for Critical Race Theory (Willis, 2017) and its extensions (such as Cabrera, 2018) to be central to preservice and inservice teachers as well as school administrators' inquiries that identify manifestations of anti-Blackness in literacy practice and beyond as well as those that reinforce hegemonic whiteness. Fourth, it is critical that teachers, school administrators, and all workers in schools be provided with a historical understanding of the intentional erasure of the language and literacies of Black peoples across the Americas (see Boutte, King, Johnson, & King, 2021) by examining how a "co-naturalization of race and language" (Rosa & Flores, 2017) has been made pervasive through associating inferiority with the languages and literacies presented and defined by Black peoples. This can be done, also, through a focus on linguistic justice, as outlined by Baker-Bell (2020). Fifth, there is a need for teachers and school administrators to identify and address variations among Black student populations to avoid monolithic representations that essentialize Black students and their literacies. This can be done by developing an understanding of how Blackness, (im)migration, and language intersect to define Blackness for Black immigrant students (see Smith, 2019, for "a transraciolinguistic approach" [p. 299]; see also Crenshaw, 2021a, on intersectionality). It can also be accomplished by exploring how the languages of African American, African, and Black "English language learners," because of their designated inferiority due to association with Blackness, remain invisible in literacy classrooms and by extension in U.S. bilingual education (Anya, 2020; Bauer, 2019; Bryan, 2020; Cooper, 2020), which has, in turn, historically tended toward anti-Blackness (Flores, 2017; Smith, 2021a, 2021b).

E—Expectations for Personnel in School Districts, Schools, and Classrooms

Unfortunately, there is a cache of online videos where Black elementary-aged children are enduring horrific treatment at the hands of administrators, school resource officers, and/or teachers. The online recordings may be the tip of the iceberg because we cannot be certain how often similar incidents occur that are not recorded. The abuse is usually followed by a uniformed law enforcement officer handcuffing Black children and leading them away to a squad car. Collectively, these incidents are examples of the dehumanization of Black children and bear witness to how early the process of attacking the personhood of Black children can occur. Too often Black children are treated as if they are Black adults, and when Black children act like children, they are victimized for doing so. There is a big push for schools to address trauma (psychological, physical, and verbal abuse) outside of school, but no similar process for addressing trauma that can occur inside schools, especially for Black students. The role of literacy in stemming the dehumanization of Black children is as critical as its role in supposedly enhancing what many seem to emphasize as their "appropriate skill set." If the very literacy meant to save Black children intellectually in schools cannot be the source of their emotional, psychological, and social freedom, indeed, then, this literacy fails in its intent, as the mind of the Black child can only find freedom when the heart and the soul are free. Free souls, free hearts, and free minds through literacy are what we long for when we envision the future of Black children. In so doing, stakeholders can draw on "intersectional awareness" (Crenshaw, 2021a, p. 6) to conduct a review of old policies and practices as well as to establish new, more equitable policies and practices.

What Does the CARE Framework Look Like for Black Parents/Caregivers?

Drawing on the notion of "standard of care" posted on the bill of rights for patients' statements in hospitals, we have crafted CARE expectations that Black parents and guardians should look for: (a) being treated with dignity and respected as informed participants in the education of their child; (b) teachers and school literacy personnel who will take the time to get to know their child as the unique person they are; (c) acceptance as advocates for their children—their queries should be answered honestly and respectfully; and (d) transparency about educational achievement as well as information about acceleration classes and programs, advanced tutoring, and test prep opportunities. In addition, we believe Black parents/guardians should minimally and reasonably expect school district and school administrators, teachers, and literacy personnel to adopt the moral responsibility to honestly and thoughtfully interact with Black children. Literacy learning that occurs, or does not occur, under their watch will require more than good intentions to develop and maintain systems of accountability. Moreover, it is reasonable to expect adults, not children, to be held accountable for literacy learning.

Black students should enter schools and classrooms where they will not be abused (emotionally, mentally, physically, psychologically, sexually, verbally), exploited, neglected, or ridiculed. As fellow humans, Black students should be welcomed, accepted, cared for, and treated with dignity and respect, free from all forms of abuse or harassment.

What Does the CARE Framework Look Like for Black Students' Literacy Learning?

- Black parents and guardians will expect that teachers and support personnel will deliver appropriate (culturally, ethnically, linguistically, and racially) and accurate high-quality literacy instruction, free from needless duplication of reading intervention strategies and assessments;
- Black parents and guardians will be active participants in decisions about their child's literacy instruction;
- Black parents and guardians will ask questions about their child's literacy progress and have their queries addressed in a professional and supportive manner;
- Black parents and guardians will be able to voice concerns about the literacy instruction without fear that their child will be retaliated against;
- Black parents and guardians will be provided with accurate and honest information about the specific literacy needs of their child;
- Black parents and guardians will be provided information about specific ways to support literacy learning at home;
- Black parents and guardians will expect that teachers and support staff will adhere to professional literacy standards and that their performance is continually reviewed;

- Black students' literacy progress data/records should be available for review in a reasonable time frame;
- Black students' literacy progress will be confidential, and the child's privacy protected; and
- Black parents and guardians, without retaliation, can and should refuse literacy instruction by researchers, interns, and students in training. (Adapted from the Hospital Bill of Rights at Carle Foundation Hospital)

We began this book after years of conversations where we voiced our dreams and hopes for the lives of our children as well as those we have taught. We framed this text by building upon our lived experiences as well as an academic foundation (epistemological, ideological, and theoretical understandings of Blackness). We also provided historical knowledge about the belief Black people held in the power of literacy to ensure freedom, liberation, and civil rights. We have shared examples of Black women activist teachers whose sacrifices to provide literacy access are unacknowledged, yet who built upon culturally, linguistically, and racially informed background knowledge to offer appropriate high-quality literacy instruction. In addition, we have shared examples of empirical research, engaged in critical conversations beyond academia and research, posed critical questions for multiple stakeholders to address, and provided additional suggested readings. Finally, drawing on this rich background, we have articulated a conceptual framework to improve literacy instruction for Black students, as well as all students. Our collaborative process offers a model for future inquiries and opportunities on how to translate research into praxis.

> Seeing race is not the problem. Refusing to care for the people we see is the problem . . . We should hope not for a colorblind society but instead for a world in which we can see each other fully, learn from each other, and do what we can to respond to each other with love. (Alexander, 2010, p. 244)

Editor's Note:

Williams, S. O. (2007). *The mis-education of the Negro continues: The connection between the beginning reading instruction delivered to three high-performing Black girls and the instruction delivered within schools designed to colonize.* University of Illinois at Urbana-Champaign, ProQuest Dissertations Publishing.

References

Preface

Evans, M. (1994). "Speak truth to the people," presented at the 1994 Furious Flower Conference. https://furiousflower.org/mari-evans/#speak_truth

Hall, S. (1980). Encoding/decoding. In S. Hall, D. Hobson, A. Love, & P. Willis (Eds.), *Culture, media, language* (pp. 128–38). Hutchinson.

Morrison, T. (2019). Invisible ink: Reading the writing and writing the reading. In T. Morrison (Ed.), *The source of self-regard: Selected essays, speeches, and meditations* (pp. 346–350). Knopf.

Pressley, A. [Ayanna Pressley]. (2020, January 28). #"We belong everywhere. Our truths deserve to be whispered in corridors of power & shouted from rooftops. We belong at every table where decisions are made about our lives, our livelihood, & our justice. Our lives, our stories, & our struggles matter." [Tweet]. Retrieved from: https://twitter.com/ayannapressley/status/1222153935764541441?lang=en

Williams, S. O. (2007). *The mis-education of the Negro continues: The connection between the beginning reading instruction delivered to three high-performing Black girls and the instruction delivered within schools designed to colonize.* University of Illinois at Urbana-Champaign, ProQuest Dissertations Publishing.

Chapter 1

Alexander, M. (2010). *The new Jim Crow.* New Press.

Barajas, J. (2019). Lessons we can learn from Toni Morrison. https://www.pbs.org/newshour/arts/lessons-we-can-learn-from-toni-morrison

Bell, D. (1980). *Brown v. Board of Education* and the interest convergence dilemma. *Harvard Law Review, 93,* 518–533.

Bell, D. (1995). Racial realism. In K. Crenshaw, N. Gotanda, G. Peller, & K. Thomas (Eds.), *Critical race theory: The key writings that formed the movement* (pp. 302–312). New Press.

Bonnick, L. (2007). In the service of neglected people: Anna Julia Cooper, ontology, and education. *Ohio Valley History of Education Society, 38,* pp. 179–197.

Bunyasi, T. L., & Smith, C. (2019). *Stay woke: A people's guide to making All Black Lives Matter*. New York University Press.

Calhoun-Brown, A. (1999). The image of God: Black theology and racial empowerment in the African American community. *Review of Religious Research, 40*(3), 197–212.

Chilisa, B., & Ntseane, G. N. (2010). Resisting dominant discourses: Implications of indigenous, African feminist theory and methods for gender and education research. *Gender and Education, 22,* 617–632.

Cho, S., Crenshaw, K. W., & McCall, L. (2013). Toward a field of intersectionality studies: Theory, applications, and praxis. *Signs: Journal of Women in Culture and Society, 38*(4), 785–810.

Cialdini, R. B., & Trost, M. R. (1998). Social influence: Social norms, conformity, and compliance. In D. T. Gilbert, S. T. Fiske, & G. Lindzey (Eds.), *The handbook of social psychology* (4th ed., pp. 151–192). Oxford University Press.

Collins, P. H. (1990). *Black feminist thought: Knowledge, consciousness, and the politics* of *empowerment*. Routledge.

Collins, P. H. (1998a). The social construction of Black feminist thought. *Signs, 14*(4), 745–773.

Collins, P. H. (1998b). *Fighting words: Black women and the search for justice*. University of Minnesota Press.

Collins, P. H. (2000). *Black feminist thought: Knowledge, consciousness, and the politics of empowerment*. Routledge.

Cone, J. H. (2000). Black liberation theology and black Catholics: A critical conversation. *Theological Studies, 61,* 731–747.

Cooper, A. J. H. (1892). *A voice from the South, by a Black woman from the South*. Negro Universities Press (original privately printed 1892, Aldine Publishing House).

Crenshaw, K. W. (1991). Mapping the margins: Intersectionality, identity politics, and violence against women of color. *Stanford Law Review, 43*(6), 1241–1299.

Crenshaw, K. W. (May 27, 2020). The unmattering of Black lives. *New Republic.* https://newrepublic.com/article/161568/white-supremacy-racism -in-america-kimberle-crenshaw

Crenshaw, K. W. [Sandylocks]. (2021, March 13). *If #Breonna Taylor's story serves as a cornerstone for a generation of activism, it will foreground something new in the freedom struggle: It will make Black women central to any analysis of and challenge to anti-Blackness.* [Tweet]. Retrieved from: https://twitter .com/sandylocks/status/1370815924974985218?lang=en

Crenshaw, K., Gotanda, N., Peller, G., & Thomas, K. (Eds.). (1995). Introduction. In K. Crenshaw, N. Gotanda, G. Peller, and K. Thomas (Eds.), *Critical race theory: The key writings that formed the movement* (pp. xiii–xxxii). New Press.

Darder, A. (2015). Decolonizing interpretive research: A critical bicultural methodology for social change. *The International Education Journal: Comparative Perspectives, 14*(2), 63–77.

De La Garza, A., & Ono, K. (2016). Critical race theory. In K. B. Jensen & R. T. Craig (Eds). *The international encyclopedia of communication theory and philosophy* (pp. 1–9). John Wiley & Sons.

Delgado, R. (1989). Storytelling for oppositionists and others: A plea for narrative. *Michigan Law Review, 87*(8), 2411–2441.

Delpit, L. (1988). The silenced dialogue: Power and pedagogy in educating other people's children. *Harvard Educational Review, 58(3)*, 280–298.

Drexler-Dreis, J. (2019). Decolonial theology in the North Atlantic world. *Brill Research Perspectives in Theology, 3*(3), 1–88.

Frazier, E. F. (1963). *The Negro church in America.* Schocken Books.

Glaude, E. (2016). *Democracy in Black: How race still enslaves the American soul.* Crown.

Hall, S. (1980). Encoding/decoding. In S. Hall, D. Hobson, A. Love, & P. Willis (Eds.), *Culture, media, language* (pp. 128–38). Hutchinson.

hooks, b. (1994). *Teaching to transgress: Education as the practice of freedom.* Routledge.

Ibrahima, A. B., & Mattaini, M. A. (2019). Social work in Africa: Decolonizing methodologies and approaches. *International Social Work, 62*(2), 799–813.

Jones, T. (2019, 9, August 9). *Beloved. Eight black female writers and thinkers on Toni Morrison's life and legacy.* https://www.washingtonpost.com/opinions/2019/08/09/eight-black-women-including-michelle-obama-toni-morrisons-life-legacy/

Khan, U., & Dhar, R. (2006). Licensing effect in consumer choice. *Journal of Marketing Research, 43*(2), 259–266.

Kidder, R. M. (2005). *Moral courage: Taking action when your values are put to the test.* Harper Collins.

Lincoln, C. E., & Mamiya, L. (1990). *The Black church in the African American experience.* Duke University Press.

Lituchy, T. R., & Michaud, J. (2017). A cultural perspective of Africa. In T. R. Lituchy, B. L. Galperin, & B. J. Punnett (Eds.) *LEAD: Leadership effectiveness in Africa and the African diaspora* (pp. 19–31). Palgrave Macmillan.

Lorde, A. (1978). Poetry is not a luxury. (Originally published *Chrysalis: A Magazine of Female Culture*, no. 3 in 1977)

Love, B. J. (2004). Brown plus 50 counter-storytelling: A critical race theory analysis of the "majoritarian achievement gap" story. *Equity and Excellence in Education, 37*(3), 227–246.

Macmillan Education Limited. (2009–2020). Moral imperative. In *Macmillan Dictionary*. Retrieved October 1, 2021, from https://www.macmillandictionary.com/us/dictionary/merica/moral-imperative

Marable, M. (2011). Marxism, memory, and the Black radical tradition: Introduction to volume 13. *Souls 13*(1), 1–16.

Matsinhe, D. M. (2007). Quest for methodological alternatives. *Current Sociology, 55*(6), 836–856.

Matsuda, M. J., Lawrence, C. R., Delgado, R., & Crenshaw, K. W. (1993). *Words that wound: Critical race theory, assaultive speech, and the First Amendment.* Westview Press.

McMillon, G. M. T. (2001). *A tale of two settings: African American students' literacy experiences church and at school.* Michigan State University, ProQuest Dissertations Publishing, 2001, 3021814.

Milgram, S. (1974). *Obedience to authority.* Harper & Row.

Miller, W. I. (2000). *The mystery of courage.* Harvard University Press.

Morrison, T. (2019). Sarah Lawrence Commencement Address. In T. Morrison (Ed.), *The source of self-regard: Selected essays, speeches, and meditations* (pp. 67–73). Knopf.

Oxford University Press. (2020). Parallax. In *Oxford Learner's Dictionaries.* Retrieved October 1, 2021, from https://www.oxfordlearnersdictionaries .com/us/definition/merica/parallax

Phelps, J. T. (2000). Communion ecclesiology and black liberation theology. *Theological Studies, 61,* 672–699.

Robinson, C. (2000). *Black Marxism: The making of the black radical tradition* (2nd ed.). University of North Carolina Press.

Rosa, J., & Flores, N. (2017). Unsettling race and language: Toward a raciolinguistic perspective. *Language in Society, 46*(5), 621–647.

Skitka, L. J. (2012). Moral convictions and moral courage: Common denominators of good and evil. In M. Mikulincer & P. Shaver (Eds.), *Social psychology of morality: Exploring the causes of good and evil* (pp. 349–365). American Psychological Association.

Skitka, L. J., Bauman, C. W., & Lytle, B. L. (2009). The limits of legitimacy: Moral and religious convictions as constraints on deference to authority. *Journal of Personality and Social Psychology, 97,* 567–578.

Stevenson, B. (2017). *The need to talk about race.* Harvard University, Tanner Lecture on Human Values. https://news.harvard.edu/gazette/story/2017 /12/bryan-stevenson-seeks-national-conversation-about-slaverys-legacy/

Walker, A. (2018). Foreword. In Z. N. Hurston (Ed.), *Barracoon: The story of the last Black cargo ship.* Amistad.

Warrican, S. J. (2020). Towards caring language and literacy classrooms for Black immigrant youth: Combatting raciolinguistic ideologies and moral licensing. *Teachers College Record, 122*(13), 1–22.

Willis, A. (2009). *Reading comprehension research and testing in the US: Undercurrents of race, class, and power in the struggle for meaning.* Lawrence Erlbaum.

Willis, A. I. (2018). Re-positioning race in English language arts research. In D. Lapp & D. Fisher (Eds.), *Handbook of research on teaching the English language arts research* (4th ed) (pp. 30–56). Routledge.

Willis, A., Smith, P., Kim, J., & Hsieh, B. (2021). Racial justice in literacy research. *Literacy Research Association.* [Commissioned]. https://www.prnewswire.com/news-releases/racial-justice-research-report-released-by-the-literacy-research-association-301256285.html

Zimbardo, P. G. (2005). A situationist perspective on the psychology of evil: Understanding how good people are transformed into perpetrators. In A. G. Miller (Ed.), *The psychology of good and evil* (pp. 21–50). Guilford Press.

Chapter 2

Alvord, J. W. (1866). *First semi-annual report on schools and finances of freedmen, January 1.* Government Printing Office, 1868; reprint, New York: AMS Press, 1980.

American Tract Society. (1865–1866). "The Freedmen's Spelling-Book." *Online Exhibitions.* https://www.virginiamemory.com/online-exhibitions/items/show/568.

Anderson, J. D. (1988). *The education of blacks in the South, 1860–1935.* University of North Carolina Press.

Asante, M. K. (1992). Afrocentric curriculum. *Educational Leadership, 49*(4), 28–31.

Atwater, D. F., & Gyant, L. (2004). A woman of vision: Dr. Bertha Maxwell-Roddy. *International Journal of Africana Studies, 10,* 117–130.

Baker, C. (2020). *A more perfect reunion: Race, integration, and the future of America.* Hachette Book Group.

Barnett, B. M. (1993). Invisible Southern Black women leaders in the civil rights movement: The triple constraints of gender, race, and class. *Gender and Society, 7*(2),162–182.

Berg, B. L., & Lune, H. (2012). *Qualitative research methods for the social sciences* (8th ed.). Pearson.

The Black Panther. (July 28, 1973).

Blakeslee, S. (1975, June 4). School for Blacks offers money-back guarantee. *New York Times, 35.* Retrieved from ProQuest Historical Newspapers: *The New York Times* with Index, June 11, 2020.

Bloom, J., & Martin, W. (2016). *Black against empire: The history and politics of the Black Panther Party.* University of California Press.

Bly, A. (2011). In pursuit of letters: A history of the Bray schools for enslaved children in colonial Virginia. *History of Education Quarterly, 51*(4), 429–459.

Brosnan, A. (2019). "To educate themselves": Southern Black teachers in North Carolina's schools for the freedpeople during the Civil War and Reconstruction period, 1862–1875. *American Nineteenth Century History, 20*(3), 213–248.

Brown, C. S. (Ed.). (1991). *Septima Clark. Ready from within: A first person narrative.* Africa World Press.

Brown v. Board of Education I, 347 U.S. 483 (1954).

Brown v. Board of Education II, 349 U.S. 294 (1955).

Browne-Marshall, G. J. (2013). *Race, law, and American society 1607–present* (2nd ed.). Routledge.

Charron, K. M. (2009). *Freedom's teacher: The life of Septima Clark*. University of North Carolina Press.

Chotiner, I. (2020, 1 June). *Bryan Stevenson on the frustration behind the George Floyd protests*. https://www.newyorker.com/news/q-and-a/bryan-stevenson-on-the-frustration-behind-the-george-floyd-protests

Clemons, K. M. (2014). "I've got to do something for my people": Black women teachers of the 1964 Mississippi Freedom Schools. *Western Journal of Black Studies, 38*(3), 141–154.

Cobb, C. (n.d.). *Some notes on education*. https://www.crmvet.org/info/cobb_education.pdf

Cobb, C. (1963). *Prospectus for a summer Freedom School Program in Mississippi: A proposal*. http://www.educationanddemocracy.org/FSCfiles/B_05_ProspFor FSchools.htm

Collins, M. (1991). Why I teach. *The Educational Forum, 55*(2), 135–138.

Collins, M. K., & Tamarkin, C. (1982). *Marva Collins' way: Returning to excellence in education*. J. P. Tarcher, Inc.

Collins, P. H. (1990). Black feminist thought in the matrix of domination. In C. Lemert (Ed.), *Social theory: The multicultural and classical readings*. Westview Press.

Collins, P. H. (2000). *Black feminist thought: Knowledge, consciousness, and the politics of empowerment*. Routledge.

Dillingham, M. (1893). Pleasant letters from Calhoun. *The Southern Workman, 23*, 12.

Douglass, F. (1995). *Narrative of the life of Frederick Douglass: An American slave*. Dover Publications (original published 1854).

Forten, C. (1864). Life on the Sea Islands. *The Atlantic Monthly.* Retrieved July 2020: https://www.theatlantic.com/magazine/archive/1864/05/life-on-the-sea-islands/308758/?gclid=CjwKCAjw9vn4BRBaEiwAh0muDCwoI-Sxb77N cgDrvndQGvxoVAtIqL5EJI0-XXnB6AyyPfBi_cee1BoChYgQAvD_BwE

Foster, M. (1997). *Black teachers on teaching*. New World Press.

Freedom School Teacher Orientation Memorandum. (1964). *Memorandum to Freedom School Teachers*. https://www.crmvet.org/docs/fs64_memorandum.pdf

Georgia Women of Achievement. (1992). *Who is Lucy Craft Laney?* https://lucylaney.mpls.k12.mn.us/history_of_lucey_craft_laney

Hale, J. (2011). "The student as a force for change": The Mississippi Freedom Schools and student engagement. *Journal of African American History, 96*(3), 325–347.

Hall, S. (1980). Encoding/decoding. In S. Hall, D. Hobson, A. Love, & P. Willis (Eds.), *Culture, media, language* (pp. 128–38). Hutchinson.

Harris, V. J. (1992). African-American conceptions of literacy: A historical perspective. *Theory into Practice, 31*(4), 276–286.

Heim, J. (2021, February 24). *At William & Mary, a school for free and enslaved Black children is rediscovered.* https://www.washingtonpost.com/education /bray-school-william-mary/2021/02/24/d7888cc8-76c8-11eb-948d -19472e683521_story.html

Hilliard, A. G. (1976). *Alternatives to IQ testing: An approach to the identification of "gifted" minority children. Final report to the California State Department of Education, Special Education Support Unit.* Columbia University. (ERIC Clearinghouse on Early Childhood Education, ED 146–009).

hooks, b. (1994*). Teaching to transgress: Education as the practice of freedom.* Routledge.

Hoover, M. E. R. (1978). Characteristics of Black schools at grade level: A description. *The Reading Teacher, 31*(7), 757–762.

Hoover, M. E. R. (1992). The Nairobi Day School: An African American Independent School, 1966–1984. *Journal of Negro Education, 61*(2), 201–210.

Huggins, E. (2007). *The Liberations Schools, the Children's House, the Intercommunal Youth Institute and the Oakland Community School.* Oakland IYI/OCS Photo Gallery.

Huggins, E. (2020). *Erika Huggins: The Official Website.* https://www.ericka huggins.com/bio

Huggins, E., & LeBlanc-Ernest, A. D. (2009). Revolutionary women, revolutionary education: The Black Panther Party's Oakland Community School. In D. Gore, J. Theoharis, & K. Woodard (Eds.), *Want to start a revolution?: Radical women in the Black freedom struggle* (pp.161–184). New York University Press.

Jackson, T. O., & Howard, T. C. (2014). The continuing legacy of Freedom Schools as sites of possibility for equity and social justice for Black students. *Western Journal of Black Studies, 38*(3), 155–162.

Jacobs, H. A. (1861). *Incidents in the life of a slave girl: Written by herself.* Post.

Johnson, S. T., & Anderson, D. K. (1992). Legacies and lessons from independence schools. The *Journal of Negro Education, 61*(2), 121–124.

Johnson, W. B. (1991). A Black teacher and her school in Reconstruction Darien: The correspondence of Hettie Sabattie and J. Murray Hoag, 1868–1869. *The Georgia Historical Quarterly, 75*(1), 90–105.

Kendi, I. X. (2016). *Stamped from the beginning: The definitive history of racists ideas in America.* Bold Type Books.

Kendi, I. X. (2019). *How to be an anti-racist.* One World.

King, J. E. (2017). Education research in the Black liberation tradition: Return what you learn to the people. *Journal of Negro Education, 86*(2), 95–114.

Klass, K. (2017, August 7). Keeping "an era alive": Georgia Washington remembered. *Montgomery Advertiser.* https://www.montgomeryadvertiser.com /story/news/2017/08/07/keeping/529717001

Ladson-Billings, G. (1994). *The dreamkeepers: Successful teachers of African American children.* Jossey-Bass Publishers.

Ladson-Billings, G. (1995). But that's just good teaching! The case for culturally relevant pedagogy. *Theory into Practice, 34*(3), 159–165.

Lockwood, L. C. (1862). *Mary S. Peake: The colored teacher at Fortress Monroe.* American Tract Society. http://www.loyalbooks.com/download/text/Mary-S-Peake-by-Lewis-C-Lockwood.txt

Lomotey, K. (2010). Black Panther Party Liberation Schools. *Encyclopedia of African American Education.* Sage.

Ludlow, H. W. (1893). Georgia's investment. *The Southern Workman, 36*(3), 219–235.

McCluskey, A. T. (1997). "We specialize in the wholly impossible": Black women school founders and their mission. *Signs, 22*(2), 403–426.

McKamey, P. (2020, June 17). *What anti-racist teachers do differently.* https://www.theatlantic.com/education/archive/2020/06/how-be-anti-racist-teacher/613138

Menkart, D., & View, J. L. (2021). *Exploring the history of the Freedom Schools: Freedom Schools curricula.* https://www.civilrightsteaching.org/exploring-history-freedom-schools

Monaghan, E. J. (2005). *Learning to read and write in colonial America.* University of Massachusetts Press.

Newton, H. P. (1975). Oakland Community School opens fifth year. *The Black Panther, 24*(1), 1, 25.

The Official Site of the Black Panther Party Worldwide. (2021). *Children of the revolution: About Oakland Community School.* http://www.itsabouttimebpp.com/Children/Children_index.html

Palo Alto Weekly. (May 15, 2002). Gertrude Wilks: Trying to change the world. https://www.paloaltoonline.com/weekly/morgue/2002/2002_05_15.gertrudewilks.html

Paris, D. (2012). Culturally sustaining pedagogy. *Educational Researcher, 41*(3), 93–97.

Payne, C. M. (1997). *Education for activism: Mississippi's Freedom Schools in the 1960s.* Paper presented at the Annual Meeting of the American Educational Research Association. https://files.eric.ed.gov/fulltext/ED410653.pdf

Peavy, L. (1993). *Promoting liberation literacy: A grassroots solution. Cultural keepers: Enlightening and empowering our communities: Proceedings of the First National Conference of African American Librarians* (pp. 212–215). Black Caucus of the American Library Association.

Perlstein, D. (2005). Chapter 2: Minds stayed on freedom: Politics and pedagogy in the African American freedom struggle. *Counterpoints, 237,* 35–65.

Phillips, M. (2014). The educational studies feminist leadership of Ericka Huggins in the Black Panther Party. *Black Diaspora, 4*(1), 187–221.

Phillips, M. (2015). The power of the first-person narrative: Ericka Huggins and the Black Panther Party. *Women's Studies Quarterly, 43*–3/4), 33–51.

Ramsey, S. (2012). Caring is activism: Black Southern womanist teachers: Theorizing and the careers of Kathleen Crosby and Bertha Maxwell-Roddey, 1946–1986. *Educational Studies, 48*(3), 244–265.

Reynolds, J., & Kendi, I. (2020). *Stamped: Racism, antiracism, and you*. Little, Brown and Company.

Rickford, R. (2016). African restoration and the promise and pitfalls of cultural politics. In *We are an African people: Independent education, Black power, and the radical imagination* (2nd ed., pp. 100–138). Oxford University Press.

Robinson, R. P. (2020). Until the revolution: Analyzing the politics, pedagogy, and curriculum of the Oakland Community School. *Espacio, Tiempo y Educación, 7*(1), 181–203.

Rofel, L., & Tai, J. (2016). A conversation with Ericka Huggins. *Feminist Studies, 42*–1), 236–248.

Siddle-Walker, V., & Tompkins, R. H. (2004). Caring in the past: The case of a southern segregated African American school. In V. Siddle-Walker & J. R. Snarey (Eds.), *Race-ing moral formation: African American perspectives of care and justice* (pp. 77–92). Teachers College Press.

Simkin, J. (2020). *Education of slaves*. https://spartacus-educational.com/USA Seducation.htm

Smith, C. A., Williams, E. L., Wadud, I. A., Pirtle, N. L., & The Cite Black Women Collective. (2021). Cite Black women: A critical praxis (A Statement). *Feminist Anthropology, 2*(1), 10–17.

Taaffe, L. (2019, 23, January). *East Palo Alto educator dies at 91*. https://www.paloaltoonline.com/news/2019/01/23/east-palo-alto-educational-pioneer-dies-at-91

Washington, G. (1893). Letters from Hampton graduates: A letter from the Calhoun School. *The Southern Workman, 23*, 11.

Wilkerson, I. (2010). *The warmth of other suns: The epic story of America's great migration*. Vintage.

Wilks, G. (1990). The Nairobi Day School, Gertrude Wilks. In M. Hoover, N. Dabney, & S. Lewis (Eds.), *Successful Black and minority schools: Classic models* (pp. 26–31). Julian Richardson & Associates.

Williams, H. A. (2005). *Self-taught: African American education in slavery and freedom*. University of North Carolina Press.

Williamson, J. A. (2005). Community control with a Black nationalist twist: The Black Panther Party's educational programs. *Counterpoints, 237*, 137–157.

Willis, A. I. (2002). Literacy at Calhoun Colored School, 1892–1943. *Reading Research Quarterly, 37*(1), 8–44.

Wong, C. (2012). *The pedagogy and education of the Black Panther Party: Confronting the reproduction of social and cultural inequality*. Master's thesis, New York University.

Chapter 3

Collins, P. H. (1990). *Black feminist thought: Knowledge, consciousness, and the politics of empowerment*. Routledge, Chapman & Hall.

Crenshaw, K. W., Ocen, P., & Nanda, J. (2015). *Black girls matter: Pushed out, overpoliced and underprotected*. African American Policy Forum. Center for Intersectionality and Social Policy Studies. Columbia Law.

Delpit, L. (1995). *Other people's children*. The New York Press.

Dillard, C. B. (2000). The substance of things hoped for, the evidence of things not seen: Examining an endarkened feminist epistemology in educational research and leadership. *Qualitative Studies in Education, 13*(6), 661–684.

Fontana, A., & Frey, J. H. (2000). The interview: From structured questions to negotiated text. In N. Denzin & Y. Lincoln (Eds.), *Handbook of qualitative research* (2nd ed.). Sage.

Greene, D. T. (2016). "We need more 'US' in schools!!": Centering Black adolescent girls' literacy and language practices in online school spaces. *The Journal of Negro Education, 85*(3), 274–289.

Harris, V. (1995). Using African-American literature in the classroom. In V. L. Gadsden & D. A. Wagner (Eds.), *Reading among African-American youth: Issues in learning, teachings and schooling* (pp. 229–260). Hampton Press.

Henry, A. (2001). The politics of unpredictability in a reading/writing/discussion group with girls from the Caribbean. *Theory into Practice, 40*(3), 184–189.

Ladson-Billings, G. (2000). Racialized discourses and ethnic epistemologies. In N. Denzin & Y. Lincoln (Eds.), *Handbook of qualitative research* (2nd ed., pp. 257–275). Sage.

Roediger, D. (2003). *How racism becomes common sense: Media and sports in Champaign-Urbana*. The Public I. http://print.ucimc.org

Sims, R. (1982). *Shadow and substance: Afro-American experience in contemporary children's fiction*. National Council of Teachers of English.

Williams, S. O. (2007). *The mis-education of the Negro continues: The connection between the beginning reading instruction delivered to three high-performing Black girls and the instruction delivered within schools designed to colonize*. University of Illinois at Urbana-Champaign, ProQuest Dissertations Publishing.

Chapter 4

Cazden, C. (1988). *Classroom discourse: The language of teaching and learning*. Heinemann.

Handbook of research on literacy instruction: Issues of diversity, policy and equity. (pp. 137–157). Guilford Press.

McMillon, G. M. T. (2001). *A tale of two settings: African American students' literacy experiences at church and at school.* Unpublished doctoral dissertation, Michigan State University.

McMillon, G. M. T., & Edwards, P. A. (2000). Why does Joshua hate school? . . . But love Sunday school? *Language Arts 78*(2), 111–120.

O'Connor, M. C., & Michaels, S. (1996). Shifting participant frameworks: Orchestrating thinking practices in group discussion. In D. Hicks (Ed.), *Discourse learning and schooling.* Cambridge University Press.

Chapter 5

Baker-Bell, A. (2020). *Linguistic justice: Black language, literacy, identity, and pedagogy.* Routledge.

García, O., & Wei, L. (2014). *Translanguaging: Language, bilingualism and education* (pp. 5–18). Palgrave Macmillan.

Kachru, B. B. (1992). Teaching world Englishes. In B. B. Kachru (Ed.), *The other tongue: English across cultures* (2nd ed.), (pp. 355–366). University of Illinois Press.

Luke, A. (2012). Critical literacy: Foundational notes. *Theory into Practice, 51*(1), 4–11.

Rosa, J. & Flores, N. (2017). Unsettling race and language: Toward a raciolinguistic perspective. *Language in Society,* 1–27.

Smith, P. (2019). (Re)positioning in the Englishes and (English) literacies of a Black immigrant youth: Towards a "transraciolinguistic" approach. *Theory into Practice, 58*(3), 292–303. DOI:10.1080/00405841.2019.1599227

Smith, P. (2020a). Silencing invisibility: Towards a framework for Black immigrant literacies. *Teachers College Record, 122*(13), 1–42.

Smith, P. (2020b). The case for translanguaging in Black immigrant literacies. *Literacy Research: Theory Method, and Practice, 69*(1), 192–210. https://doi.org/10.1177/2381336920937264

Smith, P. (2020c). "Mr. Wang doesn't really care how we speak!": Responsiveness in the practice of an exemplary Asian-American teacher. *The Urban Review, 52,* 351–275. https://doi.org/10.1007/s11256-019-00531-4

Smith, P. (2021a). Five steps to address anti-Blackness: Black immigrant literacies. *International Literacy Research Association Literacy Now Blog.*

Smith, P. (2021b). Beyond anti-Blackness in bilingual education: Looking through the lens of the Black immigrant subject. American Educational Research Association *Bilingual Education Research Special Interest Group Newsletter,* Spring Edition.

Smith, P., Lee, J., & Chang, R. (2022, Advance online publication). Characterizing competing tensions in Black immigrant literacies: Beyond partial representations of *success. Reading Research Quarterly.* https://doi.org/10.1002/rrq.375

Smith, P., & Warrican, S.J. (2021). Critical awareness for literacy teachers and educators in troubling times. *Literacy Practice and Research,* 1–20.

Smith, P., & Warrican, S. J. (2022). Migrating while multilingual and Black: Beyond the "(bi)dialectal" burden. In E. Bauer, L. Sánchez, Y. Wang, & A. Vaughan (Eds.), *A transdisciplinary lens for bilingual education: Bridging translanguaging, sociocultural research, cognitive approaches, and student learning* (pp. 102–108). Routledge.

Smith, P., Warrican, S. J., & Kumi-Yeboah, A. (2016). Linguistic and cultural appropriations of a multilingual literacy teacher educator: An autoethnographic self-study. *Studying Teacher Education, 12*(1), 88–112. https://doi .org/10.1080/17425964.2016.1143811.

Willis, A., Smith, P., Kim, J., & Hsieh, B. (2021). Racial justice in literacy research. *Literacy Research Association.* [Commissioned]. https://www .prnewswire.com/news-releases/racial-justice-research-report-released -by-the-literacy-research-association-301256285.html

Chapter 6

Connor, J. J., & Willis, A. I. (2009). African American adolescent males reflect on critically framing: *A lesson before dying.* In L. Spears-Bunton & R. Powell (Eds.), *Toward a literacy of promise: Joining the African American struggle* (pp. 81–104). Routledge.

Literature cited

Gaines, E. J. (1997). *A lesson before dying.* Vintage.

Chapter 7

Alexander, M. (2010). *The new Jim Crow.* New Press.

Alim, H., & Smitherman, G. (2020). "Perfect English" and white supremacy. In J. McIntosh & N. Mendoza-Denton (Eds.), *Language in the Trump era: Scandals and emergencies* (pp. 226–236). Cambridge University Press.

American Psychological Association. (2021). *APA apologizes for longstanding contributions to systemic racism.* https://www.apa.org/news/press/releases/2021 /10/apology-systemic-racism?utm_source=twitter&utm_medium=social& utm_campaign=apa-press-release-racism&utm_content=apology-systemic -racism

American Psychological Association. (2021). *Historical chronology: Examining psychology's contributions to the belief in racial hierarchy and perpetuation of inequality for people of color in U.S.* https://www.apa.org/about/apa /addressing-racism/historical-chronology

Anya, U. (2020). African Americans in world language study: The forged path and future directions. *Annual Review of Applied Linguistics, 40,* 97–112.

Baker-Bell, A. (2020). *Linguistic justice: Black language, literacy, identity, and pedagogy.* Routledge.

Banks, J. A., & Banks, C. A. M. (2019). *Multicultural education: Issues and perspectives* (10th ed.). Wiley.

Bauer, E. B. (2019). Kindergartners' writing in a dual-language classroom. *Language Arts, 96*(4), 213–223.

Bonilla-Silva, E. (2003). *Racism without racists: Color-blind racism and the persistence of racial inequality in the United States.* Rowman & Littlefield Publishers.

Bonilla-Silva, E. (2012). The invisible weight of Whiteness: The racial grammar of everyday life in America. *Michigan Sociological Review, 26,* 1–15.

Bonilla-Silva, E. (2015). More than prejudice: Restatement, reflections, and new directions in critical race theory. *Sociology of Race and Ethnicity, 1*(1), 75–89.

Boutte, G. S., King, J. E., Johnson, G. L., & King, L. J. (Eds.). (2021). *We be lovin' Black children: Learning to be literate about the African diaspora.* Stylus Publishing.

Bryan, K. (2020). "I had to get tougher": An African immigrant's (counter) narrative of language, race, and resistance. *Teachers College Press, 122*(13), 1–28.

Busia, A. (1989). What is your nation? Reconstructing Africa and her diaspora through Paule Marshall's *Praisesong for the widow.* In C. Wall (Ed.), *Changing our own words: Essays on criticism, theory, and writing by Black women* (pp. 196–211). Rutgers University Press.

Cabrera, N. L. (2018). Where is the racial theory in critical race theory? A constructive criticism of the Crits. *Review of Higher Education, 42*(1), 209–233.

Chin, M. J., Quinn, D. M., Dhaliwal, T. K., & Lovison, V. S. (2020). Bias in the air: A nationwide exploration of teachers' implicit racial attitudes, aggregate bias, and student outcomes. *Educational Researcher, 49*(8), 566–578.

Cooper, A. (2020). Justice for all: Realities and possibilities of Black English learners in K–12 schools. *Teachers College Record, 122*(13), 1–24.

Crenshaw, K. W. [@sandylocks]. (2021a, February 20). *The chronic failure to confront the monsters of our past is not destiny; it's a daily choice to accept American myth in the face of so much countervailing evidence* [Tweet]. Twitter https://twitter.com/sandylocks/status/1363258931108175873

Crenshaw, K. W. (2021b). *A primer on intersectionality.* American Policy Forum. https://www.aapf.org/publications

Crenshaw, K. W. (2021c, March 22). The eternal fantasy of a racially virtuous America. *The New Republic.* https://newrepublic.com/article/161568/white-supremacy-racism-in- merica-kimberle-crenshaw

Evans, M. (1994). *Speak truth to the people* [Paper presentation]. Furious Flower Conference. https://furiousflower.org/mari-evans/#speak_truth.

Flores, N. (2017). Do Black Lives Matter in bilingual education? https://blmtraue.commons.gc.cuny.edu/2017/03/07/do-black-lives-matter-in-bilingual-education

Freire, P., & Ramos, M. B. (1970). *Pedagogy of the oppressed.* Continuum.

García, O. (2015). Critical multilingual language awareness and teacher education. *Language Awareness and Multilingualism*, 1–17. Springer.

Gay, G. (2000). *Culturally responsive teaching: Theory, research, and practice.* Teachers College Press.

Goguen, D. (2021). *What is the "medical standard of care" in a medical malpractice case?* https://www.nolo.com/legal-encyclopedia/what-the-medical-standard-care-malpractice-case.html

Guinier, L. (2004). From racial liberalism to racial literacy: *Brown v. Board of Education* and the interest-divergence dilemma. *Journal of American History*, *91*(1), 92–118.

Haddix, M. (2017). Diversifying teaching and teacher education. *Journal of Literacy Research*, *49*(1), 141–149.

Harris, C. I. (1993). *Whiteness as property.* UCLA School of Law, Public Law & Legal Theory Research Paper Series Research Paper No. 06-35, 1710–1791.

King, J. E. (1992). Diaspora literacy and consciousness in the struggle against miseducation in the Black community. *Journal of Negro Education*, *61*(3), 317–340.

Kinney, E. D. (2004). The origins and promise of medical standard of care. *Virtual Mentor*, *6*(12), 574–576.

Ladson-Billings, G. (1994). *The dreamkeepers: Successful teachers of African American children.* Jossey-Bass Publishers.

Ladson-Billings, G. (1995). But that's just good teaching! The case for culturally relevant pedagogy. *Theory into Practice*, *34*(3), 159–165.

Louis, D. A., Michel, S. D., Deranek, J. E., & Louis, S. L. (2018). Reflection, realization, and reaffirmation: Voices of Black and White faculty members engaged in cross-racial mentoring. *Multicultural Perspectives*, *20*(4), 205–215.

Marusak, J. (2021, March 14). NC school system apologized for racist student hashtags by 4th graders during Civil War lesson. *Charlotte Observer.* https://www.charlotteobserver.com › article249916698

McKinney de Royston, M., Madkins, T. C., Givens, J. R., & Nasir, N. S. (2021). "I'm a teacher, I'm gonna always protect you": Understanding Black educators' protection of Black children. *American Educational Research Journal*, *58*(1), 68–106.

McMillon, G. T., & Rogers, R. (2019). Racial literacy: Ebony and ivory perspectives of race in two graduate courses. In K. T. Han & J. Laughter (Eds.), *Critical race theory in teacher education: Informing classroom culture and practice* (pp. 46–58), New York, NY: Teachers College Press.

Medical Dictionary for the Health Professions and Nursing. (2012). Standard of care. https://medical-dictionary.thefreedictionary.com/standard+of+care

Moffett, P. & Moore, G. (2011). The standard of care: Legal history and definitions: The bad and good news. *Western Journal of Emergency Medicine*, *12*(1), 109–112.

Morrison, T. (1975, May 30). *A humanist view*. Portland State University. https://www.mackenzian.com/wp-content/uploads/2014/07/Transcript _PortlandState_TMorrison.pdf

Muhammad, G. (2020). *Cultivating genius: An equity framework for culturally and historically responsive literacy*. Scholastic.

Nasir, N. S., Lee, C. D., Pea, R., & McKinney de Royston, M. (Eds.). (2020). *The handbook of the cultural foundations of learning*. Routledge.

Paris, D., & Alim, H. S. (Eds.). (2017). *Culturally sustaining pedagogies: Teaching and learning for justice in a changing world*. Teachers College Press.

Rosa, J., & Flores, N. (2017). Unsettling race and language: Toward a raciolinguistic perspective. *Language in Society, 46*(5), 621–647.

Roxas, K., Dade, K. B. M., & Rios, F. (2017). Institutionalizing internationalization within a College of Education: Toward a more critical multicultural and global education perspective. In Y. K. Cha, J. Gundura, S. H. Ham, & M. Lee (Eds.), *Multicultural education in glocal perspectives* (pp. 201–213). Springer.

Sealey-Ruiz, Y. (2021). *Racial literacy*. A policy research brief. National Council of Teachers of English.

Skutnabb-Kangas, T. (1988). Multilingualism and the education of minority children. In T. Skutnabb-Kangas & J. Cummins (Eds.), *Minority education: From shame to struggle* (pp. 9–44). Multilingual Matters.

Smith, P. (2019). (Re)Positioning in the Englishesand (English) literacies of a Black immigrant youth: Towards a 'transraciolinguistic' approach. *Theory into Practice, 58*(3), 292–303. DOI:10.1080/00405841.2019.1599227

Smith, P. (2021a). Five steps to address anti-Blackness: Black immigrant literacies. International Literacy Research Association Literacy Now Blog.

Smith, P. (2021b). *Beyond anti-Blackness in bilingual education: Looking through the lens of the Black immigrant subject*. American Educational Research Association Bilingual Education Research Special Interest Group Newsletter, Spring Edition.

Smith, P., & Hajek, S. (2021). Prism of promise: Towards responsive tools for diverse classrooms. In G. Li, J. Hare, & J. Anderson (Eds.), *Superdiversity and teacher education*. Routledge.

Smith, P., Karkar, T., Varner, J., Nigam, A., & Finch, B. (2020). Making visible awareness in practice: Literacy educators in diverse classrooms. *Review of Education, 8*(2), 380–415.

Smith, P., Kumi-Yeboah, A., Chang, R., Lee, J., & Frazier, P. (2019). Rethinking (under)performance for Black English speakers: Beyond achievement to opportunity. *Journal of Black Studies, 50*(6), 528–554.

Smith, P., Lee, J., & Chang, R. (2022). Characterizing competing tensions in Black immigrant literacies: Beyond partial representations of success. *Reading Research Quarterly. Reading Research Quarterly*, https://doi.org/10.1002 /rrq.375

Smith, P. & Warrican, J. (2021). Critical awareness for literacy teachers and educators in troubling times. *Literacy Practice and Research, 46*(2), 1–20.

Tanghe, S. (2016). Promoting critical racial awareness in teacher education in Korea: Reflections on a racial discrimination simulation activity. *Asia Pacific Education Review, 17*(2), 203–215.

Willis, A. I. (2002). Dissin' and disremembering: Historical and cultural knowledge needed in middle school language arts. *Reading and Writing Quarterly, 18*(4), 293–319.

Willis, A. I. (2017). Re-positioning race in English language arts research. In D. Lapp & D. Fisher (Eds.), *Handbook of research on teaching the English language arts* (pp. 30–56). Routledge.

Willis, A. I., Lewis, K. C., & Ladson-Billings, G. (1998). A conversation with Gloria Ladson-Billings. *Language Arts, 75*(1), 61–70.

Willis, A., Smith, P., Kim, J., & Hsieh, B. (2021). Racial justice in literacy research. *Literacy Research Association.* [Commissioned]. https://www .prnewswire.com/news-releases/racial-justice-research-report-released -by-the-literacy-research-association-301256285.html

Index

Academic achievement, 54, 59, 80, 131–133
Academic assessment, 62, 71–72, 96, 154
Access to education. *See* Education access
Adultification, 156
Aesha case study
  analysis, 64–67
  authors' discussion, 68–72
  conclusions, 67–68
  discussion questions, 72
  first-grade development, 61–64
  kindergarten experience, 59–61
  methods, 55–56, 63
  preschool experience, 57–59
  research culmination, 63–64
  researcher background, 53–54
  student background, 56–57
  suggested readings, 72–73
African American speech, 47
Afrocentric schools, 45
Alexander, M., 158
Alim, H., 154
Alim, H. S., 147
Alvord, J. W., 27
American Missionary Association (AMA), 26, 28
American Psychological Association (APA), 147–148
American Tract Society, 29
Anderson, D. K., 45
Anderson, J. D., 19, 28, 29
Anya, U., 156
APA (American Psychological Association), 147–148
Asante, M. K., 45

Assimilation, 29, 31
Athletic ability, 80–81
Atlantic Monthly, 27
Atwater, D. F., 33, 34
Audience in writing, 114–118
Awareness of anti-Blackness, 153–154

Baker, C., 23
Baker-Bell, A., 101, 155
Banks, C.A.M., 146
Banks, J. A., 146
Barajas, J., 2
Barnett, B. M., 51
Bauer, E. B., 156
Bauman, C. W., 5
Bay, B., 43
Behavior management. *See* Disciplining youth
Bell, D., 13
Berg, B. L., 20
Bible, the, 22–23
Black boys' literacy, 126, 134–135, 137
Black churches. *See* by name; Religion
Black English, 47
Black feminism, 10–12, 142
Black girls' literacy. *See* Aesha case study
Black-immigrant-youth research study
  authors' discussion, 119–122
  guiding questions, 122–123
  Jorge case study, 107–110
  researcher background and reflections, 102–107, 110–111
  researcher's work in Texas (outreach), 110–111
  structure of chapter, 101–102
  suggested readings, 123–124

Black-immigrant-youth research study
    (continued)
  youth perspectives on literacy,
      112–118
Black independent schools.
    See Independent Black
    institutions (IBIs)
Black Liberation schools, 40, 41–42
Black liberation theology, 8–10
Black male culture, 94–95, 98–100
Black Panther, 44
Black Panther Party (BPP), 40–45
Black Power movement, 47
Black radical tradition, 12–13, 142
Black subordination. See White
    supremacy
Black Vernacular English, 47, 84–85
Black women activist teachers, 19–24,
    50–52. See also by name
Blakeslee, S., 46
Bloom, J., 41
Bly, A., 23
Bonilla-Silva, E., 144
Bonnick, L., 10
Boredom, 92, 93
Boutte, G. S., 155
Brosnan, A., 27
Brown, C. S., 36
Browne-Marshall, G. J., 22, 34
Brown v. Board of Education, 32
Bryan, K., 156
Bullying, 78–79
Bunyasi, T. L., 13
Bureau of Refugees, Freedmen, and
    Abandoned Land. See Freedmen's
    Bureau
Busia, A., 155
Bussing, 34

Cabrera, N. L., 155
Calhoun-Brown, A., 8
Calhoun Colored School (CCS),
    28–29, 30, 31
CARE framework
  background, 148–150
  elements of, 150–156
  parents and caregivers, 156–157
  students' learning, 157–158

Cazden, C., 88
Centering Blackness, 122–123, 150–153
Chang, R., 110, 154
Charlotte Observer, 145–146
Charron, K. M., 36
Child, L. M., 25
Chilisa, B., 15
Chin, M. J., 152
Cho, S., 11
Chotiner, I., 21
Christianity. See Religion
Christ Presbyterian Church, 31
Church role in education. See Religion
Cialdini, R. B., 4
Citizenship Schools, 36–37
Civil rights, 32, 35–40
Classroom management. See
    Disciplining youth
Clemente case study
  authors' discussion, 134–139
  focal student description, 129–130
  guiding questions, 139–140
  researcher reflections, 133–134
  research methods, 128–129
  study background, 126–127
  suggested readings, 140
Clemons, K. M., 39–40
Cobb, C., 37–38
Code-switching, 85
Collins, M., 49
Collins, M. K., 48–50, 49, 50
Collins, P. H., 11, 32, 54
Colonialism, 14–16, 29, 41, 67, 142.
    See also Decolonial theories
Community schools. See Independent
    Black institutions (IBIs)
Cone, J. H., 8
Connor, J. J., 127
Cooper, A., 156
Cooper, A.J.H., 10
Cotton production and school
    schedule, 37
Crenshaw, K., 11, 12, 14
Crenshaw, K. W., 11, 12, 13–14, 68,
    142, 144, 146, 153
Critical lens
  multicultural awareness, 151–153
  multilingual awareness, 152–153

racial awareness, 13–14, 141, 151–153, 155
reader response theory, 128
Critical race theory, 141, 155. *See also* Critical lens: racial awareness
Crosby, K., 33–35
Cultural dissonance, 91–92, 95
Culture, 93–94, 129–130, 132, 143–147. *See also* Black male culture; Cultural dissonance
Culture versus *race*, 143–146
Curricular materials, 29, 40, 44, 47, 135, 154–155
Curriculum, 28–29, 36, 38–39, 40, 43–45, 48–49, 59, 132. *See also* Curricular materials

Dade, K.B.M., 152
Daniel Hale Williams Westside Preparatory School, 49–50
Darder, A., 15, 16
Decolonial theories, 14–16, 141
Deficit perspective, 97, 154, 155–156. *See also* Deficit theories
Deficit theories, 66, 67–68, 94
Dehumanization, 68, 78–79, 144, 156. *See also* Humanization
De La Garza, A., 14
Delgado, R., 13, 14
Delpit, L., 7, 67
Deranek, J. E., 153
Desegregation, 32, 33–35
Dhaliwal, T. K., 152
Dhar, R., 5
Dillard, C. B., 54
Dillingham, M., 30
Disciplining youth, 61–62, 64, 67, 83, 86–87, 88–89, 94
Distrust, 66
Dominant ideology. *See* White supremacy
Douglass, F., 23
Drexler-Dreis, J., 15

East Palo Alto (CA), 46
Ebonics, 47
Education access, 19, 21, 22, 24, 87–88, 142, 144–145. *See also* Isolation

Educational control, 45
Educational neglect, 54, 64–67, 68, 69, 70, 76, 94
Education policy, 54, 72, 100, 122–123
Edwards, P. A., 84
Emotional maturity, 138–139
Empowerment, 35, 40–45, 47
English-language learners, 59
Enslavement of Africans, 21–23
Equity in education, 32, 146–147, 154–156
European norms, 118
Evans, M., 141
Exclusion. *See* Education access
Expectations for ability, 31, 54, 69, 86, 97, 107, 129–130, 134–135, 136–137
Expectations for behavior, 89, 90
Expectations (of care) for educators, 145, 149, 151–152, 156

Faith-based schools. *See* Religion
Finch, B., 152
First-grade classroom research study
authors' discussion, 93–99
classroom design, 83–84
communication style, 84–85
conclusions, 92
participants: Tony, 77–80
participants: Travis, 80–83
pedagogy, 86
questions for discussion, 99–100
researcher background, 75–76
research setting, 76–77
social norms, 86–92
suggested readings, 100
Flores, N., 6, 110, 155, 156
Fontana, A., 56
Forsythe, R. M., 32–33
Forten, C., 27
Forten, C.L.B., 26–29
Fortress Monroe, 26
Foster, M., 31, 32–33
Fragmented instruction, 65
Frazier, E. F., 9
Frazier, P., 154
Freedmen's Bureau, 26, 28
Freedmen's Speller (American Tract Society), 29

Freedom Schools, 37–40
Frey, J. H., 56

Gaines, E. J., 128, 131
García, O., 110, 152
Gay, G., 147, 149
Georgia Women of Achievement, 31
Gertrude Wilks Academy. *See* Nairobi
    Day School
Gifted education, 62, 71–72
Giftedness, 62, 68, 71–72, 77–82, 92,
    94, 96
Givens, J. R., 145
Gladney, I.M.B., 37
Glaude, E., 4, 6, 16
Goguen, D., 149
Gotanda, N., 11, 13–14
Greene, D. T., 37
Guinier, L., 155
Gyant, L., 33, 34

Haddix, M., 152
Haines, F.E.H. (Mrs.), 31
Haines Normal Institute and Industrial
    School, 31
Hajek, S., 153
Hale, J., 38
Hall, S., 19
Hampton Institute, 30
Hampton-Washington model of
    education, 28, 29
Harris, V., 66
Harris, V. J., 19
Head Start, 34
Heim, J., 22
Henry, A., 37
Hilliard, A. G., 47
Historical knowledge of anti-Blackness,
    153–154
Historical research methodology,
    20–21
Home language, 47
Home literacy practices, 81–82, 93
hooks, b., 10, 34–35
Hoover, M., 47
Hoover, M.E.R., 47–48
Howard, T. C., 37
Howard University, 34

Hsieh, B., 7, 107
Huggins, E. (née Ericka Cozette
    Jenkins), 42, 43, 44
Huggins, J., 42
Humanization, 99, 108, 132–133,
    142, 149–150, 157. *See also*
    Dehumanization

IBIs (independent Black institutions),
    45–50
Ibrahima, A. B., 15
Identity, 68, 69, 79, 97, 107–108,
    109–110, 146
Imperialism. *See* Colonialism
Implicit rules of behavior, 91, 118, 138
Inadequate instruction. *See*
    Educational neglect
Incarceration, 54
Incidents in the Life of a Slave Girl
    (Jacobs), 24
Independent Black institutions (IBIs),
    45–50
Instructional methods. *See* Pedagogy
Integration, 32, 33–35
Intercommunal Youth Institute. *See*
    Oakland Community School
Intersecting identities, 107–108, 146
Isolation, 87–88, 98

Jackson, M., 24
Jackson, T. O., 37
Jacobs, H. A., 24–25
Jenkins, E. C. *See* Huggins, E. (née
    Ericka Cozette Jenkins)
Jenkins, S. W., 53–54. *See also* Aesha
    case study
Johnson, A., 100
Johnson, G. L., 155
Johnson, S. T., 45
Johnson, W. B., 27, 28
Johnson C. Smith University, 34
Jones, T., 18
Joy, 142

Kachru, B. B., 101
Karkar, T., 152
Kendi, I. X., 31, 40
Khan, U., 5

Kidder, R. M., 4
"Killing" of the self, 98
Kim, J., 7, 107
King, J. E., 32, 38, 155
King, L. J., 155
King, M. L., Jr., 40
Kinney, E. D., 148
Klass, K., 30
Kumi-Yeboah, A., 105, 154

Labels, 49, 97
Ladson-Billings, G., 45, 54, 146–147,
    150
Laney, L. C., 31–32
Language
  and audience, 114–118
  development, 84–85
  multilingual identity, 109–110
  and racial justice, 85, 155–156
  in schools, 47–48
  use, 84–85, 97, 109–110, 122
Lawrence, C. R., 14
Learning styles, 86
LeBlanc-Ernest, A. D., 42, 43
Lee, C. D., 143–144
Lee, J., 110, 154
Lesson Before Dying, A (Gaines), 128,
    132–133, 134
Lewis, K. C., 150
Liberation and literacy, 40–45, 141, 142
Liberation theology, 142
Lincoln, C. E., 8
Lincoln University, 42
Literacy access. *See* Education access
Literacy and slavery, 21–23
Literacy as liberation, 40–45, 141, 142
Literacy development, 99, 101,
    102–103, 107–108
"Literacy test," 36
Literate identities, 109
Litucky, T. R., 15
Lockwood, L. C., 26
Lomotey, K., 41
Longitudinal study. *See* Aesha case study
Louis, D. A., 153
Louis, S. L., 153
Love. *See* Care
Love, B. J., 14

Lovison, V. S., 152
Ludlow, H. W., 28–29, 30
Luke, A., 118
Lune, H., 20
Lytle, B. L., 5

Macmillan Dictionary, 3
Madkins, T. C., 145
Mamiya, L., 8
Marable, M., 13
Martin, W., 41
Marusak, J., 145–146
Matsinhe, D. M., 15
Matsuda, M. J., 14
Mattaini, M. A., 15
Maturity, 82
McCall, L., 11
McCluskey, A. T., 32
McKamey, P., 50
McKinney de Royston, M., 143–144,
    145
McMillon, D. B., 100
McMillon, G.M.T., 9, 84
McMillon, G. T., 153
*Medical Dictionary for the Health
    Professions and Nursing,* 148
Medicine and standard of care,
    148–149
Menkart, D., 40
Mentors, 139
Michaels, S., 84
Michaud, J., 15
Michel, S. D., 153
Milgram, S., 5
Miller, W. I., 4
Misalignment of education and school
    goals, 64
Mississippi, 37–38
Moffett, P., 148
Monaghan, E. J., 23
Moore, G., 148
Moral courage and responsibility, 51,
    142, 149
Morrison, T., 3, 147
Mothers for Equal Education (the
    Mothers), 46
Motivation, 69, 137
Mouton, B., 46, 47

Muhammad, G., 153
Multilingual identity, 109–110
Myles Horton's Highlander Folk
    School, 35–36

Nairobi Day School, 46–48
Nairobi High School. *See* Nairobi Day
    School
Nanda, J., 68
Nasir, N. S., 143–144, 145
National Council of Black Studies, 33
Neutrality, 54
Newton, H., 40
Newton, H. P., 44
New York Times, 46
Nigam, A., 152
Ntseane, G. N., 15

Oakland Community School, 42–44
Ocen, P., 68
O'Connor, M. C., 84
Official website of the Black Panther
    Party Worldwide, 44
Ono, K., 14
Oxford University Press, 7

Palo Alto Weekly, 48
Parents
    and CARE, 157–158
    child advocacy, 72, 99, 122, 156–157
    and childcaring norms, 98–99
    frustration of, 86–87, 89–90
    relationships with teachers, 60,
        62–63, 65–67, 86, 95–97
Paris, D., 45, 147
Pawleys Island's Holy Cross Faith
    Memorial School, 32
Payne, C. M., 37
Pea, R., 143–144
Peake, M.S.K., 25–26
Peavy, L., 37
Pedagogy, 47, 59, 107, 127–128. *See
    also* Equity in education
Peller, G., 11, 13–14
People's Village Public School, 30
Perlstein, D., 44
Personality, 79
Phelps, J. T., 8

Phillips, M., 44
Phonics, 48
Poverty, 54
Power, 55, 67, 92, 118, 144, 147
Pressley, A., xi
Privileged literacies, 118
Professional development, 72, 99,
    119–121
Pull-out programs, 59

Quinn, D. M., 152

Race versus *culture,* 143–146
Racial justice, 128, 142–143,
    154–156
Ramsey, S., 33, 34
Reading research, 16–18, 54, 72. *See*
    research study by name
Reimagining literate Blackness, 98–99,
    142, 143f
Religion, 21–23, 26, 31–32, 45, 101,
    125
Research studies. *See* Aesha case study;
    Black-immigrant-youth research
    study; Clemente case study; First-
    grade classroom
Responsibility, 54, 95, 156–157
Retention threat, 80
Reynolds, J., 31
Rickford, R., 46
Rios, F., 152
Robinson, B. V., 36
Robinson, C., 13
Robinson, R. P., 45
Roddey, B. M., 33–35
Roediger, D., 67
Rofel, L., 42
Rogers, R., 153
Rosa, J., 6, 110, 155
Roxas, K., 152

"Saving" Black children, 103–104
Scaffolding language development,
    84–85
School organization and structure, 65
Seale, R. G. (Bobby), 40
Sealey-Ruiz, Y., 155
Segregation, 32, 33–35

Self-identity, 68, 69, 79, 97
Self-knowledge, 41, 105
Siddle-Walker, V., 51
Simkin, J., 22
Sims, R., 66
Skitka, L. J., 5
Skutnabb-Kangas, T., 152
Slavery, 21–23
Smith, C., 13, 101
Smith, G., 43
Smith, P., 7, 104, 105, 106, 107, 110,
    111, 152, 153, 154, 156, 174
Smitherman, G., 154
Social justice. *See* Racial justice
"Some Notes on Education" (Cobb), 37
South Carolina, 36
Southern Workman, The, 29, 30
Standard Black Language, 47
Standard of care, 148–150
Stefanic, J., 13
Student outcomes. *See* Academic
    achievement
Student resistance, 62
Student-teacher ratio, 65
Student-teacher relationships, 91–92,
    121–122
Subordination. *See* White supremacy

Taaffe, L., 45, 47
Tai, J., 42
Tamarkin, C., 48, 49, 50
Tanghe, S., 152
Teacher-parent relationships.
    See Parents: relationships with
    teachers
Teacher preparation, 61, 155
Teacher-student ratio, 65
Teacher-student relationships, 91–92,
    121–122
Teaching norms, 98–99
Ten-Point Program, 40–41
Testing focus, 49
This work
    author's literacy experiences
        (Arlette), 119
    author's literacy experiences
        (Gwen), 121

author's literacy experiences
    (Patriann), 105–106
epistemology and ideology, 2
introduction to the authors, 1
theoretical foundations, 2–4, 7–16,
    141–142
Thomas, K., 11, 13–14
Tompkins, R. H., 51
Trauma, 97–98, 128, 138
Trost, M. R., 4

Unteaching of anti-Blackness, 141–142
"Uplift suasion," 31
U.S. Supreme Court, 32

Validation of educators, 133–134, 136
Valuing Black students, 132, 135
Valuing education, 19, 50–51, 101
Varner, J., 152
View, J. L., 40
Virginia Slave Law of 1667, 21–22
Volunteer teacher corps, 34
Voting, 35, 36, 37

Walker, A., 1
Warrican, S. J., 5, 6, 104, 105, 152
Washington, G., 29–31, 30
Wei, L., 110
Well-being sense, 79
White supremacy, 19, 29, 55, 118,
    142, 144, 145, 147, 154
Whole-child approach, 51, 151
Wilkerson, I., 37
Wilks, G., 47
Wilks, G. D., 45–48
Williams, H. A., 23, 24
Williamson, J. A., 44–45
Willis, A., 7, 107
Willis, A. I., 17, 28, 30, 127, 146, 150,
    152
Women's Department of the
    Presbyterian Church USA, 31
Wong, C., 44
Writing in school, 106–108, 112–114,
    122

Zimbardo, P. G., 4

About the Authors

Arlette Ingram Willis is a professor at the University of Illinois at Urbana-Champaign in the Department of Curriculum and Instruction, in the division of Language and Literacy. Her scholarship consists of interrogating how conceptions of race are framed in reading research, examining secondary preservice English teacher education, and applying critical theories to literacy policy and research. Willis is a University Scholar (2000), a 2020 recipient of the Reading Hall of Fame Award, a past recipient of the John J. Gumperz Award (2019), the Outstanding Researcher Award (1998), and the LRA Oscar S. Causey Award for Outstanding Contributions to Reading Research.

Gwendolyn Thompson McMillon is professor of literacy in the Department of Reading & Language Arts at Oakland University in Rochester, Michigan. Her research examines literacy practices in the Black Church and other out-of-school learning environments, and develops ways to help students negotiate the cultural borders between their out-of-school and in-school literacy learning, She is the 2020–2021 president of the Literacy Research Association, Project Director of the Wolverine State Missionary Baptist Convention's *I Read, I Lead, I Succeed* Statewide K–5 Reading Initiative, and a Spencer Dissertation Fellow (2000). McMillon and co-authors Edwards and Turner received the 2011 Literacy Research Association Edward B. Fry Book Award for *Change Is Gonna Come: Transforming Literacy Education for African American Students.*

Patriann Smith is associate professor of literacy in the Department of Language, Literacy, Exceptional Education, Ed.D. and Physical Education at the University of South Florida. Her research emerges at the intersection of race, language, and immigration. She explores the cross-racial, cross-linguistic, and cross-cultural experiences of Black immigrants in literacy instruction, assessment, and transcultural teacher education. Smith is a 2013 International Literacy Association (ILA) Reading Hall of Fame Emerging Scholar Fellow, 2017 Literacy Research Association (LRA) STAR Fellow, and the 2015 recipient of the American Educational Research Association (AERA) Language and Social Processes Emerging Scholar Award.